AS VARIOUS AS THEIR LAND

THE EVERYDAY LIFE IN AMERICA SERIES

EDITED BY

RICHARD BALKIN

As Various as Their Land

The Everyday Lives of Eighteenth-Century Americans

STEPHANIE GRAUMAN WOLF

HarperPerennial
A Division of HarperCollinsPublishers

The Library of Congress has catalogued the hardcover edition as follows:

Wolf, Stephanie Grauman.
    As various as their land : the everyday lives of eighteenth century Americans / Stephanie Grauman Wolf. — 1st ed.
       p.   cm. —(The Everyday life in America series)
    Includes index.
    ISBN 0-06-016799-8 (cloth)
     1. United States—Social life and customs—To 1775. 2. United States—Social life and customs—1775–1800. I. Title. II. Series.
E162.W83   1993
973—dc20   92-54754

ISBN 0-06-092537-X (pbk.)

   96 97 98 ❖/RRD H 10 9 8 7 6 5 4

For my children and their partners
For my grandchildren: Emma
Jacob
Stella
Zoë
Reiss
Tyler
etc., etc., . . .
But especially for Ted

CONTENTS

Part III • The Public Domain

Illustrations follow pages 48, 144, and 240.

ACKNOWLEDGMENTS

When a work has been "in progress" for as many years as this one, the number of people who have been helpful is legion. Many of them may not even remember their contributions in discussing, reading, and criticizing (constructively, of course) the bits and pieces of this manuscript as it has emerged over the course of time. I would, therefore, like to extend a few generic thank-yous embracing many of those whose names may not appear here, but whose comments have been valued nevertheless: The staff of the Winterthur Museum; members of the History, Art History, English, and Museum Studies faculties of the University of Delaware; members of the staff and faculty of the Hagley Program at the Eleutherian Mills Hagley Museum and Library; and most particularly the graduate students in the Winterthur Program for Early American Studies during the years 1977 to 1984. All taught me far more than I taught them. I am particularly grateful to my colleagues in the Department of Advanced Studies—Scott Swank, Ken Ames, and the late Benno Forman—who were the first to help me understand the importance of using material objects to understand the everyday life of the past.

In the past several years, the Philadelphia Center for Early American Studies at the University of Pennsylvania has provided me with an intellectual home for the best of all possible scholarly activities, the free and exciting interchange of ideas. Participants in the formal Center seminars and the informal discussions at brown-bag lunches and "evenings at Mike's" have provided a cornucopia of facts, theories, and analyses that have shaped both my thinking and this manuscript, as well as opportunities for close professional support and/or personal friendship with, among many others, Richard Beeman, Wayne Bodle, Karen Calvert, Lois Carr, Thomas Cochran, Elaine Crane, Richard Dunn, Jerry Frost, Michael Harris, Susan Klepp, Emma Lapsansky, Susan Mackiewicz, Judith Ann McGaw, John Murrin, Gary Nash, Alison Olson, Lucy Simler, Billy G. Smith, Lorena Walsh, Marianne Wokeck, and Michael Zuckerman.

I am grateful to the libraries and their staffs at the Historical Society of Pennsylvania, the Library Company of Philadelphia, the University of Pennsylvania, the Germantown Historical Society, and the Winterthur Museum and Gardens for their knowledge of their great collections and their willingness to share it. For providing the hours needed to transfer the bulk of the manuscript to the computer my thanks go to Heather Sneff, and real gratitude is extended to Rob Krulak, who came in late in the game but has been of inestimable help in the final research and acquisition of the illustrations. Wini Blacklow has been not only a friend but a painstaking research assistant whose intelligent understanding of the material often expanded my horizons. My appreciation to Rebecca and Walter Roshon for their willingness to take the time and trouble to help me become computer-semiliterate, and for their endless patience in answering questions and walking me through a variety of procedures.

Finally, there is my family: my husband, Ted; our children and their partners, Debby and Andy, Martha and Chris, Jim and Margaret, Dan and Heidi, Becky and Walt; and *their* children, Emma, Jake, Stella, Zoë, Reiss, Tyler, and others (several, I suspect) yet to come. They never (well, hardly ever) complained about the constant looming presence of THE BOOK. They are what everyday life is all about.

American Muse, whose strong and diverse
heart
So many men have tried to understand
But only made it smaller with their art,
Because you are as various as your land.
—Stephen Vincent Benet,
John Brown's Body, Invocation

AS VARIOUS AS THEIR LAND

Faces in the Crowd

INTRODUCTION:

VOICES FROM THE PAST

Sat. 18th to Fri. 31st: Continuing . . . building our huts . . . very cold
& almost Starved for Want of Provision & as the mens huts was near
completed moved up into one of the Serjeants Huts, puting them
amongst the men till our Hut could be fit to move into . . . at the same
time to work on my hut when the wether would admit of it . . .

   DIARY OF A SOLDIER AT VALLEY FORGE, DECEMBER 1779

They live in so happy a Climate, and have so fertile a Soil, that no
body is poor enough to beg, or want Food.

   ROBERT BEVERLEY, GOVERNOR OF VIRGINIA, 1705

You have had the best of me and you and yours must have the worst.
Where am I to go in sickness or old age? No, Master, your slave I am,
and always will be, and I will belong to your children when you are
gone; and by you and them I mean to be cared for.

   MASSACHUSETTS SLAVE WHEN OFFERED HIS FREEDOM, 1783

When we came to a small creek we had to cross the girls tucked up
their petticoats above their knees and forded it with the greatest
indifference. Nothing unusual here, tho' these are the First people
in the Country.

   DIARY OF A TRAVELER IN FRONTIER PENNSYLVANIA, 1775

In general I rise at five o'Clock in the morning, read till seven, then
take a walk in the garden or field, see that the Servants are at their
respective business, then to breakfast . . .

   LETTERBOOK OF ELIZA LUCAS PINCKNEY, WIDOW OF A
   PLANTER AND MANAGER OF THE ESTATE,
   SOUTH CAROLINA, 1742

1

[Pennsylvania is the] best Country in the World for Labourers and handycrafts, the worst for what may be called half bred Gentlemen, without some Capital . . .

IMMIGRANT TO HIS BROTHER IN IRELAND, 1768

My dear mother was in raptures to see us arrive with the babe. . . . My dear sister, seeing my mother so much elated, said, "take care, . . . this is all uncertain bliss, and may soon be changed." I have often heard my mother reflect . . . that she was . . . stupid at the time . . . never to have once thought that the babe was mortal.

REMINISCENCES OF A CONNECTICUT WOMAN IN 1800,
ON AN EVENT THAT OCCURRED IN 1760

All you that have bad masters
And cannot get your due;
Come, come, my brave boys,
And join our ship's crew.

SAILORS' RECRUITING SONG: SUNG WHILE PARADING
THROUGH THE STREETS WITH FLAGS AND MARTIAL
MUSIC, LATE EIGHTEENTH CENTURY

. . . it is a wretched country and a mere barren land, on a flat and bleak sea coast; the last place on earth where one would expect to meet with any mortal and above all with Christians.

JOURNAL OF A FRENCH TRAVELER TO FLORIDA, 1708

Friends and relatives! . . . I am myself come to bid you rise and go with me to a secure place . . . where your fields shall yield you abundant crops; . . . where your women and children . . . will live in peace and safety; where no long knife [Virginian] shall ever molest you. . . . If you stay where you now are, one day or the other, the long knives, will in their usual way, speak fine words to you, and at the same time murder you!

TRANSLATION OF A SPEECH BY A CHIEF OF THE
DELAWARE INDIAN NATION TO A TOWN OF
CHRISTIANIZED INDIANS, 1781

Our mechanics and tradesmen are very dear [expensive] and sometimes great bunglers.

RESIDENT OF UPSTATE NEW YORK, LATE EIGHTEENTH
CENTURY

I invited . . . Servants and Slaves to come to be instructed in the Church; . . . I am sorry I can give no satisfactory Account of Success . . . I am not blamed openly, . . . but it seems by their Whispers . . . they wou'd not have me urge of Contributing to the Salvation, Instruction and human usage of Slaves and ffree [*sic*] Indians.

LETTER FROM A MINISTER IN SOUTH CAROLINA, 1706

Admitted John Douglass an Ordinary Chap, has been in and out several times before this. He is not sick but Poor and ragged and is come in at this time as usual for Winter quarter to be cloathed and kept warm, and in the Spring go out and continue till autumn, when cold Boreas perhaps will blow him here again.

RECORDS OF THE PHILADELPHIA ALMSHOUSE,
DECEMBER 1800

[Davenport] not only gave an unrestrained liberty to *noise* and *out-cry,* both of *distress* and *joy,* in time of divine service, but promoted *both* with all his might . . . by extending his own voice to the highest pitch, together with the most violent agitations of body, even to the distorting of his features and marring his visage. . . . And all this, with a strange, unnatural *singing tone* . . .

TRADITIONAL MINISTER DESCRIBING AN ITINERANT
PREACHER, CONNECTICUT, MID-1750S

On the farm which I purchased . . . there were some hundred loads of rich manure which had been collecting for several years, to the great damage of the buildings. [I was advised by the former owner] to move the barn, as this would be an easier way out of difficulty than moving the manure.

LONG ISLAND FARMER, LATE EIGHTEENTH CENTURY

Hagar [female], 14, . . . a Scar under one of her Breasts, supposed to be got by Whipping: Had on . . . an Iron collar about her Neck, which it is probable she may have got off, as it was very poorly rivetted; she is supposed to be harboured in some Negroe Quarter, as her Father and Mother encourage her in these Elopements, under a Pretence that she is ill used at home.

RUNAWAY SLAVE AD, *PENNSYLVANIA GAZETTE,*
NOVEMBER 6, 1766

Were it in my power I promise you I should like to take the World easy [but] you know I like to live genteelly, tho' not extravagantly,

and it takes all my industry to accomplish it, and with great fatague
I have hitherto been able (thank God) to live well, but have not been
able to lay up such a Stock, as would maintain me without dayly
labour.

PHILADELPHIA MERCHANT,
LETTER TO HIS BROTHER, 1768

I have been doing my housework and Nursing my cow. Her bag is
amazingly sweld . . . I have been picking wool till [11 hour Evening].
A womans work is never Done as the Song says and happy shee
whose strength holds out to the end of the rais [race].

DIARY OF A MIDWIFE, AUGUSTA, MAINE,
NOVEMBER 26, 1795

I would not confine you to Palatines [Germans]; if they are good
workmen, they may be from Asia, Africa, or Europe; they may be
Mahometans, Jews or Christians of any sect, or they may be Atheists.

GEORGE WASHINGTON, LETTER TO HIS AGENT, SEEKING
SKILLED LABOR FOR MOUNT VERNON, 1784

. . . About Seven the Ladies & Gentlemen begun to dance in the
Ball-Room—first Minuets one Round; second Giggs; third Reels, And
last of All Country Dances. . . . The Music was a French-Horn and
two Violins—The Ladies were Dressed Gay, and splendid, & when
dancing their Silks & Brocades rustled and trailed behind them! . . .
[In other rooms some of the gentlemen played] at Cards; some drinking for Pleasure; some toasting the Sons of america; some singing
"Liberty Songs" as they call'd them, in which [they] put their Heads
near together and roar.

JOURNAL OF A TUTOR IN A VIRGINIA PLANTER'S FAMILY,
JANUARY 1774

These are the voices of eighteenth-century Americans as they
reveal glimpses of their everyday activities, their thoughts and
their opinions. Some of the voices seem eager to provide a
record of their times for those who come after them, publishing
their experiences for that very purpose. Others speak to each
other or themselves, allowing history to eavesdrop by saving
their letters, journals, and diaries. Still others have no intention
of making contact with the future, and the circumstances of

their lives are found, as it were, in the margins of history, where wills, tax lists, records of poorhouses, runaway slave ads and personal columns in the newspapers, dockets of the criminal court, and other such flotsam and jetsam from the past await our attention.

No single thread runs through the revelations of our colonial predecessors, nor is there anything immediately similar about their situations in life or the conditions under which they lived it. By 1700, some parts of England's New World possessions had been settled for almost one hundred years; others were still wild and untamed, at least in the eyes of the colonists. To native Americans, the picture was undoubtedly different. White immigrants saw rich and exciting new possibilities; third-generation sons in New England already felt that the land was overcrowded and used up, and that they had to move on to achieve success. A multitude of such overlapping visions and perceptions continued to prevent a clear-cut American self-image even after 1725, when the majority of the population became, once and for all, native-born.

In 1700, there were a quarter of a million Europeans and blacks in ten individual colonies, strung precariously along one thousand miles of coastline from New England to the Chesapeake. By 1800, a nation of sixteen states containing almost five million citizens and slaves stretched as far south as Georgia, as far west as Kentucky and Tennessee. The maps included here provide raw data on topography, political boundaries, and population density. More complex visual aids could provide greater detail about specific issues concerning land and people, but none could give the sense of what it was like to have been a child in the Chesapeake at the beginning of the century when dense forests separated one's home from the nearest neighbor, only to realize as an old man that not only could one now see easily from one place to the next, but also that timber had become a scarce and expensive commodity.

The differences in daily life created by time were less significant than those produced by the enormous diversity of the American experience at any single point in time. The sheer size of England's territorial claims on the continent resulted in a

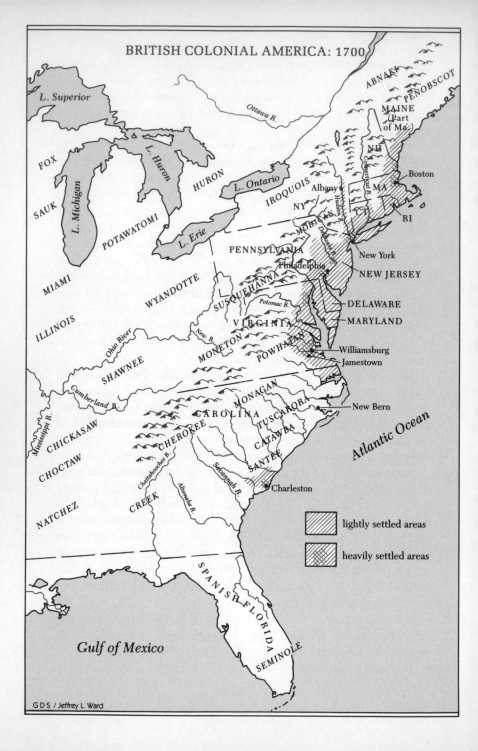

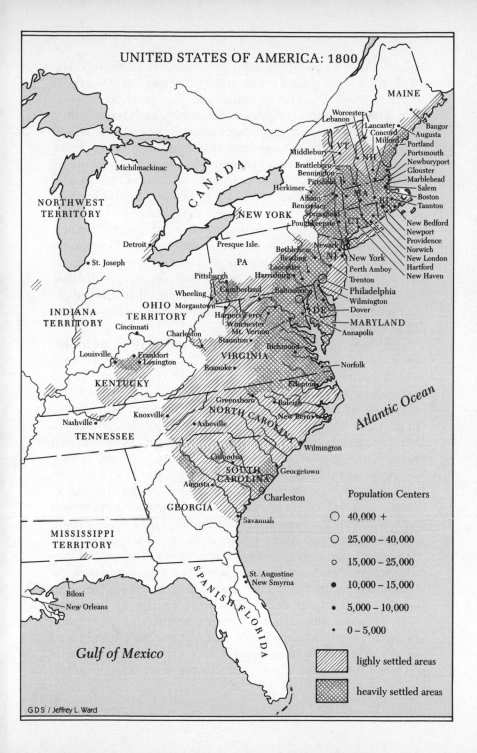

UNITED STATES OF AMERICA: 1800

MAINE

NORTHWEST
TERRITORY

CANADA

Michilmackinac

NEW YORK

Worcester
Lebanon
Middlebury
VT
Brattleboro
Bennington
Herkimer
Pittsfield
Albany
Rensselaer
Poughkeepsie

Lancaster
Concord
Milford
NH
MA
RI
CT

Bangor
Augusta
Portland
Portsmouth
Newburyport
Glouster
Marblehead
Salem
Boston
Taunton

New Bedford
Newport
Providence
Norwich
New London
Hartford
New Haven

Detroit
St. Joseph

Presque Isle.

PA

Bethlehem
Reading
Lancaster
Harrisburg

Newark
NJ
New York
Perth Amboy
Trenton

INDIANA
TERRITORY

OHIO
TERRITORY

Pittsburgh
Wheeling
Morgantown
Cumberland
Baltimore

Philadelphia
Wilmington
DE
Dover
MARYLAND
Annapolis

Cincinnati
Charleston
Harpers Ferry
Winchester
Mt. Vernon
Staunton

Richmond

Louisville
Frankfort
Lexington

VIRGINIA
Roanoke

Norfolk

KENTUCKY

Nashville

Knoxville

Edenton

TENNESSEE

Greensboro
NORTH CAROLINA
Asheville

Raleigh
New Bern

Wilmington

Columbia
SOUTH
CAROLINA

Georgetown

Augusta
Charleston

GEORGIA

Savannah

Atlantic Ocean

Population Centers

⬭ 40,000 +

◯ 25,000 – 40,000

○ 15,000 – 25,000

● 10,000 – 15,000

• 5,000 – 10,000

· 0 – 5,000

MISSISSIPPI
TERRITORY

St. Augustine
New Smyrna

Biloxi
New Orleans

SPANISH FLORIDA

Gulf of Mexico

▨ lighly settled areas

▩ heavily settled areas

GDS / Jeffrey L. Ward

variety of regions where the climate, soil, and topography made the daily lives of farmers totally unlike one another. Divergent groups of people from incompatible cultures, races, or religions lived either separately or intermingled with each other; but in either case, even when adapting to the culture and language of their neighbors, they retained enough of their old ways to make them seem strange or foreign to those of other backgrounds. As in all human society throughout history, the lives of the rich and the poor, although often bound up in ties of neighborhood or patronage, seemed to be taking place in separate worlds. In the three overlapping circles of everyday life—the home, the work-place, and the community—material conditions and human in-teraction were dependent on the who and where of history as well as the when. Yet, over the course of the century, still other factors were at work, developing parameters that made eigh-teenth-century Americans resemble each other more than they did those who came before or after.

First, there were the limitations of technology: while a vari-ety of innovations occurred in ways of doing things and there were a number of changes in the organization of work in the home, the shop, and the field, the 1700s were, primarily, still part of the earlier "age of wood," as one historian has called it. On the other hand, the virtual explosion of material goods avail-able to more levels of society than ever before broadened and changed the scope of everyday life, pointing it toward the fu-ture rather than the past. While less spectacular than the enor-mous changes wrought by the industrial revolution in the nine-teenth century, a so-called consumer revolution provided eighteenth-century Americans, along with their European con-temporaries, a whole new set of expectations, goals, and values.

Above all, the development of a system of perpetual enslave-ment for African-Americans alongside the achievement of po-litical freedom for the United States as a nation set the eigh-teenth century apart from all other centuries in American history. Slavery, although in practical operation during the sev-enteenth century, became codified, rationalized legally and morally, and brought to its finished form as a system of inherited servitude for people of color during the eighteenth century.

From the 1730s to the time of the Revolution, it was part of the lives of the inhabitants of all thirteen colonies. Then, within the very same century that had seen its universal adoption, it began to crumble, as one by one the northern states, starting with Pennsylvania in 1780, revoked their laws and opted for abolition, however gradual. The effect on the everyday lives of African-Americans was less immediate than might be thought, and the cataclysmic significance for the nation as a whole was underestimated. While one observer noted in 1781 that there was a distinct possibility of "a separation of the federal union into *two parts* [emphasis added] at no distant day," it was unclear to him whether it would split north-south or east-west.

It was the Revolution, of course, that was *the* defining event of the eighteenth century, and in any political history, it is here that the break between the world of British colonists and that of American citizens begins. But while history is written backward, it is lived forward, and for the people who experienced it, the War of Independence was really just one more interruption of their daily routines similar to many that had gone before. The absence of the menfolk, runaway inflation, shortages of essential goods, increased numbers of widows and orphans—all these were part of the War of Jenkin's Ear or the French and Indian War, just as surely as they were part of the Revolution.

The difference was one of degree, rather than of kind: The War of Independence ranged far more widely over time and space, and the number killed or ruined was inconceivably larger. When the British marched through farm after farm, taking corn, cattle, and anything else that they could move and burning the rest (or, for that matter, when the Americans did the same); when Indians, in confederation with the government in London, rampaged along the frontier; when slaves were encouraged to escape and take up arms against their former masters; when successful blockades created widespread areas of distress and poverty in the cities—the changes and disruptions affected nearly all Americans. The economic depression that followed the war lasted even longer than the war itself. Burned-out barns and houses and increased numbers of poor and homeless were more visible than they had been after other wars.

For many young men, service in the American army gave them their first glimpse of the world beyond their farms and villages and, together with the rhetoric of liberty which was part of the revolutionary fervor, set their feet on paths they would never have contemplated otherwise. Many thousands of blacks made their own declarations of independence and either fled to the British, believing the promises of emancipation, or escaped masters who, they later alleged, were Tories, to enlist in the Revolutionary ranks. Thousands of families who were British sympathizers fled to England, giving up their roots and their possessions. Everyday life was changed greatly for these individuals, but less for the population as a whole.

During the 1790s, following the adoption of the Constitution, changes in daily life occurred with increasing rapidity and might really be considered part of the story of the nineteenth century. The end of the depression that had hung on since the Revolution, the huge population explosion, a quickening of the pace of technological development, and increased accessibility of the frontier resulted in frenzies of building—roads, houses, factories, public institutions, and ships—and, most particularly, the foundation of systems of organization and management that opened up whole new careers and opportunities. A sense of optimism was abroad in the new nation, fueled by the improved economic situation, and expressed in a rising self-conscious pride in national identity.

It was an identity that remained, for the rest of the century, political rather than cultural. Before the Revolution, it can safely be said that America was a place, not a people, and while independence theoretically created a single nation out of a disparate collection of colonies, nothing immediately replaced the unifying umbrella of the British Empire. As George Washington wrote to General Lafayette shortly after the Constitutional Convention, "It appears to me . . . little short of a miracle, that the Delegates from so many different States (which States you know are also different from each other), in their manners, circumstances and prejudices, should unite in forming a system of national Government so little liable to well-founded objections."

Those who felt that the long-term stability of the union could only be assured through the development of an "American way of life" began an intellectual search for the American family, American literature and art, and American character traits such as simplicity, honesty, and pragmatism. Noah Webster wrote in 1790: ". . . independence and union render it necessary that the citizens of different States should know each others characters and circumstances; that all jealousies should be removed; that mutual respect and confidence should succeed, and a harmony of views and interests be cultivated by a friendly inter-course . . ." His suggestions for achieving the goal were educational: the development of schools and curricula that would promote American values, and the "fixing" of a distinctively American language. Most Americans at the end of the century, however, even while adopting the patriotic symbols of the new nation and participating with vigor in its rites and ceremonies, continued to live in their various ways and speak in their various accents.

The center stage of history has always been occupied by great events—political upheavals at home, wars abroad, impassioned debates in the chambers of government—and the great men who acted in them. But for every Cotton Mather, Samuel Adams, Benjamin Franklin, or George Washington there were hundreds of assemblymen, clergymen, and judges; thousands of people who made up mobs, polls, and armies; and tens of thousands of farmers, artisans, laborers, women, children, servants, and slaves. The daily lives of all these people, from the stars to the bit players to the walk-ons, formed the real web of the eighteenth century, creating the setting and condition for history's dramatic changes, as well as responding to those changes. It is only by listening to the voices of all of these eighteenth-century Americans that we can begin to understand the links that bound them to each other and, in the end, to ourselves.

Part I

THE HOME FRONT

1

A REPUTABLE individual—alone—was almost unthinkable in the everyday world of America in 1700. From a practical point of view, a solitary human being had little chance of survival on the wild frontier or in the thinly settled agricultural regions and rural villages that made up the vast majority of the colonial lands. Even in rapidly growing cities such as Boston, New York, Philadelphia, or Kingston, Jamaica, where laborers were in short supply and desperately needed, newcomers were suspected and disliked. It is not surprising. Although the computer age gives us numerous ways of checking on a stranger's identity, from passports, driver's licenses, and other picture IDs to social security cards and credit cards, we still get fooled by a sharp line of talk or an ingratiating smile.

How much easier it was in the eighteenth century to prey on the gullible when most people had no "papers" at all to prove their identities. There were only a few documents that might be expected of a newcomer, and any of these could easily be forged, faked, or altered. The most common forms of legitimation included: signed indentures that indicated the satisfactory completion of an apprenticeship; redemption papers given to those who had finished the labor required when they sold themselves to gain passage to the New World; proof of freedom dues paid by blacks who had bought their way out of slavery; certificates of removal offered by some religious groups like the Quakers to ease the introduction of their members to a new community of worshippers; or a letter of introduction from a well-known person to a local resident.

Occasionally, there were less trustworthy, one-of-a-kind written documents attesting to the worthiness of a stranger. Such was the "parchment" carried by John Hill in 1733, when he attempted to earn a living as a panhandler on the streets of Boston. His "wife" Rachel did his speaking for him since, the parchment testified, he had been captured by the Turks and tortured, his arms burned by irons and his tongue torn out by the roots. Their act fooled many respectable Yankees despite the reputation of New Englanders for sharp judgment. It was not until one of the Hills' potential victims became suspicious, grabbed him by the throat, and forced him to "produce his Tongue or be choaked" that the couple ended up in the Boston prison, convicted of fraud. Perhaps they served their time alongside Molly Kemp, a.k.a. "No Mouth'd Molly," who, the newspapers reported, without any bona fides at all, had collected a "great deal of Money (some say Pockets full) [by] deceiving charitable and well disposed People" from Philadelphia to Boston.

The Hills and Molly Kemp are but petty examples of the grifter or "stroller," as the con artist was called in the eighteenth century. The elite of the trade were almost always men, virtual international celebrities whose whereabouts and exploits were breathlessly reported in newspapers, taverns, and coffeehouses from France to England to the colonies. They wore good clothes and possessed educated vocabularies and a smattering of culture expressed in genteel accents, with a few Latin or foreign words thrown in to impress the provincials. As one historian has put it, "By virtue of his lively discourse, nimble wit, and daring or effrontery (or both), [the confidence man] passed as a man of distinction, and high society, as well as low, accepted him." Most characteristically, strollers never stayed long in any one place; they bilked the local populace for what they could, and then got out of town as fast as possible. The prototype of the romantic scoundrel was Macheath, or Mac the Knife, the fictitious hero of John Gay's popular *Beggar's Opera*, performed on the London stage in 1728 to great applause and laughter.

While the true exploits of run-of-the-mill con men were far from amusing to their many victims, it was not merely fear of being swindled or laughed at that made unattached individuals an anathema to eighteenth-century Euro-Americans. A conviction that people belonged in families was basic to their deepest culture. As an institution, the family in Europe had always been on a par with the church and the state, the third pillar on which the whole social system rested. Like the church and the state, the organization of families was patriarchal, headed by a man who not only controlled the private lives of those who depended on him, but also represented them in the public arena. Not all men shared in this power, however; those who were not at least the head of an individual family were considered subordinates along with all women and children.

If the duty of the state was to keep the peace and that of the church was to protect the soul, the family was charged with responsibility for the basic necessities of everyday life. Within the parameters of the walls and fields of the "Domestick oeconomie," crops and goods were produced, the young were educated in practical skills and moral behavior, and social services for "unproductive" members of the community—the old, the orphaned, the handicapped, the insane, and the just plain unruly—were provided. The first full-blown economic census of England, taken in 1688 by "Gregory King, Esqr, Lancaster herald at Armes," was organized by family, subsuming all individuals with the exception of "Vagrants; as Gipsies, Thieves, Beggars, &c."

Over the centuries, the traditional European institution of the family had come to include, roughly, two kinds of organization: the "House" with a capital "H" as in the Royal House or the House of Gloucester, which might be called the "dynastic" family; and the "household" with a small "h," which might be referred to as the "domestic" family. While each of these frameworks incorporated some of the meanings still included in our definition of the word "family," neither was based on the cru-

cial modern criteria of a family: immediate blood ties and/or
emotional nurturance and intensity.

The concept of the dynastic family was derived from both
biblical and feudal ideas and practices. Essentially rural in nature, it embraced a complex set of relationships, functions, and
responsibilities best characterized by the three "L's": land, lineage, and labor. It had less to do with our definition of blood
relationship than it did with land and economics; more to do
with power and control than it did with modern concepts of
intimacy and affection. While the head of the House as well as
his dependents recognized the special affinities of blood and
emotion expressed by the titles of wife and child, parent,
brother and sister, grandparents, aunt, uncle, or cousin, these
were "relatives" rather than "family." Beyond them, the preferred term for more distant relatives was "kin," a word with
no deeper overtones than "kith" (neighbor, friend, or ally), with
which it was often paired.

The law stood behind the continuation of Houses through the
apparatuses of primogeniture and entail, by which only the
oldest male heir could inherit the lands and title. He, in turn,
held them in trust for the next generation, and was legally
forbidden to sell out or abdicate responsibility for the rest of his
family. This family of obligation was made up of all those who
lived on his land: his wife and children, of course; domestic
"live-in" servants; farm laborers, bound or free; husbandmen
who lived on scattered farms around the estate, and their live-in
servants and laborers; and cottagers and artisans who lived in
villages on the property. Whether or not the landowner even
recognized them by sight, they were all considered to be part
of his "family." In return for their labor and submission, all the
members of the dynastic family down to the lowliest disabled
and widowed cottager, in theory at least, were protected at the
most basic level by an economic and social safety net of the
master's devising.

In the everyday world, the dynastic family model was, for the
most part, an ideal rather than a reality. Most members of
Western society lived in domestic households—the alternative
form of traditional family—circumscribed by the single farm-

stead, the craftsman's house and workshop, or the shopkeeper's apartments and store. Family members included those who lived and worked within these confines: the head of the household, his wife and resident children, his servants and apprentices. The grand alliances of dynastic families were mirrored on a small scale by the rural cooperation of neighboring farm households through resource sharing, labor pooling, and intermarriage. Urban merchant families did business with relatives, in-laws, and coreligionists in far-off places because they were felt to be known, and therefore more reliable and trustworthy than strangers.

The idea of "family" as blood or affectionate relationship was nearly as irrelevant to the domestic household as it was to the dynastic House. Individuals came and went, leaving one family and joining another as they grew from children in their fathers' houses to apprentices or servants in the houses of their masters; became heads of their own households when they finished their training, married, and went into business on their own; and finally, when widowed or elderly, entered the families of others, as dependents. They were always "kin," of course, to their birth relatives, emotionally and nostalgically attached, perhaps, but that was not part of the family domain.

While the dynastic family was based on the three L's of land, lineage, and labor, it was the third of these—labor—that really defined the parameters of the domestic household. The position of every member was determined by his or her ability to contribute to the economic goals of the enterprise. While the man at the head of the house was not necessarily the oldest male, he was the publicly acknowledged economic man of action, of legal maturity and in the fullest flower of his abilities, vigor, and energy. He headed the family unit as husband, father, and employer; his wife was wife, mother, manager of domestic arrangements, and, usually, a worker or supervisor in the business as well. The sons and daughters of the family were workers in the domestic economic venture as well as children of the household; apprentices and servants were usually young, and were treated as children of the household as well as workers.

"Out-servants"—adult journeymen or farm laborers who

were married and lived outside the household walls—received
some cash wages, but they, too, got much of their pay in "kind,"
taking their meals at the household table and regarded as quasi-
members of the family. At either end of the life cycle were the
inevitable, but less productive, members. Everyone loved the
baby perhaps, but there was no "fat" in the budget for unproductive mouths and that baby had better get working as soon
as possible. The elderly widow or, more rarely, widower who
had given or lost control of the farm or workshop to a son or
son-in-law occupied once more a position of dependence, assigned whatever tasks he or she could still manage, but of less
significance even than the infant, who would eventually improve with age.

These bald outlines of dynastic House and domestic household, as well as the basic relationship of family to state and
church, applied in most areas of the Western world from which
settlers to the new colonies emigrated. Many of them brought
with them the ideal of institutional families along with the actuality of a society largely made up of individual, autonomous
households. When they came—from early in the seventeenth
century to late in the eighteenth—and where they came from
determined the cultural baggage they carried and influenced
the kinds of family patterns they established in America. Where
they settled, in terms of geography, climate, and isolation from
other communities and from the Old World, was of prime importance as well. But who they were, the nature of their cross-
ing and their reasons for undertaking it, were factors that
loomed at least as large. Did they arrive with a group of friends,
neighbors, and relatives from the Old Country, hoping to reestablish a purified form of Old Testament society that they felt
had been abandoned or debased in Europe? Did they come in
large, well-established households with enough money to guarantee settlement on their own land with plenty of equipment,
intending, perhaps, to create a new nobility in the feudal style?
Were they young married couples, with perhaps a baby or toddler in tow, whose plans included an economic sufficiency and
independence they could never have achieved on the overcrowded soil of their homelands? Were they underage children

of the poor, selling themselves or being sold into servitude for the price of their passage or convicts who considered indentured servitude abroad preferable to prison for crimes and misdemeanors? The mixture of all these elements created many varieties of ideal and real families with traits that shared some common values within regions, classes, and ethnic/religious identities and were loosely tailored to American experiences, but never to a single American pattern.

Totally different patterns of family life existed among the indigenous people of the American continent. While staple crops, living arrangements, and even population growth varied widely across the Western hemisphere, and the term "Amerindian" subsumes a great number of language groups, confederations, and tribes—Tlingits in the Northwest, Hopi in the Southwest, Iroquois in the Northeast, and Muscogulges in the Southeast, to name just a few—they possessed the same kind of basic similarities that united Swedes, Germans, English, French, Italians, or any of the other nation/state/language groupings under the single rubric "European." Anthropologists refer to this similarity where peoples share a common cultural heritage, if not a collective culture, as a "grammar of culture."

Generally, relationships within Native American families, clans, and tribes were far more supportive than were the frequently adversarial activities of landed families and nation-states in Europe. Extended families among the Amerindians carried most of the responsibility for organization, order, and diplomatic decisions. While women were surely not "leaders" in our sense of the word (this kind of linguistic problem is what makes cultural differences so hard to discuss), they clearly played an important, sometimes central, role in Amerindian public affairs. Among the Iroquois in the North, for example, family membership was determined through the mother rather than the father, in what we call a matrilineal pattern. Groups of families related through the mother's side made up *ohivarcheras;* several of these made a clan; a number of clans constituted a village; and constellations of villages made up the Iroquois Nation, or "kinship state." The ohivarcheras and the senior women who headed them had real political power. They

chose the men who represented the clans in the larger meetings of villages and tribes, and who, in turn, picked the chiefs
of the ruling council of the Nation. These men were always
subject to being "dehorned," or removed, if they ignored the
wishes of the women who had appointed them. Among the
people in the Southeast, political succession followed matrilinear clan lines, so descent was through the eldest child of the
eldest sister of the chief, leading to a number of women becoming chiefs in their own right.

Within the household, Amerindian women also wielded considerable power. While membership in the clan or totem of the
Chippewas was inherited through the father, domestic life was
organized through the bloodline of the mother. The important
events of everyday life were controlled by hunting bands made
up of matrilineal family units who lived next door to each other
in individual wigwams belonging to the wife. When the son of
an Iroquois family married, he left his own mother, sisters, and
cousins to join his wife's household. If the couple could not work
out a successful union, it was up to the wife to initiate divorce
by setting her husband's belongings outside the door of their
house. Muscogulge husbands were not themselves members of
their wives' clans, but their children were, and while husbands
might leave or be sent away, the children remained and were
educated and disciplined by the mother's brother or another
male relative.

Increasingly frequent intrusive and brutal contacts with
European explorers and settlers forced alteration in the everyday family lives of Amerindians to meet the new situations. By
the time the Muscogulge peoples—who were among the first to
greet de Soto when he arrived in the southeastern part of the
continent in the sixteenth century—had been renamed Creeks
and Seminoles by the English in the early eighteenth century,
their way of life had diverged far from its original settled agricultural patterns. They had, in fact, become professional hunters, closely tied to the international fur market. On the other
hand, at the end of the century, the Mississauga tribes in the
Great Lakes region learned through hard experience that they
could only survive the European tidal wave by transforming

their economy, and therefore their cultural patterns, from hunting and gathering to herding and farming.

The newcomers were not even aware of the deepest ways in which they influenced Amerindian life. By the time the Pilgrims landed in New England in 1620, the technology of the resident Algonkian tribes had already begun to be displaced by European trade goods, and the issue was far more serious than a taste for a few new consumer items like beads, bells, rings, and mirrors. Goods that had once been manufactured within the domestic economy of the village were replaced by imports that served the same purpose but were made of materials considered more desirable. For example, brass and iron kettles were deemed preferable to vessels of soapstone or birch-bark, and glass bottles were selected over gourds and wooden bowls. Iron-edged tools and guns were clearly superior to flint axes, spears, and arrow points; while fashion dictated the replacement of dressed rawhide and fur clothing with woven textiles. While such substitutions were cultural adaptations rather than changes, the loss of the productive economic function of the family within the tribe struck a decisive blow at Amerindian domestic life.

The radical differences between Native American definitions of family and those of European colonials played a large part in the settlers' opinion that Indians were "savage" and "uncivilized." Since cultural relativism as a mode of thinking played virtually no part in the eighteenth-century mentality, neither side was able to recognize underlying similarities even when they existed. William Penn, for example, could not see (although we may) how closely the native custom among the Delaware Indians of refusing young men the right to marry "[until they had] given some proofs of their Manhood by a good return of Skins" paralleled the insistence by Western society that marriage had to be delayed until one could support a wife. Native Americans relied principally on oral traditions of religion and myth, and on ritual performance of rites and ceremonies as the underpinning of their government. In a way, they lived within a system that was just the opposite of Europeans, downplaying the status of wealth, birth, and gender; rewarding individuals who were, at once, independent yet loyal to the tribe. These basic values of Indian society, when combined with power sharing between men and women, permissive methods of child-rearing, and a legal process that did not "rationalize" nor write down its laws and decisions, created the impression among Europeans that Indians had no social controls, rules, or regulations at all. The very word "Indian," used as a verb, suggested terrifying anarchy: "Now, is it not . . . an Horrible Thing, for so many English . . . to Indianize [by adopting] the Indian Vices of Lying, and Idleness, and Sorcery, and a notorious want of all Family-Discipline . . . ," wrote Cotton Mather in *Things for a Distress'd People to Think upon,* at the dawn of the eighteenth century.

It was possible for some colonists to discern elements of nobility in Amerindians and to regard their savagery or lack of civilization as merely a function of their failure to be converted to Christianity. As early as 1700, on the other hand, blacks were found to be—as Thomas Jefferson later expressed it—"inferior to whites in the endowments both of body and mind, [which] inferiority is not merely the effect of their condition of life (slavery)." Added to this growing racial rationale for the justification of slavery was a lively perception of the danger posed to white society by a large population of slaves joined by strong family ties and kinship networks within their own communities. Although white colonists failed to suppress the complex, supportive patterns of domestic and personal relationships that flourished among blacks during the eighteenth century, the twin evils of theoretical racism and actual slavery tainted much of the process of family formation among African-Americans.

Attempts to prevent the transmission of African patterns of culture to the New World derived initially from fears of shipboard uprisings such as the one that took place on the *Ferrar Galley* when "[three hundred] Negroes of one Town Language" mutinied three times between Africa and Jamaica, killing the captain in the process. It was considered worth the slavers' while to wait four months or more, enduring the terrible conditions of the African shore, to assemble a cargo from different places since, as one mariner explained in his travel report: "[We choose the Negroes] from severall parts of ye Country, of different Languages; so that they find they cannot act joyntly, when they are not in a Capacity of Consulting on an other, and this they can not doe, in so far as they understand not one another." These tactics frequently failed, as the runaway slave ads in the *Virginia Gazette* repeatedly testified. In 1770, for example, within one month of his sale to an owner in Amherst County, Virginia, the slave Charles ran away to join three other African men who had arrived with him on the slave ship *Yanimarew,* but had been separated from him and sent to Richmond. This must have required a fair amount of preplanning, and Charles's master reported that "it is imagined that [he was] seen some time ago (along with three others of the same cargo) on Chickahominy, and it is supposed they are still lurking about the skirts of that swamp."

In their effort to keep blacks from communicating with each other, white slavers showed an understanding of divide-and-conquer, but an ignorance of the grammar of culture underlying much of the diversity of specific African tribes and nations. While there were some eleven hundred languages spoken in the belt of the continent from which most of the captives were taken, many were quite similar, differing in vocabulary but sharing grammatical systems. In addition, arriving slaves were already often bilingual or multilingual because of the fragmentation of language in their own homelands, and there was widespread use of Wolof or Mandingo, which were the *lingua francas* in many parts of West Africa. Finally, on the Guinea Coast, pidgen (trading language) based on English "navy talk" is thought to have been available to those who passed through, allowing mutual intelligibility far greater than their European captors would have suspected.

In general, our knowledge and understanding of the development of African-American life in the eighteenth century is hampered by the white observers and recordkeepers who either lacked interest in the everyday life of their slaves (except insofar as it affected their ability to work) or whose own cultural blinders caused them to misinterpret what they saw. Still, even through the veil of indifference, self-interest, and ethnocentricity, we can discern black determination to create unique domestic patterns that drew from elements of the European culture of their enslavers as well as from similarities among their varied African backgrounds. We must not forget, however, that their lives were also significantly shaped by the cruelties, vagaries, and arbitrary nature of both the individual slaveholder and the general laws governing slavery.

The grammar of African culture provided a surprising number of similar patterns of family life among blacks who, by the eighteenth century, not only lived under a wide variety of conditions but whose relationship to their roots diverged sharply from one another. There continued to be immigrants newly arrived direct from Africa, or those who had been briefly "seasoned" by a stay in Jamaica or the Indies; there were more and more Creoles, blacks born in colonial America with an African descent that was generations removed from their original roots; and there were those first-generation Africans who were "Creolized," adapted or assimilated to New World life by years or decades of residence among native African-Americans.

Continuities were often subtle and inexplicable, such as those found in the small community of Parting Ways, just outside of Plymouth, Massachusetts. Known to contemporaries as New Guinea, the ninety-four-acre plot contained four closely huddled, tiny houses, scarcely more than shacks, apparently without hearths or fireplaces. They were home to four families of black Americans, headed by former slaves who had fought for their country during the Revolution and been rewarded with their freedom and this stony, unproductive land on which they might live and try to support themselves by farming. That they were unsuccessful is indicated by their applications in 1818 and again in 1820 for hardship pensions available to veterans of the Revolution. All four of the men bore names of African or slave derivation: Cato, Prince, Plato, and Quamany. Their surnames and the known first names of their wives and children were all European. Long abandoned, the sites were a part of an archaeological dig undertaken to amass information for the celebration of the bicentennial of the Declaration of Independence. The researchers expected, of course, signs of poverty, and they thought in terms of assimilation, particularly since a photograph of the last surviving house on the site showed the typical wooden face and double-sash windows of a New England cottage. What they found, unexpectedly, were such Africanisms as redware jars of West Indian or African origin, usually used to store tamarind, a West African fruit; building dimensions, organization, and construction that were far more akin to those of West Africa than of the surrounding cottages of colonial New Englanders; and even fragments of bone that bore witness to African diet and cookery.

Many basic family patterns of African life were apt to be directly attacked or contradicted by white owners or by the conditions of slavery itself. Most important for family formation was the ability to create stable marriages, whether in the African or European mode. On the one hand, the Christian morality of white Americans would seem to have argued for European marriage rites, and it is known that in New England such marriages were celebrated by African-Americans as early as the 1650s. Yet the African custom of polygyny (multiple wives for one man) and the fact that it was sometimes difficult to ascertain whether an African immigrant had, in fact, already been married before his or her capture and transportation led to an easing of sexual codes and matrimonial practices as they applied to blacks in the New World, although Yankee clergymen tried desperately to prevent such sinful behavior. In other colonies, the concern was more that slave marriage might be a "desecration of the Holy Rites," as one New York Anglican minister worried when his literate slave "got the trick of marrying slaves with the office in the Common Prayer Book."

In the South, throughout the century, there was acceptance, if not actual encouragement, of the use of African marriage ceremonies. One North Carolinian, in the first half of the century, described the rite in a somewhat amused and condescending way: "Their Marriages are generally performed amongst themselves, there being very little ceremony used upon that Head; for the Man makes the Woman a Present, such as a *Brass Ring* or some other Toy, which she accepts of, becomes his wife; but if ever they part from each other, which frequently hap-

pens, upon any little Disgust, she returns his Present. These
kinds of Contracts no longer binding them, then the Woman
keeps the Pledge given her. . . ."

It is not surprising that there was reluctance on the part of
African-Americans to make lifelong commitments when they
had no control over their ability to remain together. While
white owners, like Zephaniah Kingsley, a Florida planter, insisted that they "never interfered in [slave] connubial or domestic affairs, but let them regulate those after their own manner,"
slavery itself created the most intense interference, of course.
Black couples were separated for a multitude of reasons that
made sense only to the owners: as part of an inheritance settlement; to rationalize the business development of a distant,
newly purchased quarter; to pay off debts; or just to cash in on
the capital investment of a slave with top market value. Sometimes separation of a man and his wife was effected to punish
the one or the other, commonly when they lived on neighboring plantations and persisted in visiting each other without
permission. Many owners who did not actually follow through
threatened to split husbands and wives as a way of exacting
obedience.

Although slave masters frequently expressed sorrow at having to break up families, they also expressed amazement that,
as Edward Shippen of Lancaster, Pennsylvania, put it, "blacks
have natural affections as well as we have," and the Boston
Evening Post, in 1746, headlined it "A very surprizing Tragedy" when a black couple carried out a suicide pact on hearing
that the woman was to be sold "into the Country." Most seemed
to take an attitude like that of Charles Ball's master when he
turned down the slave's request for travel time to visit his wife
and children on a nearby plantation before he was sold hundreds of miles away. It was a waste of time, the master decided,
since "[Ball] would be able to get another wife in Georgia."

More perceptive masters understood more clearly the fear-
some nature of the separation of slave families. When Thomas
Jefferson decided to make an example of his slave, Cary, who
had deliberately injured another slave, he explained that if
"[Cary] was sold in any other quarter so distant as never more

to be heard of among us, it would be to the others as if he were put out of the way by death." Slaves saw the issue in exactly the same light, as Frederick Douglass, once a slave himself, expressed it many years later: "[He] was like a living man going into a tomb, who, with open eyes, sees himself buried out of sight and hearing of wife, children, and friends of kindred tie."

These "friends of kindred tie" were far more important across African cultures than Europeans could have possibly imagined. In the Old World, griot castes devoted themselves entirely to the perfection of memory skills to keep track of the significant dates, events, and members of enormous extended families. All of this richness and meaning in life were wiped away in the very instant of capture and transportation, but slowly and painfully over the course of generations in the New World, new kinship patterns were woven, unwittingly extended by the nature of slavery itself. Between 1740 and 1780, carefully constructed naming patterns began to establish special relationships that could be sustained through repeated household destruction and reformation. Whenever masters moved, or set up married children on new estates, or died, dividing their slaves among their heirs, new networks of extended slave families including aunts, nieces, nephews, and cousins developed across ever broader geographical boundaries. For many African-American families, memory and blood ties played the part in their lives that land and lineage fulfilled for the dynastic houses of Euro-Americans.

The idea of the dynastic family in its pure form, although it was rare and growing rarer in its original European setting, had a certain theoretical charm for some proprietors, recipients of large colonial land grants in the New World. The prospect of enormous tracts of unclaimed land that might be organized from scratch suggested that feudalism might be resurrected and given a fresh start. The eight wealthy noblemen who received title to all the land of the Carolinas from Charles II created a constitution based on just this concept. With the help of the famous philosopher John Locke, they devised an elaborate hierarchy of hereditary "seignors," "land-graves," "caciques," and "commoners," for those who actually settled in the colony, while the proprietors, who remained in England, retained control under such titles as "Lord Palatine" or "Lord High Chamberlain." In New York, settled first by the Dutch, investors in the Dutch West India Company tried to lure settlers by setting up their own version of the feudal system of "lords and manors," promising a huge "patroonship," or land grant, to anyone who would come with at least fifty workers and establish a working estate. Maryland implemented an early system of land grants in the form of medieval baronial manors.

The failure of these schemes to achieve their ideal societies only highlighted the fact that the New World was scarcely fertile soil on which to reestablish the moribund conventions and expectations of the institutional feudal family. There was no tradition of ties to the land, no ancient relationships of patronage and deference that had made family more indicative of dependency than of kinship. Even the great families of New York were unwilling to adopt the legal strictures of primogeniture and entail, and took pride in providing large inheritances for every one of their children rather than availing themselves of those rules necessary for the maintenance and perpetuation of fiefdoms. Stephanus Van Courtlandt, one of the most prominent of New York's patroons, stipulated in his will, written in 1700, that his oldest son, Johannes, was to receive a share that was no more than "equall in worth" to those of his brother and nine sisters. In recognition of his position as the oldest, however, Johannes was given first choice of the gristmills, sawmills, farms, and city houses, as well as of the millions of acres of real estate investment that made up his 9 percent share of his father's property.

A distinctively American pseudo-dynastic family type did, indeed, develop and flourish on the large plantations of the southern colonies, and while we may see, with the benefit of hindsight, an almost grotesque transmogrification of the English model, eighteenth-century slaveholders saw nothing false or inappropriate in their identification with the medieval/Christian ideal. Like their counterparts in the Old World, the underpinnings of these upstart dynasties were rural, dependent on the ownership of large tracts of land from which they derived both economic wealth and political power. Interwoven networks of kin, based on notions of lineage rather than personal affection, held offices at every level of government—sheriffs or vestrymen at the local level, justices of the peace at the county level, and assemblymen and burgesses at the colony level—to protect their wealth and their social control of the less well-connected yeomen and small planters around them.

Great landed southerners were, perhaps, the only colonists who continued to extend their concept of family to all who lived on their property, however far-flung their quarters from the home plantation, however temporarily or impersonally connected to the household. In the early part of the century, William Byrd II, a member of one of Virginia's most influential dynastic families, kept a diary that provides a rare glimpse into the mind of at least one of these planters. We must remember, however, that the very act of keeping such a diary probably made Byrd atypical; his lack of emotional involvement may have been merely part of his personal psychology. He was able, for example, to report in 1710, with great equanimity, that "I had my father's grave opened to see him [six years postmortem] but he was so wasted there was not anything to be distinguished. I ate fish for dinner." In the brief three-year period between 1709 and 1712, Byrd referred to over ninety members of his family, several of whom he could not even name, such as "the Frenchman" or "the old joiner." He made it quite clear that while his definition of family did not exclude his wife and children, it certainly did not accord them any particular distinction. Not only were they mentioned far less frequently than retainers, servants, and slaves, but they were also referred to in exactly the same terms, including concern for their illnesses and grief over their deaths.

It was the substitution of a family of slaves of a different race and from an alien culture for servants, however circumscribed by old obligations, that separated dynastic family structure in America from its Old World model. An uneasy recognition of the incongruity led many southerners to refer to the Bible for their precedent, where slaves were common, rather than to feudal Europe, where they were not. As William Byrd II explained in a letter to the Earl of Orrery in 1726: "I have a large family of my own. . . . Like one of the patriarchs, I have my flocks and my herds, my bond-men and bond-women. . . . I must take care to keep all my people to their duty, to set all the springs in motion, and to make everyone draw his equal share to carry the machine forward. . . ." It was not until one hundred years later, when the last vestiges of feudalism were disappearing from England and southern slavery was thoroughly institutionalized by generations of plantation masters with a work force entirely made up of Creole African-Americans, that an English visitor could note with some nostalgia: "There is an hereditary regard and often attachments [of the slaves to their owners] more like that formerly existing between lords and their retainers in the old feudal times of Europe. . . ." Eighteenth-century planters knew better as they worked unremittingly to protect themselves against poisonings, arson, and uprisings among their black slaves.

In many ways, after all, it was slavery that made it possible for a rural dynastic social and economic organization to remain viable in the increasingly fast-paced economy of an industrializing world. While English landlords rethought the family nature of their relationship with their tenants and laborers, cutting them off from ancient rights and evacuating them from the land to rationalize the business of agriculture and produce the wealth they needed to maintain social and political power, southern slave owners could make business decisions secure in the knowledge that they could reorganize and manipulate their workers to suit changing economic opportunities and needs. Although it required some tact, some blinking at infringement, and the frequent use of coercion and force, to say nothing of continual vigilance for sabotage and violence, the masters could, more or less, make decisions free of labor constraints.

After the Revolution, for example, many planters in the Chesapeake saw the need to move from a staple crop of tobacco to mixed farming in cattle raising and grain production. Since this change allowed use of the plow instead of the hoe, planters were able to reduce the number of their field hands. Some workers were transferred to nonagricultural tasks and others were hired out to neighbors as carpenters, millers, or the like, but since plow culture used male slaves predominantly, the successful plantation required a new mix in the work force, involving a higher proportion of men. This purely business decision had a devastating effect on the black family. Prime adult male slaves were retrained to use the plow, while women and children who were no longer needed were disposed of through sales to distant places where hoe culture was still practiced, or retrained for town work, particularly in home or shop service. Those planters who were reluctant to break up slave families faced the prospect of diminished profits.

Nothing could seem further removed from the dynastic plantation family of the colonial south than the vision and actuality of the domestic household in Puritan New England, although here, too, it had its grounding in the Bible. The earliest colonists in Massachusetts had no interest in perpetuating feudal ideas, but were intensely committed to returning to the purity of the Old Testament vision of family and community. Isolated men or women were seen to tear at a social fabric based on the sixth verse of Psalm 68: "God setteth the solitary in families." If God worked from this principle, surely New Englanders could do no less. An early law of Plymouth Plantation stated that "Whereas great inconvenience hath arisen by single persons in the Colony being for themselves and not betaking themselves to live in well-governed families, it is enacted by the Court that henceforth no single person be suffered to live of himself. . . ." In Massachusetts Bay, groups of unattached white male servants were organized into artificial family units, while stray "bachelors and maids" were placed under the discipline of local households, Connecticut ordered that "no young man that is neither married nor hath any servant . . . shall keep house by himself. . . ." John Littleale of Haverhill was found by the Massachusetts Court in 1672 to "lay in a house by himself contrary to the law of the country, whereby he is subject to much sin and iniquity, which ordinarily are the companions and consequences of a solitary life." He was ordered to get out of town, find himself some "orderly" family, accept that one that the selectmen found for him, or be placed in the house of correction.

Local communities in New England also kept a close eye on family units once established, continuing to support the older English system where governance, socialization, social welfare, and economic activities all fell within the purview of the domestic household. Town fathers felt free to interfere when a family seemed unable to manage on its own. In 1667, for example, in Springfield, Massachusetts, they had found it necessary to take James Osborne in hand after he had spent several years making bad deals and incurring debts he could not pay. It was reported at a town meeting that it was "mutually aggreed by the Inhabitants that . . . James Osborne doth prejudice him self and his family by disadvantagious bargaynes. It is . . . voted and concluded that none of the Inhabitants of this Town shall or will make any bargayne with the said J----O------ without the consent of two or three of the Select men that shall amount to above 10s[hillings] value." While this kind of intense oversight waned during the eighteenth century, the ideal continued to be sought and partially practiced in many newly "planted" or isolated rural settlements.

The Puritan church was organized by families as well, with the head of each domestic household held responsible for the moral and religious well-being of each member, along with his or her economic viability. Servants, therefore, received baptism into the Christian covenant as part of the master's family, and this applied to black slaves as well, as Cotton Mather, the quintessential New England Puritan, noted in 1706: "[Our black slaves are] of our own household . . . [and] more clearly related to us than many others are." Although the primacy of Puritan thought and control sank under the diverse pressures of population increase, new economic priorities, fragmented religious organizations, and political fractiousness that increasingly penetrated the fastness of New England throughout the eighteenth century, many of the early ideals and a fair number of seventeenth-century practices continued to dominate family life, particularly in the more rural areas of the region. The word "family" remained a term of household intimacy rather than blood relationship, while "kin" referred to those of near or distant blood or marriage ties on whom one could count for co-operation. Neighbors were often more important than "kin," although in the context of small isolated rural towns and villages the two were frequently the same.

New England farm households contained a fairly large number of people under one roof, perhaps as many as seven or eight at any given time, some blood relatives, some not. The basic labor force of the domestic economy most commonly included one's own children and those of neighbors, although the family could also traditionally contain one or another kind of servant, attached more or less permanently and due differing kinds of compensation. The nature of the servitude and the acceptance of nonblood household residents as "familiars" varied both over time through the eighteenth century and according to the rural, village, or urban setting of the household. In all times and places one could find apprentices, youngsters living in a family to learn the "art and mystery" of a craft or trade, from husbandry to silversmithing. At the beginning of the century, families in rural communities or villages regularly contained servants who received only the necessities, and were working to pay off debts or as punishment for crimes committed. One also found numbers of indentured servants who could look forward to a set of tools and a suit of clothing at the end of their terms, which were most often set at seven years. Both of these types of family laborers became less and less frequent during the century and were largely replaced by hired servants on yearly contract, who received not only the basic room and board, but additional compensation in the form of wages. Sometimes the cost of their upkeep was subtracted from their wages, sometimes not. Particularly where there were no children left in the household, or where there were no boys old enough, the "hired hand" became a family fixture, remaining year after year, growing old, dying, mourned, and buried within the domestic household of work, even if he had blood relatives in the vicinity. This became, along with the labor of one's own children, the most lasting, characteristic form of rural labor on small farms in New England, described as a still-existing phenomenon in an early twentieth-century poem by Robert Frost, "The Death of the Hired Man."

The unmarried female "retainer" was an even more ubiquitous and integral part of the New England family circle, since every farm household needed at least one woman to do jobs outside the male domain such as laundry, cleaning, and needlework. In general, the women received less than half the wages of the men. Hired male servants who were married were, as they were in England, in a somewhat anomalous position, since their wives and children were expected to live elsewhere and were not generally part of the family in which the servant himself was accepted. He stood as head of his own blood household, a marginal one at best, probably with few roots in the community; one of the many throughout New England who could be seen in April if he failed to negotiate a contract for the coming year, moving along the country road with his family, goods piled high on a cart, hoping to find work in another community to carry him through the next harvest.

Slaves, whether Amerindian or black, formed only a tiny part of the New England family scene—2 to 3 percent by the time of the Revolution—yet their place in those families and the manner of their lives is significant for an understanding of the vast gulf that lay between the cultural style and values of northern and southern states by the end of the eighteenth century. Their numbers would be truly insignificant if they had been spread out evenly across the population, but, in fact, they clustered in ways that made them a noticeable part of life in some areas of New England and allowed them contact with one another, while they were almost totally absent from the scene and isolated from each other in most other places. Concentrated in the Narragansett region of Rhode Island where large horse-raising plantations made gang labor profitable, along river systems, and in coastal urban centers, by the time of the Revolution they comprised up to 10 percent of the populations of Boston, Massachusetts and New London and Fairfield, Connecticut, and close to 20 percent of Newport, Rhode Island.

As far as Amerindians were concerned, outside of those who labored on whaling boats out of Nantucket, there were only a few indigenous native Americans left in New England by the eighteenth century, and they tended to live together—poor but free—in pockets out of the direct oversight of the Anglo-colonials. Early in the century, there had been a brisk business in Amerindian slaves imported from the Carolinas, but the "malicious, surly and revengeful" nature of these captives, along with "divers conspiracies, insurrections, rapes, thefts, and other execrable crimes" that they committed, forced at least three of the northern colonies to ban their import by 1715. For the rest of the century, enslaved Native Americans, particularly women and children, served as artisans and house servants in some of the towns: at the time of the Revolution, for example, one-third of all the Indians living in Rhode Island were boarding in white families, employed as servants.

Since wealth was not to be dragged from the stony soil in the harsh climate of the northern colonies, the question of large plantation dynasties arose only infrequently, and slaves made little sense as capital. Wealthy merchants frequently got rich trading in blacks as merchandise, but rarely by exploiting them as labor. New Englanders, attempting to provide for their heirs through business as southerners did through landholding, needed new financial instruments—testamentary trusts, charitable foundations, and holding companies—rather than easily destructible human beings who required constant upkeep in the form of food, clothes, and shelter. However, while slaves were of little use *en masse* to the New England merchant, a few were trained for specialized business purposes, and status was given a boost through a quaintly dressed black slave acting as coachman, footman, doorman, or butler. Blacks held by rural masters, artisans in town or country, or those of few pretentions who merely needed an extra pair of working hands around the place usually did the same work as grown children, white retainers, or hired help, and were similarly regarded as members of the family. For the most part, even where there were several blacks living in a neighborhood, there were never more than a very few in any single household. As a result, northern slaves lived lonely lives as enslaved members of white families rather than more sociable ones as part of whole families of slaves on southern plantations.

This difference seriously hindered the ability of northern

blacks to form the strong family ties and patterns that gave southern slaves a modicum of independent choice and control over their own destinies. On the other hand, it was more likely that individual blacks in the north were treated like human beings by their white owners and had at least some feelings of self-worth as members of their household families. Some, like Violet, who entered the Parson family when she was a small child, eventually even acquired a certain position of respect. She was described in patronizing fashion in a family memoir as "the autocrat of her family, and the presiding genius of her household . . . who called the boys by their familiar names, even after they had become important men . . . was indulged with all the spending money she wanted and was considered the best dressed member of the parsonage circle." Identification with the family could become so complete that one old slave, for example, left his valuable silver shoe and knee buckles to his master's children, bequeathing only his ordinary ones to a fellow slave. Those who came to feel themselves integral parts of their master's families must have taken a fair amount of satisfaction from the story of Samuel Gipson. Arriving in Connecticut as a slave, Gipson not only earned his freedom but became a successful merchant. He took on his old master's son as a clerk in his business, and when Gipson died in 1795 at the age of thirty-four, he left his entire estate to the fortunate young man.

Exceptions only prove the rule and there is no doubt that the indifference and injustice of slavery as a system left its indelible handprints on those blacks who were held in servitude in eighteenth-century New England. Many of the babies or young children bought as slaves were taken from grieving mothers whose masters did not wish to support an extra member of the family, and were often given away "like puppies or with a cash bonus." Slaves who presumed too much on a "family" relationship might find themselves threatened with separation, like the "young Fellow" whose master explained the decision to sell him: "His fault is, being born in the Family with me, he thinks I am not to use the same government with him as with one who wasn't, . . . and knowing my Disposition, that I cannot flog him, for the aforesaid Reason, he has at length got the upper hand of me. . . ." Some owners were so intimidated by their slaves that they arranged to have them taken away secretly before they could become violent, escape, or appeal to the community; but whatever this may indicate about the kind of power a slave could command, the fact is that when the deception was completed, the slave was gone, uprooted from home and family, suffering the same living death described by Frederick Douglass as the lot of southern slaves who were "sold down the river."

The best description of the violation of black family life that occurred in the north is found in a petition for freedom presented to the Massachusetts General Court by a group of slaves in 1774:

> . . . we are deprived of every thing that hath a tendency to make life more tolerable, the endearing ties of husband and wife we are strangers to for we are no longer man and wife than our masters or mistresses thinkes proper married or onmarried. Our children are also taken from us by force and sent maney miles from us wear we seldom or ever see them again there to be made slaves of for Life which sumtimes is vere short by Reson of Being dragged from their mothers Breest . . . how can a slave perform the duties of a husband to a wife or parent to his child How can the wife submit themselves to their husbands in all things How can the child obey thear husbands in all things. . . .

In their plea for freedom, these Massachusetts slaves presented another definition of "family" that neither relied on the ideal of the great southern planter's biblical dynasty nor on the model of domestic household expressed by the Puritan farmer. It was a definition that had begun to be articulated in the midseventeenth century in England when the *Oxford English Dictionary*, ultimate arbiter in the search for the meaning of words and their change through time, first dropped all reference to outsiders working within a household as part of the family, and included only "the group consisting of parents [and] their children whether living together or not." What this left was a core or nucleus: a father, mother, and their children, tied together by blood rather than by economic necessity and organization.

It was this so-called nuclear family that became the reality of most of America, and the wave of the future. It was not the nineteenth-century sentimental vision of cuddly babies, loving, selfless mothers, and proud, protective fathers, but a new ordering of personal relationships that read children and parents into an inseparable unit even when the children no longer lived at home, and read strangers out even when they passed their lives on the premises. By the end of the eighteenth century, it had become the common form of family life in every corner of the new nation, although pockets of New England farmers and southern planters hung on to their old ways into the nineteenth century and beyond.

The desire to remove unrelated household members from the bosom of the family came early in the Chesapeake, among the small planters of Maryland and Virginia, and had to do with feelings about race and class more than it did with wage labor. In fact, the workers they so assiduously excluded right from the start of the eighteenth century were not wage workers at all, but bound servants, black or white, who were legally attached to their households—either forever, in the case of black slaves, or for a long term of years, as in the case of white convict labor. Black slaves may well have fared worse than in most other colonies. Viewed through the racial prism of southern attitudes, they were isolated on small farms without the kind of support system that came from being part of a slave family on a plantation; yet they did not become a family slave in the manner of New England's single black servant within a household. As slaves became at once more skilled and more expensive during the eighteenth century, small farmers in the Upper South turned to a new kind of bound white labor, finding that they could more easily afford to buy convicts imported into the colonies under a statute of Parliament in 1717 "for the further preventing robbery, burglary, and other felonies, and for the more effectual transportation of felons. . . ." Through this law, which remained in effect until the Revolution, Maryland and Virginia absorbed most of the fifty thousand–plus convicts transported to the colonies, effectively "Draining [the mother country] of its offensive Rubbish, without taking away their lives," as the policy was described by a British pamphlet in 1731. Not only were such servants cheaper than slaves to begin with—only £11 for a seven-year contract—but they were more permanent than other indentured servants who had signed on voluntarily and were usually only committed for three to four years, while convicts were typically bound from seven to fourteen years.

On the other hand, even the least elegant, poorest colonial with enough capital to take on a servant at all was likely to look down on convict laborers. The vast majority of these unwilling immigrants were poor, unattached young men in their early twenties. Each had committed some fairly serious crime, often more than once, and had had no friend or family connection with enough influence to get the sentence commuted. Convict transports were apt to be untrained, at least in anything but criminal activity, or trained inappropriately for the needs of the masters who bought them: a small-holding, backcountry tobacco farmer had little call for a silversmith, a metal refiner, a rare-book–collecting barrister (he had "collected" a large number from the University Library at Cambridge), or the former cook to the Duke of Northumberland. Convicted felons were certainly seen as dangerous enough to keep away from one's wife and daughters, especially since, according to the *Maryland Gazette* in 1767, they were carriers of "the foulest Poluttions" and were likely to transmit all kinds of diseases, presumably venereal, through proximity to Maryland families.

Like slaves, convict laborers had little opportunity to establish stable families of their own. Since there were at least four men to every woman among those who were transported, even casual sex was difficult to come by, and marriage partners almost impossible. For the most part, bound laborers were permitted to marry only with the master's approval, which was rarely forthcoming, completing a family "catch-22" where convicts were not really part of a domestic household, yet were unable to form nuclear units of their own. The harsh nature of their treatment—they were seen to be even more exploitable than slaves, partly because they had been less expensive—and the restricted lives and opportunities available to them even after their period of servitude was over encouraged a life-style of gambling, alcoholism, and brawling. During the century, laws were enacted in both Maryland and Virginia that further restricted the convicts' access to civil rights and placed them in a position before the courts that was closer to that of slaves, although their own racism prevented them, in most cases, from seeking any kind of common cause with African-Americans.

Middle Colony farmers much preferred white labor to black, voluntary indentures to convicts, and free wage labor to any of the above; yet it was neither race nor class aversion that led to the firm establishment of the nuclear family as the basic pattern of domestic life in this region by the second half of the century. Rather, the difference was made by a complex combination of theoretical and cultural beliefs of Quakers and Germans, the changing nature of the German and Scots-Irish immigration over the course of the eighteenth century, and the development of a rationalized economy that found wage labor to be more profitable than bound labor.

Among New England Puritans, a shift to contract labor had often meant that these workers, along with any slaves, became members of the family circle. To the Quaker settlers of Pennsylvania and New Jersey, however, this kind of intimacy presented a danger. They believed that religious regeneration was manifested by an "Inner Light" aided by "holy conversation" between people who had already achieved the "Truth." Those who were not part of holy conversation not only suppressed the Light for themselves, but also tended to corrupt others, and should not be part of a household in which Quaker parents tried to protect their children from such "carnal talkers." Rich Quaker farmers, therefore, were apt to isolate their workers, slave or free, from the innermost circle of the hearth, and although the reason for exclusion was spiritual rather than social, the effects on the servants themselves were not dissimilar to those of the Chesapeake. Quakers made some use of slaves in their fields, houses, and shops until the predominance of wage labor was clearly established and scruples concerning the system of bondage caused the Meeting to put teeth into their abolitionist rhetoric.

German immigrants, within their own cultural frame of reference, had no background of contact with either Africans as a race or slavery as a system. Their distaste and unfamiliarity with black bondage was clearly stated in a protest issued by a newly arrived group of German Quakers, living in Germantown, Pennsylvania, in 1688: "We hear that the most part of such negers are brought hither against their will and consent, and that many of them are stolen. Now, though they are black, we cannot conceive there is more liberty to have them slaves, as it is to have other white ones. . . . And those who steal or rob men, and those who buy or purchase them, are they not all alike?" Acculturation to the New World led to a growing incidence of racial antipathy among Germans toward such "idle, slothful people" and for this reason as much as for their earlier philosophical stance they tended to eschew slaveholding in favor of the use of white indentured servants and tenant families.

The second reason for the early development of nuclear families in the Middle Colonies had to do with the changing shape of its immigrant population. Unlike New England, where immigration almost ceased during the eighteenth century, or the Chesapeake and Deep South, where most new arrivals came as forced labor, black or convict, the key feature of Middle Colony demographic life throughout the period was an abundant flow of non-English European settlers who eventually made up one-third to one-half of the total inhabitants. In the early decades of the eighteenth century, immigrants of many ethnic backgrounds—but primarily Germans and Scots-Irish—arrived as single young men or teenagers, younger sons who could not be provided for by their families at home, and who sought, through the indenture system, to establish independent lives for themselves in the New World. Pennsylvania was particularly attractive, since a servant who worked out his time was entitled to land as well as to the traditional small sum of cash and "two suits of cloathes" as "freedom dues."

At first, these single immigrant servants could be found in both the rural and urban setting, usually living with the master's family in a relationship that bore some resemblance to the familiar form of the domestic household in Europe. Parents in the Old Country or among German and Scots-Irish newcomers, if they were in a position to do so, arranged indentures with an eye to choosing masters from the region they had just left. It was felt that, in this way, the old family customs could be maintained and the culture passed along, together with the language and information necessary for establishment in the new homeland. In 1733, a visitor from Germany wrote home that "there are few houses in the City or Country where the people are at all well off that do not have one or two such Children." Where there were ethnic differences between servant and master, a German worker on an Anglo farm, for example, the underlying European grammar of culture might make the relationship more familiar than if the servant were black, but it still tended to hinder true inclusion of the outsider in the family circle.

Beginning in the 1730s, poor economic conditions in Germany and Ireland caused the migration of whole families rather than healthy young men looking to improve their lot. Called "redemptioners" because they usually sold themselves into servitude to redeem the loan for their passage, these families were generally poorer and less well connected than earlier immigrants had been. They arrived in small units: Most commonly families consisted of a young married couple with a small child or perhaps two; older couples who brought teenage children, sold separately to pay ship's passage for the whole family; or occasionally small numbers of adult siblings, hoping to save enough to send home for aged parents. During these same years, Pennsylvania ended the practice of distributing land to servants at the conclusion of their indentures, and the arrival of so many new workers caused a cyclical glut of labor on the market. The unfortunate latecomers were often moved in gangs by "soul drivers" to less settled parts of the colony where questions of ability or stamina were overridden by the consuming need to get the land cleared and planted.

By midcentury, the economic advantage of binding whole families of servants into a household was beginning to disappear in favor of hiring individuals as wage laborers, leaving immigrant families to shift for themselves, and creating what we might call cast-off nuclear families. Living separately in assigned cottages on large farms, by the end of the century these families were far from independent. Unlike tenants who merely rented land and house for a set fee, paid the taxes on it, and were free to pursue their interests, cottagers had no such control over their own lives. They received their house, a set amount of firewood, a small plot on which they could raise some of their own food, and the right "to keep a cow and run a pig in the lane" for a small sum written off against the labor they and their families provided the farmer. They could also expect to be able to "rent the use of a plow and horses in the spring for their own little patches, a wagon and team to haul their wood or, on moving day, their family goods." They were "promised wages as harvest hands," farm work by the day at other times of the year, and if they had a skill such as weaving, they were paid wages by the piece for the work they did. Their wives and children might earn extra money by helping with the harvest, by spinning, or by performing domestic services for the farmer's wife. The rates for all of this work were generally fixed by custom, as were deductions from wages for things like liquor when it was provided along with meals during work. Most importantly, the employer set the amount of work done: he had no obligation to use his "cottagers" for a guaranteed amount of time, and they were responsible for finding other jobs to tide themselves over when their services were not required. On the other hand, he could monopolize their time for low rates, leaving them no opportunity to plant their own plots or work their trades to their own advantage.

Some landowners, of course, continued to maintain old-style domestic households, sheltering within their walls and at their tables a domestic servant, an apprentice, a single laborer, and/ or a bound servant. The gulf between these workers and the farmer's own "flesh and blood" tended to be wider than it had been in the Old Country or the old days. They were regarded as "inmates" rather than intimates, and their room and board were not provided as part of a family exchange, but were charged at a commercial rate. In addition, their living spaces tended to be isolated from those of the "real" family, like "the west end of the house and garden," assigned to Greenwag and

Cuff, single farm workers on the property of Caleb Brinton in Chester County, Pennsylvania, in 1781. Frequently inmates were bedded down in barns or sheds, or even as boarders with the cottagers.

It is in the cities of eighteenth-century America that we find the greatest number of cast-off nuclear families, independent because they had been cut adrift by the changeover from term labor to wage labor rather than because they had made any conscious decision to create a home for wives and children. They occupied the lowest rungs of the economic ladder where there was no safety net in the form of a master who owed them any personal obligation. The change that had taken place in reading servants out of the domestic family, paying them a wage, and giving them the freedom to set up their own households, marry, and rear children of their own is documented in the pages of the diary of Elizabeth Drinker, wife of a wealthy Philadelphia Quaker. During the 1790s, several women who had worked for the family from eleven to twenty-one years before applied to Mrs. Drinker for help when they or their husbands became disabled, or fell on hard times and were unable to support their families. It is clear that these former servants evidently felt something of the old entitlement to membership in the Drinkers' family, but it is equally clear that the Drinkers felt no such reciprocal responsibility. Although Elizabeth treated Betty Burge, for example, as she would have done any beggar, giving her "some victuals and some money," she did not see that there was any further obligation, noting that ". . . I don't expect H[enry] D[rinker] will give her a good character [recommendation], he can't, tho' perhaps she may be recommended as a proper object of charity."

The lives of laboring families in the city were far more precarious than those of rural cottagers. They had to find their own housing and generate enough income or credit to cover their food, rent, fuel, and clothing even when they received no wages because they were laid off. Men, women, and children all worked. Children of the laboring poor often disappeared from the small core family, indentured away by the Guardians of the Poor, an eighteenth-century version of a public welfare agency, since there was no one at home to care for them. One of the vaunted advantages of nuclear families, that of privacy, was almost always denied to urban wage workers, who either took in boarders or rented space and became boarders themselves as a principal way of lowering their housing costs or acquiring a little cash. Shared housing did not, however, mean a blending of family units; there is a good bit of evidence that attempts were made to provide internal divisions within the house, and even, where possible, two separate hearths for heating and cooking. When two unrelated mariners and their families occupied the same house in Boston "under the same roof" from 1754 through 1755, one part of the house was known as "the said McCartys end of the house."

At the end of the century, the individual without a family and the couple without a home were still as unacceptable to colonial society as they had been in the early 1700s. They had become, however, an established part of a system in which families were no longer expected to number among their members all those who lived within their walls or provide housing for those who merely worked by the day in the woodworking shop or shipyard. Each of the major cities had to cope with great numbers of continually shifting, single, young people of few skills, fewer resources, and no family ties at all. Young men with jobs and mariners between voyages boarded with families in cramped back-alley tenements or in boardinghouses along the wharves. Single women, whose work was almost surely domestic, continued to live in the homes of their employers under family regulation as long as they held their jobs. Prostitutes were the principal exceptions, living on their own in the nooks and crannies of the city, from inns to stables to open alleyways.

Urban communities (rural areas as well, if they were past the frontier stage) began to come to grips with the idea that the private sector, as we would call it today, was not able to cope with the effects of unemployment and underemployment resulting from the changed institution of the family. They fell back on the old British model of the almshouse, or bettering house, as a refuge for the "perishing poor," in addition to the custom of outdoor relief whereby a cash-short family might be tided over with a judicious handout of flour or firewood. In the Old World, these institutions had been intended only for the benefit of local, worthy indigents, but in the larger, more anonymous world of the young Republic, it was necessary to provide social services, in the name of humanity, even to those who seemed clearly unworthy. So the clerk of the Philadelphia Almshouse grumbled about Ruth and Henry Kendall in the summer of 1789:

> [These are the] most Notorious Strolling Ramblers generally known from Boston to Baltimore. . . . They appear to have scarce any necessary Cloathing. But are very artful in appearance, frequently leaving their cloathes & other property at different places through the Country & though they may have Money, came here [the poorhouse] in such wretched plight & swarming with Vermin so as immediately to extort clothing. They are both lame & both subject to Fits, of which with their wretched plight extorts Commiseration and Charity.

He grumbled, but he took them in.

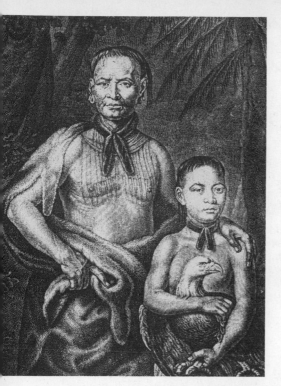

1.1 *Tomochachi and His Nephew*, painted in Carolina in 1734, illustrates the close relationship between a mother's relatives and her children in a matrilinear society. In many cases, this bond proved far more central to the child's life than contact with the father, whose presence in the household was often transitory (p. 22). *(Smithsonian Institution)*

1.2 This cartouche, from a testimonial certificate presented to a group of friendly Indians in 1770, portrays the way in which the surface or formal manifestation of cultural contact masked the different interpretations placed on these events by the participants (p. 23). *(Courtesy of the New-York Historical Society, New York City)*

1.3 A rare painting done around 1800 by an anonymous artist was discovered in South Carolina. As far as we can tell, the depiction of the event and its setting are accurate, right down to the plantation houses in the background and the musical instruments and clothing of the revelers. What we cannot understand is the true nature of the celebration taking place, although it is very likely a marriage ceremony (p. 25). (*Abby Aldrich Rockefeller Folk Art Center, Colonial Williamsburg, Virginia*)

1.4 An engraving of Phyllis Wheatley, frontispiece to her book, *Poems on Various Subjects, Religious and Moral*, published in London, 1773. As a very young black slave in a middle-class white family in Boston, Wheatley received an upbringing like that of the household daughters. She was alienated from both races by the combination of the color of her skin and the nature of her education (p. 38). (*Library Company of Philadelphia*)

2.1 In the modern era, the manipulation of consumer items is still considered to depend on cultural background, and women are still seen as the prime movers in the world of consumerism (pp. 50, 79–80). (*Tribune Media Services*)

2.2 Some examples of the variety of eighteenth-century housing as shown in nineteenth-century images (pp. 55–56). *(Dover Publications)*

B. Southern planter's house, Westmoreland, Virginia, built before 1760.

A. Massachusetts farmhouse, built in 1767.

C. Mill and house, Roxborough, Pennsylvania, built before 1695.

D. Dutch-built house, Brooklyn, New York, built in 1699.

E. A log cabin on the frontier in Ohio, built in 1800.

F. The Hancock family house in Boston, built in 1740.

G. Mount Vernon, home of George Washington, built over the years 1774–1787.

H. Middle-class housing in Letitia Court, Philadelphia, built in 1682.

A. This watercolor illustration of Broad and Wall Streets in New York in 1797 shows how many buildings, small as well as large, were essentially Georgian in design, although older homes, such as the urban Dutch example at the far right, continued to reflect the character of their origin. *(New York Public Library)*

B. The highly sophisticated architecture of Joseph Brant's last home in the late eighteenth century stands in bold contrast to the natural appearance of its surroundings. Brant, one of the most important Indian leaders during the Revolution, chose to adopt many English ways. *(William L. Clements Library)*

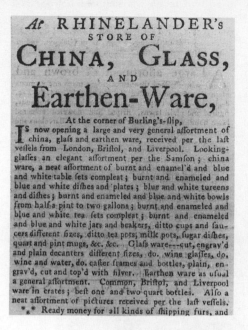

At RHINELANDER's
STORE OF
CHINA, GLASS,
AND
Earthen-Ware,

At the corner of Burling's-flip,

IS now opening a large and very general affortment of china, glafs and earthen ware, received per the laft veffels from London, Briftol, and Liverpool. Looking-glaffes an elegant affortment per the Samfon; china ware, a neat affortment of burnt and enamel'd and blue and white table fets compleat; burnt and enameled and blue and white difhes and plates; blue and white tureens and difhes; burnt and enameled and blue and white bowls from half a pint to two gallons; burnt and enameled and blue and white tea fets compleat; burnt and enameled and blue and white jars and beakers, ditto cups and faucers different fizes, ditto tea pots, milk pots, fugar difhes, quart and pint mugs, &c. &c. Glafs ware---cut, engrav'd and plain decanters different fizes, do. wine glaffes, do. wine and water, do. cafter frames and bottles, plain, engrav'd, cut and top'd with filver. Earthen ware as ufual a general affortment. Common, Briftol, and Liverpool ware in crates; beft one and two quart bottles. Alfo a neat affortment of pictures received per the laft veffels.

₊ Ready money for all kinds of fhipping furs, and

2.4 The wealth of consumer items that were becoming available to colonial Americans in a wide range of style and quality is apparent in this advertisement, which appeared in the *New York Gazette and Weekly Mercury* on May 23, 1774. It is but one of dozens of advertisements describing the variety of merchandise imported to meet growing demand. The presence of "crates" of goods suggests a wholesaling operation selling to small-town merchants for resale to country customers (pp. 65, 191–192). (*Courtesy of the New-York Historical Society, New York City*)

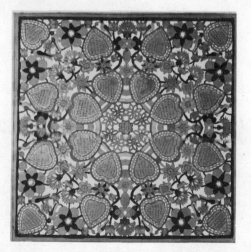

3.1 The importance of romantic love as a factor in the choice of a marriage partner can be illustrated not only by the literary expressions of well-educated elites, but in other forms appropriate to the culture of other colonials, like this cutwork love letter, produced in Lancaster County, Pennsylvania, in 1779 by Adam Dambach. Heart #15, for example, reads, "My heart which burns out of love's passion, would like to know what hers does" (pp. 75–77). (*Henry Francis du Pont Winterthur Museum*)

3.2 Changing perceptions of relationships within marriage. The first of these two illustrations, painted around 1725, presents two people who neither touch nor look at each other, while the second, dated about 1775, shows people whose physical closeness is, perhaps, emblematic of the importance of emotional factors in their relationship. The feeling of mutuality and equality is emphasized by the fact that Mrs. Purves, standing, appears of equal stature to her husband, while Johannes Schuyler's wife is portrayed well beneath him. In addition, the title of the earlier picture does not mention the wife's name, speaking to the loss of identity of married women (pp. 72, 77).

A. John Watson. *Captain and Mrs. Johannes Schuyler.* Oil on canvas, c. 1725. (*Courtesy of the New-York Historical Society, New York City*)

B. Henry Benbridge. *John Purves & Wife, Anne Prichard.* Oil on canvas, c. 1775. (*Henry Francis du Pont Winterthur Museum*)

3.3 The need for women to rally to the cause of the Revolution led to the occasional presentation of women as "heroes," capable of performing tasks beyond the usual domestic ones associated with "women of the army." It was not a role envisioned for upper- or middle-class women, and this woodcut was sometimes titled "Miss Fanny's Maid," although it appears here from a Boston broadside of 1770, labeled "A New Touch on the Times" (pp. 84–85). *(Courtesy of the New-York Historical Society, New York City)*

4.1 In 1795, James Peale presented *The Artist and His Family* in a way that summarized the middle-class model of the affectionate nuclear family. Not only are he and his wife on equal footing, standing shoulder to shoulder, but both are involved with the children, who express playfulness as well as loving relationships with their parents (pp. 104, 115). *(Pennsylvania Academy of the Fine Arts)*

4.2 While Charles Willson Peale painted only the dead child when he first worked on this picture in 1772, he added Rachel and the setting sometime around 1776. Changing the sense of the work from a study of death to a consideration of family emotions and relationships and renaming it *Rachel Weeping* is in harmony with the changing emphasis of the period (p. 109). *(Philadelphia Museum of Art)*

4.3 It is not only the slave but the young master himself who is objectified in this painting of *Charles Calvert and His Servant*, done by John Hesselius in 1761. As the child of an elite Southern family, Charles is shown practicing for his role as an adult, wearing clothes more like those of his father than like his own usual wardrobe, posing with his "property"—slave and rolling acres (p. 116). *(Baltimore Museum of Art)*

4.4 This watercolor on ivory of the Bordley brothers, Matthias and Thomas, was executed by Charles Willson Peale while the boys were studying in England at Eton in 1767. Their training in the classics, as signified by the Roman bust in the painting, was hardly the usual fare of "common" or even "middling" boys of the period, but the emphasis on book learning as a theoretical necessity for children of all ranks became one of the hallmarks of America's training of children (pp. 125–131). *(National Museum of American Art)*

2

I T TAKES a heap of livin' to make a house a home." This bit of popular twentieth-century American doggerel may not be very good poetry, but it expresses with admirable brevity the relationship between the material realities of everyday life and the ideas and sentiments that give them meaning. A house is a physical structure; a home is the vision of life and family that it embodies. During the eighteenth century, Americans molded and shaped their domestic space, within the technological limits of their times, not only to accommodate their daily habits, but also to fit the human values and relationships that were important to them.

These eighteenth-century Americans rarely discussed what they were doing, let alone what it meant. Few people bothered to record where they put the trash, how often and where they bathed, or where and with whom they made love. Nor did they explain even to themselves, perhaps, why it was important to live in a house that was "spacious and well-furnished with linen and silverplate" yet unimportant that three or four persons, including guests, slept in the same room. They assumed that those around them used similar objects, followed similar patterns, and attached the same meanings to them. It was only when travelers from another culture were surprised or confused by everyday habits that differed from their own that the mundane details of American living were recorded at all, and while their descriptions may have been factually correct, their value judgments were based on the traveler's own cultural ex-

49

pectations. A genteel Englishman from London had no way of
evaluating the degree of luxury, style, comfort, convenience, or
even cleanliness to be found in the rural home of an upstate
New York squire. Wealthy Anglo colonists traveling beyond the
borders of their own township, region, class, or ethnic group
failed to understand how others could tolerate homes so different from their own: Indians were "savage" because they slept
on skins and lay their fires directly on the floor; Germans were
"boorish" because they expended more effort on their barns
than their houses; southerners were "filthy" because they slept
together in a single room.

Most of these derogatory comments came, in fact, from those
who were raised in English ways, and middle- or upper-class
ways at that. For centuries, decent living as defined by English
culture had required that animal and human living spaces be
separate, that hearths and chimneys take the place of open fires
and roof vents, and that there be some division of the house into
rooms that served different purposes. By the beginning of the
eighteenth century, respectable English farmers, craftsmen,
and tradesmen had long participated in a domestic upheaval so
deep and far-reaching that historians refer to it as the "consumer revolution." Even common homes came to be filled with
objects of utility and display, in number, kind, and variety previously reserved only for the very rich and powerful. A house
became more than a shelter and a workshop: It became a family
center where privacy, comfort, and leisure were expected parts
of the daily routine.

It also became a measure of its owner's place in society.
Before the consumer revolution, chairs, for example, were rare
commodities, and only religious or secular rulers were entitled
to own or use them. Everyone else sat around on stools or
benches, leaned against the walls, or squatted on the floor. The
quickening pace of the English economy and the beginning of
the Industrial Revolution during the seventeenth century made
chairs more affordable and available, and they became less symbolic of power and more indicative of the economic and social
position of their owners. As more and more householders filled
their homes with chairs, mere possession was no longer suffi-

cient to establish superior status and the owner was judged by the cost of the materials and fancy decoration that went into his seating pieces, as well as by the number of specialized chairs and matched "setts" he could afford. As with chairs, so also with a host of other newly available items, from cooking utensils and tableware to luxury fabrics and looking glasses.

Eighteenth-century settlers from England carried an awareness of the new domestic standards with them to the colonies, and whether or not they had been involved in the consumer revolution at home, they generally hoped to become active participants in their new communities. Other European colonists, Africans, and Native Americans were only introduced to the English ideals of the "proper home" through association with their Anglo neighbors or masters. They often rejected these alien arrangements in favor of their own cultural traditions or were barred from involvement by economic insufficiency. By the end of the eighteenth century, however, the English model of culture had become the dominant pattern of the new nation. A vision of the ideal American home increasingly took a form based on domestic values rooted in the English housing and consumer revolutions of centuries before.

In actuality, of course, there was no typical eighteenth-century American home, just as there was no one kind of eighteenth-century American family. The domestic reality was a combination of physical necessity and cultural choice. First and foremost, the kind of house in which a family lived was dictated by its location in relation to the frontier. We tend to think of colonial frontier life as a seventeenth-century phenomenon, yet there were as many backcountry people at the time of the Revolution as there had been colonists in 1690. The first settlers in newly opened, isolated regions during the eighteenth century replicated the stages of housing typical of the previous century. Their immediate problem was to erect some kind of shelter, however temporary, and begin to clear ground for a first planting.

Many of their first houses were called "English wigwams," combining features of the rough, conical dugouts used by itinerant workers like goatherds, shepherds, and farm laborers in the

English countryside with those of the mobile shelters erected
by Amerindians like the Iroquois, MicMacs, and Delawares during the hunting season. Both had the advantage of quick construction and easily available material: forked poles, branches,
bark, turf, or animal skins. The English version also required a
handful of nails. Where feasible, eighteenth-century pioneers
created a larger, slightly more stable version of the "newcomer's wigwam" by digging into the ground to a depth of
about three feet and topping this foundation with the roof structure of a hut. The best-known of these so-called "caves" were
built in Philadelphia on the banks of the Delaware River in the
early 1680s by William Penn's first settlers. Well into the nineteenth century, the sod houses of pioneers in the Great Plains
reflected a continuing tradition of this sort.

With the exception of these cave huts, the common denominator of most impermanent houses was that they had no foundations; buildings rested directly on the ground, or were attached to posts driven into the ground. Where the crisis of total
wilderness was past, or in parts of the backcountry that were
somewhat less remote, these temporary homes bore a closer
resemblance to permanent structures, with squared walls,
roofs, chimneys, and window openings. While they were not
sturdy enough to last indefinitely—the wood next to, or directly
in, the ground was bound to rot out relatively quickly—these
second-stage houses nevertheless were capable of providing
settlers with shelter "for some years, till they find leisure and
ability to build better."

The economic status of the colonist and his ability to hire
professional workmen often determined the nature of his first
home. The merchant James Claypoole was rich enough to send
workmen ahead to his plantation in the New World. By the time
he himself arrived on the scene, they had already provided him
with a "slight house like a barn with one floore of two Chambers." Although the house had no chimney throughout the first
winter, there was a small cellar underneath for storing wine and
liquor, giving us, perhaps, some sense of his priorities. When the
prospective farmstead had neighbors already settled in the vicinity, the new owner was less pressured to provide shelter,

however rude, for himself and his family. In 1710, for example, Thomas Nairne described the steps to be taken in settling in South Carolina. It was necessary, he wrote, "after having cutt down a few Trees, to split Palisades or Clapboards and therewith make small Houses or Huts to shelter the slaves." The planter himself, his overseer, and any white indentured servants could board "without any Charges" with nearby planters, while his wife and children stayed with friends until "a suitable dwelling Place and Conveniences are provided, fit for them to live decently." On the other hand, in upstate New York where there were no near neighbors as late as the time of the Revolution, a passing English traveler noted that new settlers were "in such a hurry to get up their houses, that they pile up round trees one above another, notching them at the corners to hinder them from falling, saw out a door and windows, and bind a roof, covering it with bark instead of shingles, and plaistering up the joints between the trees with clay and straw."

The creation of impermanent houses was merely an expedient response to the necessities of frontier life; by the end of the seventeenth century New Englanders in settled regions were erecting farmhouses and town houses that they hoped would be "solid at the end of three hundred years." Permanent housing was slower to appear in the South, where climate and disease often cut life short, creating an unstable atmosphere in which families had difficulty surviving long enough to build for the future. By the middle of the eighteenth century, however, in the well-established settlements of the Chesapeake, colonists who could afford it were building to last. In the Delaware Valley, within two decades of its founding in 1681, Philadelphia boasted "several hundreds" of brick houses, and provided enough work in permanent construction to keep four brickmakers and ten bricklayers employed. As urban areas exploded, country towns were established; farmlands were taken up and filled in, and the stock of permanent housing continually increased.

The impermanent houses of the second stage often outlasted their use as dwelling space for the family of the original settler. Sometimes abandoned by their builders in rural areas, these

cottages were used by later arrivals until they, too, could get on
their feet. In 1727, John Mercer, an English merchant, arrived
in Marlborough, Virginia, and took advantage of one such abandoned hut. Within four years, he was able to provide himself
with a "fayre framed" house although it had impermanent
wooden chimneys, and sixteen years later he boasted of his "fine
brick mansion." Some settlers tore down their first shelters to
reuse the materials in something more substantial, but many
continued to use these simple structures as outbuildings—to
serve as barns or washhouses or, most frequently, as kitchens.
In New England, where buildings of unframed construction
sometimes had some sort of foundation, they were "built
around," becoming the core of the final dwelling, or were attached to the new house as a lean-to kitchen. Foresighted settlers, in fact, often placed their "small houses" with just such an
end in mind.

During the course of the eighteenth century, far from being
a matter of cultural choice, the continued use of cheap, impermanent, or ramshackle housing in settled areas became a sign
of poverty or dependency. Commercial farmers in the Middle
Colonies provided small, windowless, cellarless, wooden houses,
either free or on a sharecropping basis, for the cottagers who
worked their fields and whose wives and children labored for
them as spinners or household servants. Even on the wealthiest
showplace plantations in the South, slave housing (at least that
of field hands far from the main house, where it did not show)
continued to be built in impermanent ways: wooden houses
directly laid on the ground, with dirt floors and mud-covered
wooden chimneys connected to the house only by supports that
could be knocked away in the event of fire. Although the principal streets of colonial cities were increasingly lined with substantial brick houses, the poor continued to crowd into flimsy
wooden structures in narrow, filthy back alleys. Death came to
these "shambles" not only because of the crime and disease
occasioned by the overcrowding, but also because of fire and
the occasional sudden collapse of the buildings themselves. In
Philadelphia, long after they had been abandoned by the first
settlers, the caves along the Delaware continued to be occupied

by a long succession of the poorest, most unstable inhabitants of the city—sometimes used as taverns, sometimes as brothels. Although the city government made continual attempts to get rid of them, at least one was still known to exist as late as 1760.

The line between impermanent housing and that of a permanent nature was marked not only by the use of more substantial materials and construction techniques, but also by the appearance of elements of cultural choice. Whether small or large, simple or pretentious, eighteenth-century American houses varied tremendously in style from rural to urban and region to region according to the ethnic backgrounds of their builders, the available materials used, and the aesthetic fashion of the day. While seventeenth-century houses continued to dot the landscape, particularly in New England, their stylistic elements, such as overhanging second stories, tall gables and chimneys, and leaded casement windows gave way to newer visual effects, often through remodeling. Builders who immigrated to the New World carried in their heads a picture of the latest styles of the Continent, and in their hands the skills by which they could reproduce these fashions.

Our romantic assumption that every colonial was his own builder is challenged by the knowledge that just about every settled area included professional house-builders—carpenters, brickworkers, and stonemasons—whose training guaranteed that the roof would stay up and the walls withstand the blasts of wind and weather. Communities experiencing a population explosion, or those that had recently suffered a catastrophic fire (a common occurrence in early eighteenth-century towns where seventeenth-century buildings of wood and with wooden chimneys still stood), appealed for builders. In 1722, for example, a Boston newspaper reported that carpenters and bricklayers who were willing to travel to Charleston, South Carolina, would find "employment enough . . . by the reason of the want of such artificers there."

The continuing immigration of English-trained house-carpenters and "joyners" to all of the colonies and the desire of American elites to keep up with European fashion led to the widespread adoption of Georgian-style houses during the eighteenth century. The essence of this style is balance and decoration based on the classical models of ancient Greece and Rome. Central doors are flanked by an equal number of windows on each side, and by matching openings on the second story. They feature details like pillars or pilasters, and carved pediments over doors and windows. Another almost universal difference in the visual style of the eighteenth-century house lay in the changeover to wood-frame sash windows from the diamond-paned, lead-set casements of the earlier period. In 1705, a merchant from Newport, Rhode Island, visited Boston and noted that "sash windows are the newest Fashion." Ten years later, he had installed them in his own house, and by the 1730s they seem to have become the standard method of fenestration among those who could afford glass at all. As older houses were updated, the lead casements were replaced by wooden sashes, and by the time of the Revolution, advertisements for "Diamond Quarreys by the Crib" to repair old windows had completely disappeared from the newspapers.

Much of the regional variation in appearance of houses can be traced to the use of different building materials, for reasons both practical and cultural. The vast majority of houses throughout the colonies were built of wood, which was cheap and available everywhere; yet it was really only in New England that wood continued to be the universal choice of homeowners wealthy enough to have options. When brick acquired a high status value in the region after the Revolution, New England elites faced the front of their houses, but left the rest in traditional wood. Almost from the moment of settlement, Southerners who could afford it built in brick, as did the residents of urban centers like Philadelphia and New York, where the very real fear of fire was always uppermost in the corporate mind. In Charleston, South Carolina, and the suburbs of Philadelphia, the distinctive appearance of stucco laid over the brick was a side result of the additional warmth and weatherproofing it provided, while in eastern Pennsylvania it was availability that created the fieldstone tradition. Tiles for roofing, on the other hand, although they were very expensive and heavy to transport, represented a cultural choice in places like New

York, parts of Pennsylvania, and New Orleans where there were large numbers of settlers from European communities with a tile tradition. In other areas, slate roofs were the expensive alternative for wealthy urbanites, while wood shingles covered the homes of most Americans until the technological advances of the nineteenth century made tin roofing ubiquitous.

Although visitors to America in the early years of the republic would still have been intensely aware of a variety of architectural styles across the new nation, the ideology of the Revolution that emphasized an American connection to the republics of the ancient world had already begun to create a Federal "look" even more dependent on classical ideals than its Georgian antecedent had been. Anything else was old-fashioned and ugly. Thomas Jefferson spoke for stylistic pacesetters across the new nation in 1784, when he criticized the buildings of William and Mary College as "rude, misshapen piles, which, but that they have roofs, would be taken for brick kilns." By the end of the eighteenth century, architectural professionalism and the publication of architectural handbooks helped to spread these new, more "national" ideas that, in time, became the hallmark of Federal America. As new houses proliferated, older houses were either remodeled or torn down, and the image of the American house took on a less regional appearance.

For the most part, the appearance of the yard did little to enhance eighteenth-century American houses. Our mental picture of carefully tended flower beds, neat and gracious borders, graveled walks, and stately trees is a nostalgic dream based on a handful of wealthy models, most of them only from the very end of the century. Any land surrounding a house served a much more mundane purpose by providing space for small livestock such as chickens and pigs, for growing some table food (the effect of rotting cabbages in the border is aesthetic to neither eye nor nose); and for the disposal of trash. In newly settled areas, tree stumps two or three feet high rotted in the ground while corn grew right up to the doorstep to avoid wasting an inch of the laboriously cleared land. In urban areas, the small, open space usually contained, in addition to a mucky yard for animals, a large, square trash pit indiscriminately filled with broken pottery, seashells, glass, vegetable trimmings, and human waste. The attraction for vermin and flies can hardly be overestimated. In low-lying places like the Chesapeake, Long Island, or the crowded waterfront of Philadelphia, the high water table meant that the waste from these pits and the "necessaries" (outdoor toilets, which were the primary facility found in household yards) seeped into drinking wells located nearby, causing water pollution, which led to frequent intestinal complaint, disease, and death.

While a few wealthy householders who adopted the Georgian style in architecture also created formal, balanced gardens in imitation of European models, they kept touch with the practical nature of the yard. A visitor to Maryland late in the eighteenth century waxed highly enthusiastic over "Mr. Pratts garden" which "excelled all that I ever saw for beauty and elegance." After describing its almost obsessive division into alleys and walkways and borders, Lewis Beebe explained the way in which "the border of every square is decorated with pinks and a thousand other flowers [within which] is planted . . . beans, pease, cabbage, onions, Betes, carrots, Parsnips, Lettuce, Radishes, Strawberries, cucumbers, Potatoes, and many other articles. . . ." Strange though it may seem to our sensibilities, the trash from such households continued to be dumped out the door, thrown against the fence, or even strewn across the yard.

The organization of a house for everyday living rests, in the end, less on the style of its exterior than on the substance of its interior arrangements. The house types of both the rural North and South had developed out of the options available from English patterns at the time the settlers emigrated, but local builders responded to different conditions of life in the two environments by creating plans that clearly distinguished the everyday lives of their inhabitants. When the realities of family and economic life in the regions diverged during the eighteenth century, the changes were mirrored in the common housing of their people.

As eighteenth-century New England farmhouses were enlarged from the single-room dwelling of first settlement, they were built to provide for a household which, though large, contained no real outsiders. While the original "hall," with its great fireplace, remained the general gathering spot for sitting, eating, and, occasionally, sleeping, it shared a central chimney with a "parlor" or "chamber" where the farmer and his wife, and perhaps the newest baby, slept. This new room doubled as more formal space, where outsiders were entertained: If visitors stayed for a meal, it was taken here, in which case mere eating was elevated to the status of dining. A small entryway or lobby provided access to parlor and hall, as well as a staircase to the room or rooms above, where most of the family slept and which served as storage space for household goods and even occasional crops. What was unique about the New England farmhouse was the development of a full-blown "kyttchin" out of traditional, unheated storage space present in English hall/parlor houses. While originally a shed off the back of the hall, by the eighteenth century the "lean-to" extended across the whole back of the house and was actually incorporated into its basic framework. One end was frequently partitioned off for the storage of provisions and utensils, and the other end turned into a small chamber for the ill, the elderly, or women confined to childbed who might require attention. The central portion, however, acquired its own hearth and became the single location for food cooking and processing, moving such activities entirely out of the hall. An underground cellar for cool storage, meat-salting, and dairying completed the innovations to the English model. By the second half of the century, the New England farmhouse had become the northern norm for "decent" country living. Anything less was substandard, as John Adams noted in 1767 when he visited a poor family in Braintree. The husband, wife, and five children occupied "one Chamber, which serves them for Kitchen, Cellar, dining Room, Parlour, and Bed Chamber.... There are the Conveniences and ornaments of a Life of Poverty. These the Comforts of the Poor. This is Want. This is Poverty." By the 1790s, as New Englanders "hived out" west across the northern territories, they carried their traditional house plans with them, creating a familiar type that has become the modern symbol of nostalgic old-time domesticity.

Southern families and farm life were established on a different basis from the very beginning, and their eighteenth-century houses developed traditional forms that were adapted to these particular patterns. Most southern farmers were a far cry from the great plantation owners and their homes were nothing like our modern national image, based as it is on something like Tara in *Gone With the Wind*. They were described by contemporaries as "meane and Little," referring both to impermanent building techniques and to the fact that perhaps as many as half of all southern whites and nearly all blacks continued to occupy one-room houses right through the 1700s. The little houses of common southern planters were even smaller than those of far poorer New England contemporaries, since they lacked the second story usual in New England "hall" houses. In 1733, William Byrd commented on the "rudeness and remoteness" of the immediate backcountry. He felt "quite out of Christendom" and noted that the local farmers admired the house "of a few rooms" that Byrd had had built for the manager of his estates there "as much as if it had been the Grand Visier's tent in the Turkish army." Nor was Byrd, admittedly something of a snob, prepared to accept the hospitality of his neighbors. He preferred sleeping out of doors to sharing a room where the family "all pigged loveyngly together."

Since southern servants were not part of this "loving" domestic scene, the final form of the multiroom southern farm was a physical manifestation of this cultural reality. Some houses retained a cross passage common to one type of older English plan, where the hall lay on one side and a room for storage and farm processing, known as a "downside" kitchen, lay on the other. More and more, however, the passage in the southern house served to separate the family who used the hall for a sitting room from the servants who worked in the processing room and slept above it in a separate loft. Eventually the segregation was quite complete. The Chesapeake farmer eliminated the passage entirely, and provided detached buildings for the "drudgeries" of cooking, washing, smoking, dairying, soap boiling, and all the other heavy domestic chores of preindustrial farm life. He also provided separate "quarters" for the laborers who, under the supervision of his wife, performed these tasks. As newly settled southern, backcountry regions adopted the economic patterns of the Chesapeake, they accepted its domestic arrangements as well.

In the Middle Colonies—New York, New Jersey, and Pennsylvania—the diversity of population, family structure, and farming practice prevented the development of any single, clearly defined "machine" for daily living. Even where immigrants retained something of their Old World common culture, such as the very small number of the thousands of German immigrants to Pennsylvania who consciously chose to isolate themselves, they did not re-create the *hofs* (barn/house complexes built around a courtyard) typical of their places of origin. The true distinctiveness of their homes was often a matter of decoration and style, rather than a radically different organization of space.

It was in the many small towns of eastern Pennsylvania, as well as among middle- and upper-class families of more urban areas and rural gentry throughout the colonies, that the Georgian home came to be the standard by the 1760s. This European import was more than the ideal of exterior balance and classical decoration we have already described; it embodied an organization of interior space as well. A broad hall ran all the way through the center of the house with two rooms opening out on each side. A staircase led directly to an upstairs hall, also flanked by four rooms. Work spaces and servants' quarters could be attached to the back in urban areas, or located in separate dependencies on country estates. They could even be stuffed into the main body of the house—kitchen in the cellar, servants in the third-floor garrets, for example—without disturbing the basic symmetry of the arrangement. So perfectly was the Georgian plan adapted to the middle-class families who formed the fastest-growing segment of the American population by the end of the eighteenth century that, in one form or another, it has continued to symbolize the American home right through the twentieth century.

Initially, of course, it was the Georgian's new and fashionable "look" that attracted the rich, the near rich, and the merely aspiring. For country dwellers wealthy and sophisticated enough to have transcended the status of farmer and entered the colonial equivalent of English gentry, a new, stylish Georgian house carefully set on a rise or by a river where it could be seen and admired by neighbors and passersby made a powerful statement of the owner's "arrival." It was no accident that led Robert Carter of Virginia to locate his huge mansion on a "high spot of Ground" where its forty-foot facade could be seen "at the Distance of six Miles," as his admiring new employee, Philip Fithian, recorded in 1773. Earlier Georgian houses, like James Logan's mansion, Stenton, built near Philadelphia in 1724, betrayed the status-seeking nature of their style by keeping the balanced look only on the front, while punctuating the back of the house with windows and doors wherever they were useful, regardless of symmetry. Mansion houses like Carter's, built beside rivers where both front and back were visible to the public, were Georgian in design on both sides. For town and city residents, use of the new style communicated a similar message to an even larger audience.

The quick and long-lasting popularity of the interior Georgian house plan was due to the way that it fitted in with developing notions of specialization of the tasks and people within households. As we have seen, even ordinary rural houses were being modified to these ends. Although many farm families still cooked in the dining area, slept in the parlor or cooking area, and stored farm implements and surplus crops almost anywhere, the trend was clearly in the direction of separating spaces for special tasks and daily routines. Georgian houses, with their formal arrangement of front rooms around a central hall and back spaces appended or detached that were, in a sense, not part of the plan at all, clearly separated "working" from "living," and "living" into neat compartments. As the century wore on, plans began to specify a function for each of these spaces: parlor or sitting room, dining room, office or study, bedchamber or back parlor. The priorities involved in determining which household activities required segregation differed radically from our own. There is little question that if we could have only one private room in our houses, it would be a bathroom or, at least, a water closet. Yet, while many colonial Americans used indoor facilities rather than resorting to the outdoor necessary—as indicated by the increasing frequency of "wash basins, pitchers, chamber pots and close stools" on lists of household furnishings—they were content to locate these intimate conveniences in bedchambers which they frequently shared with others.

The most important room in the Georgian house, in terms of reflecting the changing concepts of everyday life among middle- and upper-class Americans of the eighteenth century, was the central hall. It not only maintained the segregation of function within the household by allowing access to each room without having to go through another, it performed the increasingly important task of preserving family privacy from the outside world. Privacy itself was not a concept that had had much currency in the seventeenth-century world of communal living, nor was it a luxury afforded to the majority in the eighteenth. It was, however, implicit in the growing separation of household members as we have discussed it. The desire for solitary space is perhaps best expressed by Abigail Adams in a letter she wrote to John, in 1776, while staying at her aunt's house:

> I have possession of my Aunts chamber in which there is a very convenient pretty closet with a window . . . a number of Book Shelves [and] pretty little desk or cabinet . . . where I write all my Letters and keep my papers unmollested by anyone. I do not covet my Neighbours Goods, but . . . I always had a fancy for a closet with a window which I could more peculiarly call my own.

Just as important as personal solitude, however, was a growing emphasis throughout the century on the withdrawal of the family as a whole from the rest of the world. The old one-room house allowed outsiders access to every activity of the household. Ordinary houses set off work space from living space but allowed for few subtle distinctions among visitors. The Georgian hall, however, separated callers from all household activities until they could be directed to the appropriate room, depending on the nature of their business and their degree of relationship to the family. Female intimates might be allowed upstairs to the wife's chamber, social inferiors who had business affairs to settle with the master might be taken to the office, servants or menials could be directed around to the back, and those of equal social standing who were privy to household entertainments might attain the parlor or the dining room (or be politely turned away, when the family did not care to receive them). While few reacted as strongly as Mrs. Benjamin Harrison, who fainted when a local farmer appeared unannounced in her parlor, the hall helped to prevent this kind of unexpected confrontation.

Since the hall was the place where the family met the public, its size, grandeur, and furnishings all bespoke the social position of those who lived within. High ceilings, elaborately carved doorways to the inner rooms, and stairways to the upper regions where none might penetrate except by invitation—all at once informed the visitor of the status of the family and fixed his or her own position in the social hierarchy. The slow but steady increase in the use of Georgian house plans meant that by the 1790s even those of modest means and few pretensions had adopted the ideals of household organization and family privacy that were formerly the standard only among the elite.

It took far less than a century for the consumer revolution, represented by the furnishings and accessories of everyday household life, to penetrate and change the patterns and expectations of even the very poorest and most rustic American. One need not be able to afford a Georgian house to indulge in a few porcelain plates, a teapot, or a mirror. One might live in the most impermanent of frontier huts, yet sit on a chair and sleep in a bedstead. After the middle of the century, the ownership of at least some of these objects had become almost universal: a necessity rather than a luxury. In 1700, the best-furnished house—already hall/parlor in form—in a wealthy farming county just outside Philadelphia contained, in full: a table, two forms (benches), a chest, four stools, five pewter dishes, a pewter pot, four brass kettles, a tankard, an iron pot with hooks, and a set of fire irons (a real rarity) in the hall; and two beds and bedsteads (another rarity), three chests, and two "spin" wheels in the parlor. The average householder in the same community boasted only two flock beds and bedding without bedsteads, four brass pots, and a table. Many, not considered poor, had even less. Outside the more settled, rural parts of New England and the small but thriving towns and cities across the colonies, the lack of chairs and bedsteads indicates that people well above subsistence level still squatted, leaned, and slept on the floor, ate with their fingers from a common plate, and drank from a common vessel.

Yet by 1750, what a change had taken place! Even at the very bottom of the economic ladder, such items as chairs, chests with drawers, forks, knives, plates, teapots, and an occasional clock or looking glass were regular accoutrements of life. There were regional curiosities like the chopping block found on Cape Cod that was made from the cervical vertebrae of a large whale. There were ethnic preferences like storage jugs of African design and West Indian manufacture found only in the homes of African-Americans. German settlers seem to have continued to store their household goods in top-loading chests and front-opening *schranks* or wardrobes long after other colonists had switched to chests of drawers.

Just as the rooms in houses became more specialized both with regard to how they were used and who used them, so, too, did the furniture with which they were filled. It was not enough to own a table; now there were dining tables, breakfast tables, game tables, tea tables, and sewing tables, as well as candlestands and washstands. There were water pitchers, wine decanters, teapots, coffeepots, and chocolate pots. There were forks and knives, as well as spoons—enough for each person at the table to have his or her own set of utensils. Separate sleeping rooms implied individual beds and personal bedding, at least enough to segregate adults from children, masters from servants.

Many of the rapidly proliferating items were directly related to increased physical comfort. Comfort as a concept, like privacy, existed only for the wealthy at the opening of the eighteenth century. By the end of the period, however, it was not only available to a broad segment of Americans, but it had also become one of the determinants dividing the "civilized" from the "savage." This, of course, tended to make an invidious value judgment on the lives of those with different cultural traditions who did not opt to participate in the consumer revolution, as well as on those who were too poor to do so. The first entry of a family into the world of goods was usually marked by an increase in bedding and bedsteads, providing improved warmth and comfort at the basic level of rest. Next came chairs, and it is in their changes that we can mark the increasing emphasis on comfort as a goal of American domesticity. The hard, wooden nature of the originals was mitigated by extra cushions and padding; later on, upholstered easy chairs became available to those who could afford them. "Necessary chairs" or "close-stools" were comfortable alternatives to chamber pots and outhouses. The first mention of a rocking chair appeared in 1742 when a Philadelphia chairmaker, Solomon Fussell, billed Thomas Robinson six shillings for "one nurse-chair with rockers." Although this new form did not become popular until the nineteenth century, it symbolized eighteenth-century American consumer goals of ease, comfort, and leisure.

Most of the increased ability to live an everyday life of tolerable comfort came about through the improvement and price reduction in personal consumer goods that had been around in the houses of the rich for centuries. The technological revolution that made possible our insistence on heat, light, and water as minimum necessities and turned the basic shelter of a house into the cozy domesticity of a home lay well ahead in the nineteenth century. Lighting never progressed beyond animal-derived oil or candles, and the very small number of oil dishes or candlesticks in household inventories suggests that most people went to bed when it got dark. Despite our myth of the colonial past, candles were rarely manufactured at home and they remained far too costly for the average American, particularly since they represented a continuing expense rather than a one-time purchase. In 1761, the president of Harvard College figured that a scholar who needed artificial illumination just five hours a day for his studies would need to spend the equivalent of eight dollars every month for "common" tallow candles, more than the initial outlay for a durable good like a chair or coverlet. Plumbing, of course, was almost unknown, and lugging water for household use from well, spring, creek, or urban pump might involve some six thousand miles of walking (with heavy buckets) over the course of a lifetime.

There is no doubt that the difficulty of obtaining sufficient water contributed to a rather low level of cleanliness, by our standards; the good eighteenth-century homemaker was cautioned to be "frugal" and "prudent," but not necessarily clean. Upper-class houses probably maintained a higher level of cleanliness because there were servants to carry the water and do the wash, and travelers from these homes continually complained about the great variety of vermin that lurked in the rarely washed bedclothes of other people's houses. In general, however, there was an almost fatalistic acceptance of the discomfort arising from sharing the domestic space with creatures that crept, crawled, and flew. Few technologies, even very simple ones, were developed to deal with the situation. Broom corn was not widely available until the 1790s, so houses were inadequately swept; bedevilment by ants and roaches was the unpleasant, even unhealthy result. To complete the invasion of the insect world, there were no window screens to protect against a New World plague of mosquitoes and flies. The most ingenious device proposed in the battle against these pests was to hang a wasp's nest from the ceiling, on the theory that, if left undisturbed, the wasps would attack the winged intruders of the house rather than its residents. Wealthy southern households occasionally made use of a gauze curtain arrangement called a "pavillion" that surrounded the bedstead and was useful in the war against mosquitoes if not against bedbugs and other vermin; but this was far too expensive for most colonial budgets.

There were times when cultural preferences triumphed over technological advances in consumer comfort. The standard means of heat in British homes was the open-hearth fireplace, and Anglo-American colonists carried it with them as both a physical and symbolic manifestation of home and family. Yet in the far colder winters of the new continent, it was peculiarly ill-adapted to serve its role. The English fireplace wasted fuel and was noticeably inefficient, lacking even the refinement of a rudimentary flue or damper. Most of its warmth went up the chimney and left all but the immediate vicinity cold and uninhabitable. A better technology was readily available: Settlers from Holland, Scandinavia, and Germany, where winters were cold and fuel scarce, had come to the New World from a background that made use of stoves rather than open hearths. Made of cast iron or sheet metal and decorated with tile or brick, these stoves offered efficient and frugal heating. They were noticed approvingly by Anglo travelers in the Middle Colonies throughout the eighteenth century, but they were rarely imitated. Benjamin Franklin decided that consumer resistance to the stove stemmed from the fact that there was "no sight of the fire which is in itself a pleasant thing," and designed his "Pennsylvania fireplaces" with doors that could be left open to provide a view of the dancing flames. Still, while a modest number of "Franklin Stoves" came into use in the vicinity of Philadelphia after 1760, it was decades before fireplaces were generally replaced by stoves for utilitarian purposes.

Up to a point, the ownership of consumer goods improved the quality of life. Beyond that point, it became an indicator of power, prestige, and position. True luxury by midcentury was no longer measured in the mere possession of consumer items, since they were available, at some level, to nearly everyone. Porcelain and its imitations were cheap enough to be purchased by those of very modest means and owned by those who were even poorer: the inhabitants of Parting Ways, the small community of nearly destitute, free black families outside of Plymouth, Massachusetts, possessed a considerable number of mismatched, out-of-date, fancy ceramics, no doubt obtained as gifts or "scavange" from wealthy white neighbors or employers.

On St. Simon's Island in Georgia, the lifestyle at Cannon's Point Plantation exemplified the way in which consumer goods divided people by class even more importantly than by race. Generations of planters and their white overseers lived in more spacious housing than did the black slaves in the quarters, but while both overseers and slaves used knives, forks, chairs, and other objects unthinkable early in the century, they were of local production or the mismatched assortments that signified secondhand goods. The planters' furniture, tableware, paintings, and fabrics, on the other hand, were purchased abroad in the "European taste" and in matching sets. People were expected to see and admire. In 1766, when John Adams was invited to the home of Nicholas Boylston, a wealthy Boston merchant, he confided to his diary that he "Went over the House to view the Furniture, which alone cost a thousand Pounds sterling. A Seat it is for a Noble man, a Prince. The Turkey Carpets, the painted Hangings [wallpaper], the Marble Tables, the rich Beds with crimson Damask Curtains and Counterpins, the beautiful Chimny Clock . . . are the most magnificent of any Thing I have ever seen."

The consumer revolution was not entirely bloodless. As early as 1732, Benjamin Franklin cautioned against the acquisition of luxury household goods as a way of "buying into" the rank of gentlemen and as a threat to the proper colonial virtues of simplicity, hard work, and frugality. Similar warnings concerning the loss of American simplicity sounded again and again throughout the century. One traveler at midcentury bemoaned his discovery that a common backwoodsman had "pretensions to fashion" in the ownership of a looking glass, when his reflection in a pail of water would have served as well. In the 1790s there was a particularly large outpouring of articles in the American press purporting to come from "honest farmers" condemning the vice of luxurious living that seemed to be sweeping the new nation. Most were actually written by wealthy gentlemen whose own homes were elaborately built and richly furnished, but whose political philosophies saw the self-sufficient farmer in the wilderness as a symbol of the superiority of American simplicity over European decadence.

Nostalgic longing for the plain life had virtually no effect on the growing American attachment to comfortable homes and consumer goods. By 1800, farmers or woodsmen—however remote, however impermanent their huts—would have considered it savage to eat from a common pot or squat on the floor.

Though early eighteenth-century immigrants had crossed the ocean with a couple of chests containing clothing, a few tools of their trades, and perhaps a knife or gun, it required the services of full Conestoga wagons to move their descendants, along with cook pots, bedding, clocks, teapots, and other necessities, across the prairies to the new frontier of the nineteenth century.

3

T HE SHORT pamphlet entitled *Some Fruits of Solitude,* written by William Penn, was hardly a runaway bestseller when it was first published in the 1690s. It promoted an ideal of family life that centered around an affectionate little circle of father, mother, and children, and went so far as to count the ability to live in such a household as one of the blessings of *not* being famous: "It is the *Advantage* little men have . . . they can be *private,* and have *leisure* for Family Comforts, which are the greatest Worldly Contents men can enjoy." According to Penn's vision of domestic bliss, the three L's of the traditional household—land, lineage, and labor—were joined, even superseded, by two other L's: love and learning. This newly conceived home revolved around both love and affection between husband and wife, and also love, emotional support, care, and education of children.

As one might imagine, the redefinition of an institution as fundamental to society as the family did not occur overnight. By the end of the eighteenth century, the affectionate nuclear family was still unfamiliar to most Americans, although *Some Fruits of Solitude* had been reprinted a dozen times, indicating that an emerging colonial middle class, continuously growing in size and influence, found its precepts congenial to the goal of achieving lives of economic and social security in the New World. Along with the political beliefs and structures set forth in the Constitution, presentation of the new ideal of domestic purpose and behavior for the young nation became a popular topic for social and literary moralists of the last decade of the century.

A couple—husband and wife—stood at the core of the nuclear family just as it had in older, more traditional households. The minimal duties of each spouse remained the same as well: Both were expected to engage in normal and exclusive sexual union and to cohabit peacefully for life. The husband was responsible for directing the economic affairs of the family, the wife for maintaining the basic condition of the house and care of the personal needs of its inhabitants. Although romantic love and sexual attraction were certainly not inventions of the eighteenth century, their emergence as a primary ingredient in the selection of a partner for life is one of the hallmarks of the development of the affectionate family. Dependent on the ability of young people to choose for themselves, the struggle was not easily won, particularly where the economic function of the family was paramount. Among landholding rural neighbors or wealthy merchant gentility, the marriage contract often bore many of the aspects of a twentieth-century corporate merger.

When upper- and middle-class fathers aggressively sought to augment the family fortune by engineering advantageous marriages for their daughters without regard for their wishes, the results could be tragic, as they were for Ann Shippen of Philadelphia. In 1781, her father, William Shippen III wrote to his son, justifying his refusal to allow the marriage of "Nancy," as he called her, to her chosen lover, Louis Otto, and his insistence on her acceptance of a loveless and eventually disastrous union with Colonel Henry Beekman Livingston. "[Nancy] loves ye first & only esteems the last. L——will consummate immediately. O——not these 2 years. L——has 12 or 15,000 hard [twelve to fifteen thousand pounds, English sterling, in cold cash]. O——has nothing now, but honorable expectations hereafter. A Bird in hand is worth 2 in a bush."

Other fathers allowed, if not choice, at least the exercise of a veto. Eliza Lucas, an eighteen-year-old heiress in South Carolina, responded spiritedly to her plantation-owning father in 1740 when he proposed two suitors from whom she might choose. As to the "old Gentleman," she wrote, "the riches of

Peru and Chili if he had them put together could not purchase a sufficient Esteem for him to make him my husband." She rejected the other candidate as well, although she knew him less well, hoping ". . . as I am yet but Eighteen [that] you will [put] aside the thoughts of my marrying these 2 or 3 years at least." Eliza's father evidently acquiesced, and four years later, the young heiress agreed more willingly to accept the equally eligible Charles Pinckney, a wealthy, well-connected widower over twenty years her senior.

As the century progressed, however, there were more and more parents who themselves had married for "love," and who were therefore more prepared to share, if not abdicate, the fateful decision to the new generation. John Adams bemoaned his absence from home when his daughter seemed about to choose a young man whom Adams regarded as "a reformed rake." "Take care how you dispose of your heart—I hoped to be at home and to have chosen a Partner for you." Then Adams appeared to remember that he was living in new times, and rephrased his thought: "Or at least to have given you some good Advise before you should choose."

At the other end of the social scale, we can see the ways in which looser bonds between family and household membership played a growing part in the personal choice of marriage partners. For servants in traditional households where economic production lay at the heart of family formation, the choice of who and when to marry was, technically, in the hands of the master, standing *in loco parentis* (in the place of a parent). His approval was required, usually in the form of a certificate, before any member of his "family" could be legally married by either civil contract or religious sacrament. With the increase of wage labor and the diminution of the domestic household, the responsibility for this decision theoretically devolved back on the birth father, and this was the case in the multitude of legal marriages that took place in American churches, chapels, and parlors during the course of the century. Yet, clearly, control was slipping away, as the high rates of premarital pregnancy attest. Many young people had moved far from their parents and contact with them had virtually ceased. They also ran away from work and master because, like Mary Musgrove, who "was remarkably fond of a sweetheart," they felt they had a fair chance of going it alone in the new colonial economic world of opportunity without relying on sponsors, parents, or master.

To be sure, there were ministers and congregations who struggled valiantly to maintain the institution of the family in all its authority. Beginning in 1789, the Reverend Nicholas Collin of Gloria Dei church in Philadelphia kept a record in his marriage register of what he called "Remarkable Occurrences Relative to Marriages and Especially Refusals." It was needed, he wrote in 1795, "[because of] the licentious manners which in this part of America . . . are evidently striking, and which in matrimonial affairs are so pernicious . . ." Most of his refusals resulted from the failure of both partners to provide either written permission from their fathers or freedom papers to prove that they had completed their apprenticeships, indentures, or, in the case of blacks, that they were not slaves. He kept a close watch on potential bigamists, particularly mariners like some "New England men, as well as other Americans [who] not seldom have 2 or more wives by getting married in diverse places," while protecting naive young men from "strumpets," "hussies," and "town drabs" who got them drunk in order to trap them into marriage. He was more willing to help out couples who had lived out of wedlock for some time, although he steadfastly refused to antedate certificates to make their children appear legitimate "tho' they begged very hard." Collin himself noted that he was swimming against the tide, that his ideas of propriety made no sense to young applicants in the 1790s who demanded to be married without the consent of their parents, "insisting on their capacity and right of choosing for themselves." One couple, he admitted, thought it "very odd" that he required such permission, they "having no idea of parental authority."

When couples chose for themselves, they were not necessarily as impetuous and unreflective as the Reverend Collin believed. They could, in fact, be as practical and hardheaded as any stern father arranging an old-fashioned marriage. When young men came to marry, they often followed the old adage that it was as easy to fall in love with a rich girl as a poor one and the regularity with which enterprising apprentices and farm laborers married "the boss's daughter" indicated one way of moving ahead on the road to the American dream.

While women had less control over marital choice, if for no other reason than that it was rarely up to them to do the asking, their thinking appears to have been equally practical. Black slave women in the earlier part of the century had some choice among partners since there were so many more men than women. They consistently chose Creole men who knew this strange, forbidding world and could, to some degree, maneuver within it, leaving large numbers of first-generation African men to the single life. Widows, although we might suppose them not insensible to masculine charms, appear to have been extremely reluctant to remarry if they were comfortably situated. In most colonies, they could handle their own finances, settle their husbands' estates, and conduct other business without facing the ridicule afforded spinsters, who were the only other women so empowered.

Among young people whose background, prospects, and attainments made them what we would call upper-middle or upper class, the rising interest in "romantic love" was closely connected to a growing market of literary production in poetry and novels. The theme of many of these works was that there was only one perfect partner for each person, and that mate, once found and captured, would eternally be without fault or blemish. While romance was expressly dissociated from sexuality, the plots stressed symptoms of a love that struck like a thunderbolt at first sight and overrode all thought of material considerations or other practical matters, which seems very much like a code for sexual attraction. It was this aspect of romantic attachment that young colonials constantly warned themselves and each other against, at least in public or semi-public expressions like letters and journals, but a short note from John Adams, written in 1762 to the young Abigail Smith, soon to become his wife, helps us glimpse the sexual universality

of love, even among proper Puritans and Calvinists in eighteenth-century Massachusetts. "Miss Adorable," he wrote,

> . . . I hereby order you to give [the bearer of this note] as many Kisses,
> and as many Hours of your Company after 9 O'Clock as he shall
> please to Demand and charge them to my Account: . . . I presume
> I have good right to draw upon you for the Kisses as I have given two
> or three Million at least, when one has been received, and of Conse-
> quence the Account between us is immensely in favour of yours,
>
> JOHN ADAMS.

Although direct literary evidence is rare, sexual tension and
broad humor clearly existed across the whole spectrum of colonial society. We have continual reminders by William Byrd of
the number of times he "rogered" his wife, in an unlikely number of places, often to restore "good humour." We have the
young working-class suitor who "begged" Reverend Collin to
perform the wedding ceremony, giving "as a strong reason for
his importunity, that his love was so violent that he might suffer
if he refrained from bedding with her that night." And we have
the brief entry in the log of the Philadelphia Almshouse in 1800,
noting that one of the men who worked the bakery oven had
gotten one of the inmates pregnant, and suggesting that ". . .
if he had heated one Oven only, it would have been better for
him." Given how seldom this kind of evidence appears, even
these isolated bits are useful in helping us to understand the
more concrete evidence of sexual activity suggested by the
statistic that after the Revolution, one-third of all brides were
pregnant when they married.

Most people who left information on their criteria for a perfect mate chose a blend of features, both practical and romantic, beginning with "reasonable fortune" or "circumstances,"
and including such attributes as "similarity in Taste," "liveliness
of manner," and "gentle wit." Cotton Mather wanted it all—
financial independence, companionship, and sex. In search of a
third wife, he began to court a wealthy widow as "a very valuable fish" and moved on to the conventionally stated compan-
ionate qualities, on which he so elegantly dwelt: "your bright
accomplishments, your shining piety, your polite education,

your superior capacity, and the most refined sense, and incomparable sweetness of temper, together with a constellation of all the perfections that [I] can desire to see related unto me." That he was also head over heels in love with her is obvious in his notes to "My— (Inexpressible!)," and his gushings about his "Collection of a Thousand Lovelinesses!"

Many partners who had chosen each other for love may well have enjoyed a degree of personal fulfillment unknown to their grandparents who were joined under the old system. The hundreds of thousands of lower- and middle-class couples in cities, towns, farming communities, and frontier societies were perhaps less secure than they might have been as subordinate members of large domestic households. On the other hand, their very isolation and need to rely on each other created conditions in which trust and shared authority and responsibility between husbands and wives could grow. As usual, more articulate across the years than any others, the Adams correspondence provides a picture of a lasting marriage of love and companionship, in a letter written by Abigail to John after almost twenty years of marriage. ". . . in the domestick way, should I draw you the picture of my Heart," she wrote, "it would be what I hope you still would Love . . . I look back to the early days of our acquaintance, and Friendship, as to the days of Love and Innocence; and with an indescribable pleasure I have seen near a score of years roll over our Heads, with an affection heightened and improved by time. . . ."

Still, the actuality of married life for most folks was a long way from "happily ever after." Nothing in the change from dynastic House or domestic household to nuclear family automatically implied any change in the patriarchal nature of relationships within the home. While marriage was in itself a voluntary contract, once consummated, its terms required the subordination of the wife. Her property was his, her obedience his to command; if she worked for wages, they, like those of the children, belonged to him. In many places, she, like an apprentice, was legally subject to "reasonable correction," that is, corporal punishment. The introduction of romance as a proper consideration in choosing a partner for life did, however, change to some extent the expectation of equal behavior within the basically unequal relationship. A husband was asked to do more than support his wife economically: he was also asked to protect and cherish her, and to remain sober and faithful. He was even expected to take her opinions and interest into account when forming his decisions. By the end of the century, as divorce became possible, although difficult, in most states, abusive husbands were sometimes called upon to justify their actions. Many did by noting that they had been "provoked by her scolding." "Scolding," the contemporary term for nagging or arguing, was a serious fault in a wife, probably as deserving of a beating as any other form of insubordination. Our friend Reverend Collin noted in November 1795 that "A couple came to request my parting them. He gets drunk and beats the wife. She seems to have a cutting tongue. Dismissed with proper advice."

Romantic expectations of a marriage in some ways made it more difficult for wives. While it had always been the woman's place to remain virtuous and of good disposition, keeping the home a pleasant place and dissuading her husband from anger or passionate outbursts, the ideal of a loving relationship went further. It suggested that a cheerful, gentle wife might, in fact, reform an ill-tempered, brutish husband, who would then be grateful for her guidance. Popular novels toward the end of the century, in true soap-opera style, often required that the wife die before the reform was achieved. Articles like the "Rules and Maxims for Promoting Matrimonial happiness," which appeared in the *Philadelphia Minerva* in February 1795, counseled wives not to ignore the admonition to "obey" found in the wedding service. Other authors suggested that a tactful letter from wife to husband gently urging that he not neglect her and mentioning that his behavior was noticeable to their friends and relatives would have "the desired effect" of awakening the man to his conjugal responsibilities.

Some women, however, seemed to have felt an implicit contradiction between affectionate marriage and patriarchal domestic arrangements. Sarah Harrison, a determined young woman of aristocratic southern background, insisted that the minister remove the word "obey" from the ceremony before she would proceed with her wedding to James Blair. She got her way. When Abigail Adams considered the appropriate place of women in the new republic, she commented on the irony implicit in a relationship in which the husband remained employer; the wife, servant: "Such of you [men]," she wrote, "as wish to be happy, [should] willingly give up the harsh title of Master for the more tender and endearing one of friend." While Abigail Adams was (and is) well known and her letter private, one ordinary woman, Charity Barr, was willing to go public with the failure of marriage to meet her expectations. In 1785, when she left her husband, he took out a notice in the newspaper accusing her of "desertion without cause." She replied in the public forum as well, detailing his abuse of her, and adding, "If such cruel usage, *from a man who ought to have been her best friend*, be not sufficient cause for leaving him, she leaves the impartial to judge" [emphasis added].

In some ways, quarrels between married couples, complaints, and countercomplaints were merely part of the eternal battle of the sexes common in folk tradition as well as in high literature. There is no need to look for further significance in the name of an "exceedingly noisy" stream christened "Matrimony Creek" by the eighteenth-century crew that drew the dividing line between Virginia and Carolina. While men might grumble, the need for a woman about the place was obvious: As the Puritan preacher John Cotton put it in 1699, "women are creatures without which there is no comfortable Living for man." It was the increasing emphasis on the word "comfortable," with the growth of the home as a center of consumption and emotional relationships, that focused this battle more narrowly.

The changing nature of the home reallocated discretionary funds, putting more power and control in the hands of women whose customary responsibilities involved the maintenance of the house and its operations. Throughout the century, there were more frequent, bitter references to female extravagance as the cause of everything from domestic discomfort to financial ruin and the corruption of the moral virtue of the new Republic. At the beginning of the nineteenth century, a New York paper, the *Independent Mechanic*, printed a fictitious letter from "A Tradesman" who connected his wife's foolishness to a more general concern over the greater amount of free time available to women outside of the home. After about three months of marriage, he complained, his wife "began to form a new set of female acquaintances . . . who were enabled, by foolishly squandering their husband's substance, to dress . . . in every new fashion, give tea parties . . . resort to the theatre, and, in short, to launch out into every kind of extravagance, unfitting for a mechanic's wife." "Tradesman" confessed that he had no power to stop her, for when he "lock[ed] up [his] money, and forbid her to run [him] in debt," she sulked, became a slattern, and ran the house with "slovenly neglect." In real life, husbands did not retreat quite so easily, as the divorce action between John McElwee and his wife Rebecca proves, although the very fact of the suit indicates that wives were no longer willing to regard themselves as completely subordinate. John explained to the Supreme Court of Pennsylvania that he had flown into a "great passion" and pushed and threatened his wife justifiably, since in her extravagance she had insisted on a new carpet and a shawl "which cost a guinea, because a neighbor had one." Rebecca won a "divorce from bed and board" with alimony.

In 1787, another popular Philadelphia magazine, the *American Museum,* published a critique of feminine extravagance by a "Farmer" who blamed all the problems in the economy, personal and national, on the teakettle. Drinking tea not only required family dependence on "market commodities," it wasted time as well. He vowed to reform his own household: ". . . no one thing to eat, drink, or wear shall come into my house which is not raised on my farm, or in the parish, or in the country except salt and iron-work, for repairing my buildings and tools—no tea, sugar, coffee, or rum. The tea kettle shall be sold."

His choice of the teakettle as the most important target in the battle over domestic morality was particularly telling. It was tea drinking, its ceremony and its equipage from pots to slop bowls to cups, that more than any other single ritual symbolized the new domestic world in which women were in charge of a home that was the center of social and family life. During the century, tea and its accessories had become less and less expensive, and more and more available on some level to almost everyone. The mere drinking of the beverage itself became something family members did together in unceremonial fashion, male and female together, and this increased family togetherness was an important aspect of the change to the affectionate, nuclear home. It implied parents who might someday—over the tea-cups—discuss the affairs of the day and make joint decisions concerning family strategies and priorities, including those determining the education and future directions of the children.

Less progressive men like "Farmer" saw these changes in household behavior, such as too much togetherness over the breakfast table, in a threatening light. Even John Adams, our model for the new middle-class affectionate husband and family man, is reported by one historian to have seen the domestic patterns as somewhat less than completely appealing.

> In 1759 a young lady . . . asked [Adams] if he would "like to spend your Evenings at Home in reading and conversing with your Wife, rather than to spend them abroad in Taverns or with other Company?" [He responded, diplomatically, that he] "Should prefer the Company of an agreeable Wife, to any other Company for the most Part, not always. I should not like to be imprisoned at home."

No such prison was built, certainly not in the eighteenth century, certainly not for men. Everyday life offered an abundance of public and semipublic entertainment at every social level. Taverns, coffeehouses, gaming events from billiards to fishing to horse racing, cockfighting, prizefighting, bear-baiting, and a host of less seemly pastimes were generally part of the men's world, along with the more sober pursuits of literary clubs, debating societies, and self-improvement associations. One such "conversation club" in 1766 introduced talk of women into its precincts in an all-male debate on the question, "Is it advantageous to admit women into the Councils of State?" The question was decided in the negative. It was admitted that women had abilities the equal of men, and might, with proper education, add new light to public business, but it was felt that they would exploit men through the use of feminine strategies and the result might be to "destroy the peace of Families."

The absence of women from the separate sphere of men was in fact an absence of women as a gender, not females as a sex. For example, women both owned and operated taverns, and there was no law prohibiting their frequenting them (as there was in the case of Indians and blacks), although very few "respectable" women, rich or poor, would have considered doing so. Most masculine activities could not have proceeded without the women who served the liquor, cleaned the floor and the tables, cooked and served the food, and, in many places, provided rowdy companionship and sexual favors for a price. It was as a gender—that is, as appropriate guests, customers, members, or participants in the frivolities—that women were separated from the men's world. There were some public functions in which elite women and men both participated: dancing assemblies would have been fairly peculiar affairs if women had not been included; and female guests were present on occasion at fishing club picnics, musical performances, and, of course, at the theater. Attendance at public festivals, fairs, parades, hangings, and, later, balloon ascensions and Fourth of July celebrations was not restricted by gender, and women from all ranks and stations of society enjoyed these spectacles. Those of the "better sort" were apt to be nervous in public, however, particularly if unattended. When Sarah Eve, a young Philadelphian, went with two girlfriends to see the troops muster on the Commons, they were "mortified" to get separated from their "gentlemen" and to find themselves "surrounded by people of all ranks and denominations." They only felt comfortable when they found their escorts, although Sarah candidly confided to her diary that "It is certainly more from custom than real service that the gentlemen are so necessary to us Ladies."

Of course, church services were open to both sexes, and seating was sometimes by family, sometimes separated by sex. Parallel but separate activities also took place at which families or couples gathered at a single home, then moved into different spaces to partake of gendered activities. In those social circles where "dining" took the place of mere "eating," the meal was enjoyed together; the women then withdrew to the parlor for tea, while the men remained at the table with brandy and smokes. A custom surrounding Quaker marriages in Philadelphia involved a week of visitations at the home of the newlyweds, with the women drinking tea with the bride in one room while the groom's guests joined him in another for a cup of punch.

Many of the ways in which women formed bonds of friendship or mutual assistance with each other were hidden from men's eyes, and thus from public notice. Female comradeship usually took place in the secluded arena of the home and was, in fact, of a very private nature: decades of correspondence between old school friends; quiet moments for reading or sewing or "walking out" together; times of selfless assistance when neighbors "came by turns to 'give the infant suck'" after its mother died of childbed fever. Family networks of women—mothers, sisters and others who were intimate—exchanged information on contraception and discussed issues of family planning. So firmly was this area considered part of the women's sphere in colonial America that men appear to have rarely employed those male techniques that were available: condoms or *coitus interruptus*. Rather, many merely bemoaned their wives' pregnancies as the family grew. Occasionally, a man felt so helpless and unable to control the situation that he abandoned wife and children, explaining as John Fitch did in 1769 that "fearing an increase of my family urged my departure."

The idea behind limiting marital fertility changed throughout the eighteenth century, as did the methods for achieving that goal. Before about 1730, such limitation seems to have been largely unintentional: for a variety of reasons, couples married later and therefore had a shorter time in which to produce children. By midcentury, many women appear to have given more thought to preventing pregnancy, making use of abstinence, prolonged breast-feeding, and folk medicines that produced abortions. Although no special strictures—either religious or moral—were attached to abortion, particularly before "quickening" of the fetus, most women preferred to think of these "decoctions" as ways to safeguard health by "regulating menstruation." Through the period of the Revolution, the prevention of pregnancy was considered a way to avoid having a baby during a particular crisis, rather than as part of an overall plan of family limitation. After the Revolution, however, we see the first real attempt by some middle-class urban women, frequently the wives of lawyers and the growing upwardly mobile group of bureaucratic government employees, to reduce their fertility in order to limit the size of their families. These women were part of the group that was quick to accept both the new republican ideology and the values of the affectionate nuclear family. They felt that having small families would make it possible to provide their children a better education and start in life.

Issues of family planning and of women's health were strictly part of the women's network that they could not, or would not, share with their menfolk. Mary Drinker Cope came from a family where the women discussed this part of their lives only with each other, and when, at the beginning of the nineteenth century, she became pregnant with a seventh child while her husband was in deep financial difficulties, she resorted to abortion. Even before she was out of danger of death as a result of a mismanaged procedure, Thomas Cope fulminated against her decision, made without his permission. Although theirs had been a loving marriage of shared responsibility, he now felt moved to write that "Where differences . . . occur between husband & wife, it is the duty of the latter, if she cannot think with, at least to succumb to the wishes of the former. . . ." He clearly saw Mary's personal decision as a betrayal of trust.

Loyalty, honor, fidelity, and trust were seen to be masculine virtues, often exhibited in public in aggressive situations from street brawls to the battlefield. It was generally felt (even by many women) that these attributes were contrary to the feminine constitution. While the Revolution did little, in the end, to increase the independence of women, it provided a more public arena in which to display their ability to work together for causes and principles and to stand up for themselves. There was no "women's side" in the war and while some working-class women signed the nonimportation agreements and led riots against merchants who failed to abide by them, others did not. The Cummings sisters, small shopkeepers in Boston, stood up for each other and their right to continue to do business since "it was verry trifling, owr Business, but that littil we must do to enabel us to Support owr family," and accused the revolutionaries of trying "to injur two industrious Girls who ware Striving in an honest way to get there Bread." As had been true since the sixteenth century in Europe, when war came, women made up to 10 percent of the payroll of the English and Hessian armies involved in the Revolution, while the General Orders of George Washington set the ratio of "women of the army" at one to every fifteen American male soldiers.

Elite women could also be found on both sides of the issue, although their positions almost always mirrored those of their fathers and husbands. Tory wives saw their homes and possessions destroyed and often found themselves in exile. Patriot women formed committees that raised money through such activities as the door-to-door campaign led by Esther Reed and Deborah Franklin in Philadelphia to support the troops with donations of money, foodstuffs, and various kinds of home-manufactured goods. Since boycotts against British merchandise were among the most popular and effective of the prewar strategies, it was middle- and upper-class women, purchasers of the consumer goods involved in this tactic, who were asked to carry the burden.

They were particularly active in the tea boycott, only complaining from time to time in the "letters columns" of the newspapers that it was unfair to expect them to give up such an important part of their social lives when the men were allowed to continue their consumption of imported rum. Although the South Carolina patriot Christopher Gadsden acknowledged that without this help from their wives the boycott would not have succeeded, cynical doubt that women could act together from disinterested motives was more in keeping with the accepted ideology. As the loyalist Peter Oliver explained in joking fashion: "The Ladies too were so zealous for the Good of their Country, that they agreed to drink no Tea, except the Stock of it which they had by them; or in the Case of Sickness. Indeed, they were cautious enough to lay in large Stocks before they promised; & they could be sick just as suited their Convenience or Inclination."

Even revolutionary activity undertaken by women in the public arena, however, revolved around tasks that had their root in what was perceived as "housekeeping." No job, not even farming, was as ubiquitous among men. What constituted the specific tasks covered by "housekeeping" varied according to geography, class, ethnic background, and age, but essentially involved the production of those goods and the provision of those services necessary to the basic maintenance of food, clothing, shelter, and the care of young children. Women's separate sphere of work shared certain other attributes across the dividing lines of time, place, and culture: whatever else they were, the jobs were fairly repetitious, did not call for intense concentration, could be interrupted and easily resumed, and were not, visibly at least, particularly hazardous. When their "housekeeping" tasks were actually performed outside of their own homes—for instance, as servants or day workers in the homes of others, as spinners in a factory, or washerwomen with the army—"working women" were considered to be only transitory members of the labor force by both themselves and others. The goal of almost all of them was to be fully occupied, as soon as possible, at their own hearths with their own families.

A sharp gender division of labor was basic to all cultures in colonial America, and the definition of men's work was that it was definitely *not* women's work, and vice versa. Actually, certain tasks were almost universally regarded as part of the housekeeping routine, while others were considered "not fitting" for a woman. Among all Amerindians, for example, men hunted, fished, fought, and engaged in the basic construction work of the village. Women handled most of the agriculture, made pottery, provided fabric for both clothes and houses, and ran the households. As slaves, blacks were not divided by gender in the same way, since they were set to tasks dictated by the needs of the master. Women and men worked together on precisely the same tasks of the heaviest fieldwork, and skilled males might be set to housework, like the runaway slave Simon, described by his owner in the *Pennsylvania Gazette* in 1785 as one who "understands working on a farm, but more especially house and kitchen work, is an excellent cook, can wash, spin, sew, knit, etc." In the little time left for their own lives, however, slaves returning at night to "quarters" allocated the jobs between the sexes in a traditional pattern where women attended to housework. The same held true for free African-Americans.

The skills of Simon, the runaway slave, read much like the roster of accomplishments expected of any mainstream colonial farm housewife at any time during the century, although it is a scant list with many of the most usual tasks omitted. A traveler to South Carolina in 1704 reported that "Ordinary Women take care of Cows, Hogs, and other small Cattle, make butter and Cheese, spin Coton and Flax, help to sow and reap Corn, wind Silk . . . gather Fruit and look after the House." Although he doesn't bother to mention it, a good bit of their time must have also been spent in looking after the "very large families of 10 or 12 Children" that he describes.

Oldmixon, our travel reporter, skipped lightly over "looking after the house," yet the organization, equipping, and maintenance of residential space lay at the heart of women's work. The changes that took place in house structure and space allocation over the century were primarily a result of decisions made by women on how their households should be run. While the improvement in the quality of buildings and in domestic technology made housework less arduous, it did not make it less time-consuming, rather, it challenged women to upgrade their standards. Take cleanliness, for example. Expectations rose along with the improved nature of wells and their ability to increase the availability of water; the increased production of broom corn that produced a cleaning utensil more effective than the old-fashioned "besom," or bundle of twigs on a stick, and the increase in wooden, as opposed to packed-earth, floors.

By the end of the century, there is evidence that some women had begun to turn housekeeping as a responsibility into homemaking as a vocation, and were vigorously moving to enforce their control over men within their own sphere. During the 1780s, a man writing in a popular journal described the havoc of "halves of China bowls, cracked tumblers, broken wine glasses, tops of teapots and stoppers of departed decanters" created by women in too-eager pursuit of the task of whitewashing the walls. A female "scribbler" responded by relating an incident (probably apocryphal) that occurred in her own home. Her husband had taken over the parlor and embarked on a series of "important philosophical experiments" which were "one means, and the principal one," for the mess of broken objects around *her* house. She considered herself very restrained and ". . . said nothing, or next to nothing; for I only observ'd very pleasantly . . . why philosophers are called *literary* men is because they make a great *litter*. . . ." She made a final withering indictment of men as "naturally nasty beasts," noting that the "carpet, which had suffered in the cause of experimental philosophy in the morning was destined to be most shamefully dishonoured in the afternoon, by a deluge of nasty tobacco juice—Gentlemen smoakers love segars better than carpets." That it was the woman's task to whitewash the walls was not a matter of controversy.

Nowhere do the gender divisions of work and their variations among cultures appear more vividly than in the provision of food for the household. As a general rule, fieldwork belonged to men, gardening to women. Yet among Algonkian Indians, men did none of the fieldwork associated with food crops, although they, and they alone, were in charge of growing tobacco. Fieldwork was expected of women in England well into the seventeenth century, yet as early as the settlement of Plymouth colony, Anglo women in the New World did not work the fields except in cases of extreme poverty, or occasionally at harvesttime when male labor was in critically short supply. Among German settlers, on the other hand, fieldwork was regularly expected of wives and daughters. Margaret Dwight, a New England traveler to Pennsylvania early in the nineteenth century, indicated the way in which the culture gap could exceed the gender gap when she wrote: "Women in new England are employed only in and about the house and in the proper business of the sex. I do not know that I was ever more struck with the strangeness of any sight than with the appearance and business of these German females."

Since the work was largely divided by gender, the table food provided by men and women varied as well. Men produced food grown further from the house and in larger quantities, often with the help of animal power. They cultivated grain— wheat, barley, oats, and maize—as well as pumpkins, squash, and beans that grew between the hills of corn. Animals pastured on the outskirts of the land, the cattle and sheep, were also their responsibility. It was men, too, whose guns supplied game and whose lines augmented the table offerings with fresh-caught fish. These seasonal foods bridged the gap of "scarce" times between the end of the stored food from last season's crop and the first fruits of the new year's harvest. They were doubly welcome as a treat from the monotony of what lay at the bottom of the barrel, and as a reprieve from the hunger, even semistarvation, that set in when the bottom of the barrel was scraped clean. Convenient to the house, women tended vegetables and fruits grown in relatively small quantities and cultivated with hand tools, and took responsibility for barnyard domestic animals. They fed, watered, tended, and slaughtered pigs and the so-called "dung-hill fowl"—chicken, ducks, and geese. When the cows returned to the barn for milking, women took over, and the dairy was entirely a woman's domain. She set aside some milk for drinking and processed the rest into butter and cheese. Once the cow was slaughtered, it was she who saw to the salting down and preserving of the meat, as she did with her own swine and poultry. Cultural preference played its part in determining her tasks in this area: German housewives were more apt to make *brothswurscht* and *lewerwurscht* (sausage and liver pudding) than the bacon of Anglo preference, and *schmier-case* (cottage cheese) as opposed to English pot cheese.

Women's kitchen gardens and the orchards adjacent to them produced a far more reliable and substantial part of the table fare than the occasional masculine forays into woods and streams. As the value of these gardens to the family food supply increased during the eighteenth century, husbands assisted their wives by fencing their yards against the depredations of wandering swine and chickens, and by keeping the soil "in good manure." The nature of the produce grown in the garden changed throughout the century as well. Pease for "English pease porridge" were supplanted by beans for "baked beans" in New England. Potatoes made their appearance in the 1720s and were well established by midcentury in the North; however, they were more of an innovation on the frontier until much later, and, along with tomatoes, were never really part of the southern colonial garden—sweet potatoes found favor there. And while turnips were most prized by the Germans, others thought them fit only for pigs, cattle, or slaves.

In 1748, a Boston shopkeeper advertised over two dozen varieties of seeds for sale, "all fresh and new Imported from London." The purchase of seeds involved women in a wider world of commerce than we might have supposed, and this involvement included selling their extra produce, or "truck" as it came to be called, in increasing volume through the century. By 1800, many women kept their gardens primarily for the production of market crops, from enterprising New England women anxious to improve the family standard of living to African-American slave women who were saving cash to buy their own freedom or that of a loved one. Women in Wethersfield, Connecticut, and Barnstable, Massachusetts, specialized in onions, which came to provide an important source of cash in those communities, while Indian women in many places sold herbs, berries, and nuts. Almost all farm women managed to derive income from their eggs, their salted, pickled, or smoked meat, and the butter and cheese produced in their dairies. If their production was large enough, the profit became part of the general family budget, but small sums in "egg money" or credit were often discretionary funds for their own use. This "extra" went for items that improved the family table, such as salt, molasses, sugar, rum, tea, coffee, and chocolate, along with other necessary purchases like candles, soap, thread, and needles.

What was available under ideal conditions and throughout the whole century does not tell us a great deal about actual diet. A list compiled by one historian of purchases made between 1750 and 1800 by the Pennsylvania Hospital, a largely charitable institution, sounds like a veritable cornucopia of plenty and variety: grains included wheat flour, bran, oats, barley, and rice; there was fresh and salted pork, mutton, veal, beef (including calf's head), chicken, goose, turkey, pigeon, and rabbit, as well as seafoods like shad, herring, oysters, and clams. Vegetables included white and sweet potatoes, turnips, parsnips, corn, beans, peas, asparagus, and cucumbers; fruits—apples, oranges, peaches, lemons, raisins, currants, and cranberries—were listed in season and must have frequently been imported, since many did not grow in the Philadelphia area. Dairy products such as eggs, butter, and cheese appeared, as did a long list of seasonings including salt, pepper, mustard, horseradish, sugar, molasses, syrup, and vinegar. Beverages were both nonalcoholic—milk, coffee, several types of tea, chocolate, and sweet cider—and spirituous—hard cider, rum (both local and West Indian), wine, and "small" and "strong" beer. The actual estimated daily diets of laboring Philadelphians, however, bore almost no resemblance to these possibilities—a pound and a half of grain in some form, usually bread, less than a half pound of meat, small amounts of dairy products, and almost minuscule helpings of vegetables, most often potatoes or turnips.

In fact, even where there was money enough, the dietary habits of urban Americans tended to be poor, part of a pattern of misinformation that saw raw vegetables, for example, as unhealthy, and preferred heavily salted meat as more "wholesome" than fresh. In this last belief there was probably some truth, since "fresh" was likely to be spoiled, or "strong" as they called it. Evidence (from the trash pits again) tells us that the difference between rich and poor was quality. Both primarily ate beef, with some mutton and less pork. Both ate a variety of domestic fowl. But the meat that landed on the tables of the poor was from elderly animals whose days as milk, wool, or egg producers had come to an end. The tables of the rich were graced by young animals raised for the purpose, as well as by a variety of "luxury" meats. Occasionally, during what must have been hard times, the remains of cats, dogs, and even rodents are found among the table scraps in the poorest neighborhoods. Throughout almost all of the century, the characteristic pattern involved too much meat and too few fruits and vegetables, creating diets that were high in protein, fat, starch, and sugar, but low in vitamins. Those vegetables that were used were overcooked or pickled; "sallads" did not become popular until the very end of the century. Finally, for all classes, sexes, and ages, too many of the calories consumed were in the form of alcohol: drinking began at breakfast and continued throughout the day. Doctors prescribed alcohol of all types for all sorts of medical problems: beer for nursing mothers, wine for intestinal trouble or consumption (tuberculosis), brandy for pain.

Farm families at any level of wealth probably ate better than urban families, and changes in the farm routine pointed to more healthful, tasty, and varied diets for households at the end of the century than had been the case at the beginning. The main improvement was what one historian has called "a deseasonalization" of the food supply. There were no great breakthroughs in technology that accounted for the change: The chemical processes by which meal was turned into bread, malt into beer, milk into cheese, and flesh into bacon remained relatively constant. Dried apple cores and peels were still used to brew the beer that produced the "bawm" that was used to raise the bread. Improved butter churns and gristmills may have allowed for larger production or a somewhat better product, but not revolutionary advances. The methods for preservation of food continued to involve drying, with or without smoke, and pickling in a salt or acidic solution of some sort. Canning was certainly a technique of the future, and the first icebox was not even patented until 1803.

Yet, by varying long-established Old Country routines, abundant food supplies came to characterize life in ways that made America worthy of the title "best poor man's country." By altering schedules and applying more forethought and energy to storage, the "scarce times" of late spring (when the meat barrel was empty), late fall (when the last of the cheese was used), or winter (when the vegetables disappeared from the table) became things of the past in settled communities by midcentury. Instead of assuming that their preserved meat would run out in the spring, farm wives turned to "almanacs and agriculturals" with new suggestions and recipes for salting meat "to last a month or a season or even 'to keep the year around.'" Better provisions for feeding cows during the winter, rather than allowing them to winter over in "a meane condition," allowed them to produce milk with sufficient butterfat content to make the manufacture of butter and cheese a year-round possibility. In addition, there was an interactive effect: When more meat was stored for longer periods, the butter and cheese were not so quickly used up and remained available from one season to another. Vegetables, too, ceased to be thought of as fresh food only, and "dry sauces" made from stored roots and cabbages were used to flavor pottages and stews in winter as well as summer. "Green sauces"—"green" referred to freshness as well as to the color of many of the vegetables—continued to be something of a summer delicacy. Asparagus spoiled quickly and had to be picked and eaten when it appeared in June, for example, and berries generally had to be used up, although tree fruit like apples, pears, and cherries could be dried and saved for later. The word "sauce" was even dropped in association with plant foods, as they began to appear as dishes on their own, rather than as merely part of the general flavoring of meat or grain recipes.

Once we come to recipes, the cooking and serving of food, we are almost entirely in the woman's sphere, as the husband's responsibility for food preparation and service stopped at the farmhouse door. His job was to chop the wood and get it to the house; hers was to make and tend the fire, perhaps her single most mundane but crucial responsibility since in most eighteenth-century homes the open fire was not only the energy source for cooking, but also the principal source of light and heat as well. The skillful fireplace cook knew how many small fires should be built on her cavernous hearth, so that she could prepare an entire meal at once. Our nostalgic picture of a huge fire taking up the whole chimney space must give way to the reality of several more useful blazes: a medium-sized fire over which the housewife occasionally rotated a spit; a smaller group of embers on which a skillet sizzled; another under a hanging pot of soup, pottage, or stew; and yet others for foods that cooked best when buried in embers or just needed warming.

By the end of the eighteenth century, the issue surrounding food had moved from "enough" to "well cooked and wholesome." Improvement in the variety and taste of the food went along with an increased emphasis on mealtime as a kind of sociable time for the family to get together. In 1700, most houses lacked enough chairs for the whole family to sit together, and enough dishes and utensils for them to eat at the same time, even if we consider that they may have all dipped with their hands into a central pot and passed around a communal drinking vessel. By 1800, even the poorest families—if they enjoyed stable household space at all—were provided with these former amenities, now necessities. Creation of dinnertime as family time was not only related to the development of the nuclear family, but also to women's ability to serve food that was worth lingering over. This was pointed out by S. Jean de Crevecoeur in *Letters from an American Farmer* late in the century. A man's comfort, he explained, all depended on the "sagacity" of his wife. "He may work and gather the choicest fruits of his farm, but if female economy fails, he loses the comfort of good victuals. He sees wholesome meats, excellent flours converted into indifferent food; whilst his neighbor, more happy though less rich, feeds on well-cooked dishes, well-composed puddings."

The manufacture of textiles for home and market and of clothing for the family was another area in which tasks were allocated by gender. Since the need for fabric is universal and its durability is limited, textiles used up a heavy proportion of the colonial budget. Despite attempts by England to limit cloth production in the colonies at the beginning of the century, it was well established in most settled communities by the 1730s. Flocks of sheep tended by men and patches of flax and hemp grown in women's gardens provided the woollen, linen, burlap, and "duck" that clothed most Americans, covered their beds, and provided storage for their "dry goods" and sails for their ships. Men saw to the shearing of the sheep and the combing of the wool, as well as to the heavy work of "breaking" and "hackling" flax and hemp, that is, separating the fibers from the stems of the plants and softening them to make them ready for spinning.

Women spun the fibers to turn them into yarn or thread

suitable for making cloth: this was a job perfectly suited to the concept of women's work as relatively light, easily interruptible, and requiring some—but not too much—skill and training. Spinning was, in fact, so quintessentially an appropriate labor for young girls that the word for an unmarried woman was "spinster." Throughout the eighteenth century, spinning became less a task for all women and more one for certain groups of women: farm women whose own homesteads produced the raw material; and poor women and children of both sexes who lived in urban communities and were provided with the raw materials by "clothiers" who acted as middlemen in the production of cloth.

On the other hand, the craft of weaving—which required skill, concentrated blocks of time, and a fair amount of investment in the equipment, as well as a good deal of space in which to set up the looms—had long been a man's job. Most rural communities supported at least one professional male weaver to "make up" cloth from the locally spun yarn, although he frequently worked at his craft only part-time while farming in season, perhaps raising his own sheep and flax from which he could make cloth to sell on the open market. Urban weavers purchased their raw materials or obtained them from clothiers under the same conditions as female spinners. Full-time weavers were skilled professionals who could produce cloth in a wide "variety of widths of yardage of both wool and linen in a variety of weights and patterns, as well as more specialized fabrics such as 'bedtickin,' 'blanketin,' 'shirten,' 'meal-bags,' and 'coverlets,' " as did John Gould in Topsfield, Massachusetts, in the first quarter of the century. Once the fabric was woven, it still required several stages of "finishing," from fulling to napping or shearing, and these, too, were done by men.

By the middle of the eighteenth century, women on well-established farms where the frontier stage of building was past and there were enough children or servants to help with the regular household tasks began to break the gender barrier and weave their own fabric, or set their female servants and slaves to do it for them. They did not compete with the professionals like John Gould nor, of course, did they try to replicate fine

imported fabrics like rainbow-colored silks and satins and vel-
vets. Homemade goods were usually the simple, coarse materials used within the household for servants' clothing or children's shirts, and very occasionally sold in the local market to
poorer neighbors who lacked the time or extra hands to weave
their own.

When it came to making household items and clothing out of
textiles, tight gender divisions continued in operation. Women
were expected to be skillful with shears for cutting cloth, and
with the needle for sewing it together. It was they who made
the sheets, napkins, bed-curtains, and cushions used in the
house; they who made the basic family clothes. Women made
their own shifts and those of the children, as well as their husbands' shirts. Whether the fabric for these items had been
bleached snowy white, or was merely less expensive un-
bleached linen, it was undyed and served many uses, since
there was no such thing as underwear or nightclothes, as we use
the terms, for either men or women. Women were also responsible for working clothes like farmers' smocks and the simple
one-piece garments worn by the slaves. Finally, below the level
of *haute-couture,* they made their own and their children's
outer garments—petticoats, overskirts, bodices, and even
cloaks.

What all products of women's manufacture had in common
was that they required very little shaping or fitting, and were
fastened with ties and pins rather than with buttons, snaps, or
hooks. Only tailors—again, specialized male craftsmen—acquired the tools and the training to make buttonholes, cover
buttons, and do the kind of complicated fitting that went with
men's breeches and coats. And only men worked with that
other common clothing material of the eighteenth century:
leather. The exception occurred among Native Americans,
whose women produced all garments, whether of leather or
cloth. In urban areas, male upholsterers covered furniture in
leather as well as in fine, often imported, high-line materials.
Women's role in the decorative end of textile conversion involved embroidered marks or designs on garments and household goods, done either as an occupation or as a genteel skill

pursued as a kind of art form by women with leisure time.

No matter who made the clothes and sheets, no matter how simple or fancy, maintenance was the woman's responsibility. Repairing rips and tears, remaking out-of-date or outgrown items, experimenting with special "receipts" for removing stains, and boiling, beating, starching, and ironing the "white wash" were so clearly eschewed by real American men that a foreign observer at Bunker Hill blamed the "ragged and unkempt" appearance of American soldiers on a lack of washerwomen and seamstresses. "Americans, not being used to doing things of this sort, rather to let their linen, etc., rot upon their backs than to be at the trouble of cleaning 'em themselves," he wrote, while another reporter noted, "They wore what they had until it crusted over and fell apart."

Tending only to the upkeep of one's own home and the comfort of one's own family was a luxury afforded to comparatively few colonial women. Most family economies required that, in addition to production for home consumption, women produce for the market as well. Farm wives not only supplemented the family income with the processed goods and "truck" of their kitchen gardens and dairies, but also wove straw hats from Caribbean straw provided by local shopkeepers and baskets from reeds they found by the river. The shopkeepers collected the finished products and paid off in merchandise from their shelves. Urban women had fewer opportunities to trade in "produce," since meager city lots offered, at best, space for a small garden with which to supplement the family food supply, and no opportunity for overage at all. They did spin yarn and thread from wool or flax provided to them by cloth merchants, in much the same way that straw was available to their rural sisters through shopkeepers. Service of some sort, however, provided urban women with the best opportunity to augment the household income. They took in boarders, washing, and sewing. They did cleaning and cooking and looked after children in the homes of the wealthy.

Up the social scale, housewives had to develop another set of skills. Managing servants and slaves, keeping the household stocked, always bearing and caring for children, and playing

hostess to the friends who increasingly gathered in the consumer atmosphere of the house were less physically draining,
perhaps, but just as demanding. Southern wives, in particular,
carried the burden of patterns of "southern hospitality" as they
developed. We can be sure that the fifty or more people who
stayed with William Byrd each month, either on his plantation
or at his home in Williamsburg, were not cared for by him in
anything but the figurative sense; their bed linens, their wash,
their food, and any incidental sewing was done or prepared by
the women of the house. It might seem that in a society that ran
on slavery, none of these household tasks was really the problem of the planter's wife, whose real job was to make polite
conversation and manage the slaves. Yet the plantation owner
frequently economized on the household servants, providing
his wife with too few helpers who were also too young, too old,
or too untrained to allow her to devote her full time and attention to charming her guests. Genteel northern girls prepared
for lives as helpmeets to rising lawyers, merchants, or government officials by mastering the arts of domesticity—cooking
and sewing—and gentility—music, dancing, drawing, and some
(but not too much) knowledge of literature and current event".
In a way, their genteel skills were part of their housekeepir
tasks, since their roles as status symbols assisted their husban‹
to rise in the world.

The distinct but interdependent roles of men and women
eighteenth-century America suggest that they did not rea
inhabit separate spheres, but rather hemispheres, each of whicn
required the other to make a single, complete way of life. Men
without women were, of course, in bad shape (like the ill-clad
soldiers on Bunker Hill); yet, generally speaking, if he had any
means at all, a man could hire a housekeeper's services, or
marry one. But, as the old drinking song goes, if "a man without
a woman / is like a wreck upon the sand . . . there is one thing
worse / in the universe [and] that's a woman without a man."
The intent of the song is ribald, perhaps, but its literal meaning
applies to colonial life. A woman, in theory, needed a man to act
for her since she had no place and no standing in the public
arena and her economic opportunities and options were

severely limited. Yet, while almost all women married at some point in their lives, they also spent a number of years at either end of their adulthood single, dependent first on fathers, then on sons.

Even women who were midstream in their married lives spent some time in charge of the household as "deputy-husbands." It might be just for a few nights while their farmer-husbands took the crops to market or went to the nearest good-sized town to lay in supplies not available in the neighborhood. It might be for months while he prepared a new homestead on the frontier before returning for the family and whatever goods they could manage to accommodate in a cart or wagon. Or it might be for years, as it was for women like Abigail Adams and Deborah Franklin, whose husbands were caught up in the great affairs of creating or running a new nation. Quaker women both in England and the colonies had, possibly, the widest experience of this life—keeping their country homes, shops, and farms solvent while their husbands were on their frequent traveling ministries. On the other hand, since Quaker women also went on distant missions, their husbands had the unique experience, unfamiliar to most men, of managing the day-to-day affairs of housekeeping and childrearing.

Wives and husbands who coped with separation the most consistently were those whose living was earned on the sea, and in the northern colonies this represented a very large part of the population. Coastal towns in New England were almost completely dominated by the ocean and, whether as merchant mariners or fishermen, the men spent months, often years, away from home. During their absence, their wives handled everything from the financial management of family property and market production to the daily tasks of breadwinning, which, according to Lydia Almy of Smithfield, Rhode Island, at the end of the century included "whitewashing, keeping live-stock, carting wood, bringing in hay and . . . Childcare [which was] just one duty, no more or less important, among many," to quote her historian. Lydia's responsibilities, however, took place in a community where almost every married couple experienced a similar situation at some time in its life cycle. Neigh-

bors, who were frequently relatives as well, expected to pitch
in: One neighbor who sawed and split wood for Lydia refused
to even consider the repayment that Lydia promised ". . . if my
husband lived to return." He said that he "would not take anything for it because he thought it was right for him so to do."

The situation was far more grim for a sailor's wife in a setting
where she was on her own. The Philadelphia Almshouse records for October 7, 1800, provide one of many instructive examples: "Admitted Mary Wright hath Legal residence, is twenty
years of age, born in this City. Her husband Dominick Wright
twelve months ago went to sea in the Ship Jane Brown to London (the Owner nor Captains Name she cannot tell) and heard
only once from him since, and as she says, never received one
farthing of his Monthly pay. (The reason is obvious, he neither
gave Power of Attorney or Orders for her to receive any part
thereof). However, unfortunate it is that she was taken with a
Fit & contiguous to the fire place, she fell into the Flames and
got burnt in a most distressing manner."

Wealth, training, family connections, and luck all played a
part in how women coped when they found themselves on their
own. Abandoned, divorced, or widowed women, if they had just
a little property, might scrape by—particularly in a small
town—on an independent income derived from taking in
boarders, doing occasional nursing, hiring out as domestics, or
even in leasing out small parcels of inherited land. These were,
of course, pretty much the same opportunities they possessed
if they were providing a second income for a household in
which the husband was present but unable to make ends meet.
In some cases, "independent" women were better off, since
they could make their own decisions about spending what they
earned.

With a little more capital, a little more experience, a network
of friends or kin, and better luck, there were suddenly many
more options for the spinster, widow, or wife of an insufficient
provider. Middle-class rural widows whose husbands left the
real estate to their sons were often better off if the will stipulated that the heir provide them with an annual stock of "grain"
or "apples" or some other marketable goods in lieu of a cash

bequest. This kind of inheritance, in addition to being ongoing, was also adjustable for inflation; thus, the widow did not have to worry about having too little to support her old age, at least as long as her son's luck and ability at farming continued.

Urban widows of similar status who had been the wives of successful artisans frequently carried on their husbands' shops: They advertised themselves as silversmiths, printers, upholsterers, and even blacksmiths until their sons were old enough to take over. Having worked alongside their husbands, many continued to work with their sons, and sometimes carried the whole burden if the son proved unequal to the business end of affairs. Still other women, not necessarily widows, found the capital to begin their own workshops in one of the "feminine" crafts or to open retail establishments. The most successful of these might in fact become very large dealers in a wide spectrum of goods, buying directly from merchants, exchanging instruments of credit, and investing in a part of a ship or cargo themselves.

Prosperous "she-merchants," as they were called, if they decided to marry, were well advised to sign prenuptial agreements. Henrietta Maria East, who ran a thriving millinery shop in Boston in the 1740s, found this out to her sorrow when her husband of four years, Hugh Caine, turned out to be a fortune hunter and bigamist who "dissipated a great part of her Estate and carried away the remainder," according to her testimony before a judge. She was forced to go to court to get the marriage dissolved, because no one wanted to "supply her with goods to carry on her business" as long as the marriage contract was still outstanding, lest Hugh come back and legally strip her of her assets once again.

The wealthiest, best-connected widows lived lives not unlike those that their husbands had enjoyed. Mary Marshall Bolling, the wealthy wife of a wealthy husband, became head of the "most powerful household" in the small Virginia town of Petersburg when her husband died in 1777, leaving her a widow at forty. She ran her family with an iron hand, managed her property, and attended to her civic duties. She not only directed the financial activities of the tobacco plantation, but also invested in real estate and bank stocks, promoted public projects like the paving of Petersburg's streets, and subscribed alike to the Anglican Church, the Female Orphan Asylum, and Thomas Wade West's theater company. Elizabeth Powel, widow of Samuel Powel, erstwhile mayor of Philadelphia and one of its wealthiest citizens, clearly thought of herself as her husband's replacement and not merely as his deputy when she lectured a tenant who was delinquent in his rent that "[As a] Man of business [I] must be sensible,—that if I wish to preserve integrity in my own engagements I take care that others are punctual in their payments to me."

Connections, along with money, education, and luck, were just as important to the intact nuclear family as they were to women on their own. While there were more opportunities for minimum-wage jobs for men who could do heavy labor, these were not opportunities that fully supported families or provided children with the chance to "amount to something." Because the new style of family was a unit of relationship, not of economy, it depended on relationships for its survival. As a structure it was not only fragile, but short-lived. In some respects, it began to break up as soon as the children grew up, married, and left home. When the original couple died, the break was complete, and each child formed a new family unit of his or her own. Once this occurred, economic success really depended on the ability of these new families to maintain contact with each other. Those who owned land near each other and continued to participate in broader community social life together had a better chance of establishing themselves on a stable footing.

The best hope of family achievement lay in economic cooperation. New England merchant families like the Cabots, Higginsons, and Lowells did business with their uncles, brothers, and cousins. Since there were no banks, insurance companies, or corporations, individual family members spread the risk by going into partnership with other branches of the family and training the next generation for employment in the family enterprise "in positions commensurate with their abilities." In a way, they developed an economic family that was the reverse of the old domestic household: instead of nonrelatives living together as an economic unit, relatives now lived apart but worked together. Small New England towns were often dominated by a few such families of incredibly complex, interrelated lineage. By the beginning of the eighteenth century, in Windsor, Connecticut, for example, all of the major politicians were sons or grandsons of the most distinguished early settlers. Among southern planters the same kinds of connections created great landed families with branches that spread across a county, often across an entire colony. These kin not only monopolized the wealth, but also controlled the legislatures, the courts, and, if they thought it important, the churches as well.

More modest nuclear families, ones that gave each of the children a chance through education, love, and a comfortable existence, were only just emerging by the end of the century as the ideal. They were, in a way, the right kind of family structure for the new nation with its emphasis on individual attainment. Some of the second generation who grew up in these families made use of their start to form successful families of their own. Others failed and went elsewhere to start again, disappearing, more or less, from the family tree. In the end, the nuclear family existed to serve the individual and provide a start, not to be served by the individual as the security of the future. Benjamin Franklin, whose own birth family provided just such a stepping-stone, saw that the individual had to make his or her own way in a republican world that lacked hereditary honors when he wrote to his daughter in 1784: "Honour worthily obtained . . . is in its nature a personal thing and incommunicable to any but those who had some share in obtaining it." The old revolutionary Sam Adams said it best, perhaps: "The cottager may beget a wise son; the noble, a fool . . . the rank of rulers is from the good they do, and the difference among the people only from personal virtue. No entailments, no privileges. An open world for genius and industry."

Iɴ 1768, Mrs. Hannah Winthrop of Boston, Massachusetts, wrote from her summer home in Cambridge to her good friend Mrs. Jonathan Belcher: "Can there be a happier Seene, than nature display'd in Rural life . . . surrounded with your Little ones, Tasting the sweets of domestic peace." At almost the same time, Margaret Parker, wife of a southern gentleman, wrote to her absent husband: "I endeavour as much as possible to guard against [spoiling our young son] but find it requires more resolution than I am mistress of to help doting on him." Nor were those men who were involved in modern, affectionate eighteenth-century marriages immune to something like offspring worship. Edward Chandler of New York was overwhelmed with the sentiment when he unburdened himself to his brother-in-law: "Oh Samy, she is the loveliest Child that ever god Created. There is nothing in this world half so dear to me as my Child."

These parents did not, of course, invent a new, modern kind of child, but rather a different expectation of childhood. While seventeenth-century parents had tried to make their children into adults as quickly as possible, more and more middle- and upper-class couples in the eighteenth century were coming to feel that their children were entitled to be children. This does not mean that earlier generations of youngsters didn't laugh and cry, run and play, or act silly and mischievous. In fact, their daily lives may not have varied too much from those of children of their station in life a hundred years later. What changed was the way in which adults perceived the basic nature of children and arrived at a different understanding of human development, one which stimulated new methods for achieving the same old goal of turning irresponsible and incapable babies into responsible and productive members of society.

Although seventeenth-century European scholars and philosophers were breaking new ground with a scientific perspective on the material world and man's place in it, most settlers in the New World interpreted the universe from a religious point of view. The underlying assumption was that the natural world and its creatures were somehow part of Satan's empire of chaos and evil, while the order of Heaven and the angels represented the true goodness of God's handiwork. Between these two visions—the dark, threatening world of nature, and the light and radiance of Heaven—man was dangerously and uneasily poised, mired in the clay of the world, but with a chance of salvation. His redeeming task was to tame and civilize the chaos of nature, build orderly communities, and subdue the savage instincts with which all men were born. He possessed three attributes which placed him above all other earthly creatures: he could walk upright on two legs, he could talk, and he could reason.

Since babies at birth fulfilled none of these qualifications, serious parents worried that without outside help they might never do so. Parents worked hard at turning their infants into real human beings using tightly bound swaddling clothes, corsets, and high collars to achieve an upright position, and rushing them into walking, toilet training, and talking. The Puritans, fearing that children who were unconverted would burn in hell for all eternity, coaxed or frightened their youngsters into conversion experiences as early as possible. Pride and relief were expressed by the Massachusetts mother who overheard her four-year-old daughter speaking "in her childish manner . . . crying, and wreathing her body to and fro [and saying] I am afraid I shall go to Hell! . . . til at lenth she suddenly ceased crying and began to smile, and presently said with a smiling countenance, Mother, the kingdom of heaven is come to me!"

By the beginning of the eighteenth century, many literate

colonials had accepted a new "scientific" approach to the world: While the universe followed God's rules and regulations, it was removed from His active and continual intervention. Humans, as part of this natural universe, were morally neutral, adaptable to training in either appropriate or inappropriate behavior. As far as children were concerned, explained English philosopher John Locke, they were ignorant rather than evil, "travelers newly arrived in a strange country." Although basic human nature might contain antisocial traits such as pleasure-seeking, selfishness, vanity, and laziness, youngsters who were started early enough could be trained to understand that the restrained, productive life was more satisfying than submission to the immediate pleasures of mere animal passions.

In 1690, Locke wrote *Some Thoughts Concerning Education,* which was based on his theories of human psychology. While his goal of turning out adults of good character was not particularly revolutionary, his concept of human nature and his methods of bringing out the best in children were decidedly novel. He suggested that parents did not have to worry so much about getting an early start: maturation would occur naturally. "Never trouble your self about those faults in them, which you know age will cure." Babies will eventually assume human form, walk upright, talk, and even reason. More radically, Locke regarded the desires to play, laugh, run around, and ask questions as natural attributes of childhood and good signs of potential intelligence to be encouraged, always with the proviso that they be steered in rational and productive ways.

The notion that "kids will be kids" was further transformed from an accepted inevitability to an ideal state of affairs by the romantic movement of the late eighteenth century. According to this worldview, expressed most importantly by the French philosopher Jean-Jacques Rousseau in his "educational romance" *Emile* (1762), nature was neither evil, as evangelical religion proposed, nor neutral, as the Enlightenment scientists countered. It was, in fact, a positive good—the true creation of God that was only debased and degraded by the accoutrements of civilization. Therefore, the best and most noble people were the "savages" who lived in harmony with nature and without all of the corrupt institutions of modern European culture. Standing the values of both religion and reason on their heads, romanticists argued that it was those who remained unsophisticated, uneducated, and lacking in the social graces who exhibited the real hallmarks of purity and divinity.

The excellency of "nature in the raw" as a general proposition, much less as a blueprint for raising children, was not quickly adopted by Americans. Perhaps it was easier to romanticize nature in Europe, where it did not impinge on daily life, than it was on the colonial frontier, where success was measured by the extent to which the "wilderness" was subdued, the "noble savage" eliminated. By the time of the Revolution, however, and in the years of independence that followed, Americans found the romantic identification of European civilization and corruption more appealing, and at least one educator argued, in the 1790s, that American youth was too innocent to be sent abroad for education where it would be exposed to degenerate overcivilization.

In the end, how much did the theories of the great philosophers affect the everyday lives of real children in the eighteenth century, when the communication of ideas moved with glacial slowness? The answer is probably very little, in the short run. Yet the ideal of childhood did indeed change among wealthy, literate Americans over the course of the century, and eventually the lives of all children were touched by the laws and institutions of a society created after the Revolution by men who had accepted these theories and principles. For most eighteenth-century youngsters, however, the changes were subtle and a matter of degree rather than of kind. The daily life of a child depended far more on the individual accident of birth. Colonial America was first and foremost a multicultural society. Conditions varied according to geography, ethnic and racial background, economic status, and religion far more than they did across time. The experiences of a German child in Philadelphia whose father was an artisan differed significantly from those of a wealthy merchant's son in Boston, a native-born farm child in New York, a black slave on a plantation in South Carolina, the daughter of a wealthy planter in Virginia, or the child of a Scots-Presbyterian

frontier squatter. Still, there were certain constants, facts of
social conditions in eighteenth-century colonial America that
applied to almost all children, poor or privileged, urban or rural,
male or female. The first of these was that the place of the child
was at the bottom of the family hierarchy. The words "child,"
"boy," and "girl" were all derived from Old English derogatory terms for servants, and even the legal word for youth—
"minor"—was literally defined as "less," a social rather than an
age designation.

As long as the primary function of the family was economic
and its goal physical survival rather than emotional support, age
was reckoned by ability and situation rather than by chronol-
ogy. In the first part of the eighteenth century, Cotton Mather,
the New England minister and scholar, acknowledged only
three stages of life: childhood, youth, and old age. Youth, as a
period of life, was prolonged until domestic and financial independence was reached. In rural New England, men over thirty
were still called "youths" if they still lived as single persons in
their fathers' homes, while in other parts of the colonies, teens
were on their own and treated as adults. In the South during the
same period family structure was less stable and youngsters
assumed adult roles before they reached the legal majority of
twenty-one; the frontier and the port cities were crowded with
young people who were unattached to traditional patriarchal
homes, either as children or as servants, and who were responsible for themselves.

No one doubted that infants were a special case: they were
not only dependent in a financial and social sense, but also
physically helpless. In colonial times, babies seemed especially
fragile and vulnerable. Under the best circumstances, perhaps
one in every six children was fated to die before its second
birthday and in some places the number rose above one in four.
Although these figures are only approximate, a terrible toll in
infant mortality was exacted to some degree from rich and
poor, slave and free, black and white, urban and rural. In fact,
medical misinformation being what it was, cossetted babies of
the rich were just as much at risk—if not because of inadequate

food and shelter, then because of lack of knowledge concerning nutrition and disease.

The response of a parent to the death of an infant might reflect deep grief, but it also required resignation to the inevitable. In 1713, Cotton Mather lost three of his children and his wife to a measles epidemic within a two-week period. He particularly mourned his two-year-old daughter, Jerusha: "I begg'd, I begg'd that such a bitter Cup, as the death of that lovely child, might pass from me. Nevertheless!—My glorious Lord, brought me to glorify Him, with the most submissive Resignation." Although the chances of infant survival did not improve much during the eighteenth century, parents began to focus on illness as a condition of the body that might be cured by proper treatment, although neither they nor the doctors on whom they relied had any effective knowledge of what constituted such treatment. Less than ten years after the tragedy in his family, Mather was urging Bostonians to try the new English inoculation procedure against smallpox, the greatest killer of children (and, for that matter, of adults) of the day. Since patients stood a certain risk of death from the serum itself, the treatment remained controversial throughout the century. Scientific "moderns" continued to promote inoculation, and when there were rumors that Benjamin Franklin's infant son had died of the procedure in 1739, he inserted an announcement in the *Pennsylvania Gazette* that his child had not been inoculated, but had died of a naturally contracted case of smallpox. He blamed himself for leaving his child unprotected. In the early 1770s, when Charles Willson Peale painted *Rachel Weeping* over her dead baby, she gazed at heaven in resignation and perhaps for comfort, but the nearby table held a medicine bottle, indicating that earthly remedies had at least been tried.

The life of an infant almost literally hung on the life of its mother, since breast milk was its only reliable source of nourishment. Lack of understanding about nutrition prevented the development of healthy alternatives, as did the state of technology before the invention of bottles and nipples as delivery systems. A small number of surviving curiosities like bowls with attached metal tubes indicate that desperate families tried to

compensate for a failure of the baby's natural food supply. The
very young might be presented with semisolid starchy mixtures, such as boiled "Indian bread and milk," but the only real
alternative was to find a woman with a baby of her own and
extra milk to spare. In the isolated rural context of colonial
America, such women were hard to locate. One Chesapeake
father went from neighbor to neighbor seeking a woman who
might be able to feed his motherless child, but the only offer he
received was from a woman who was willing to "dry nurse,"
that is, to take care of the baby and attempt to feed it by the
procedure described above.

During the eighteenth century, city newspapers carried occasional advertisements by parents seeking wet nurses, or, conversely, by women who offered their services in that capacity.
The emphasis in these ads was not only on the abundance of
supply and health of the supplier, but on her character as well.
Scientific and religious theory both agreed that morality, disposition, and temper traits were actually transmitted through the
physical properties of the milk. Very wealthy plantation wives
in the South with a large number of children might also have
recourse to black slave women as wet nurses, but this was less
prevalent in the eighteenth century than it appears to have
become later on. The recognized necessity of keeping mothers
and infants together meant that this was the one family unit
among slaves that was rarely violated. Although the nursing
black baby may have had to travel into the fields with its mother
when she was required to return to the labor force, the pair was
unlikely to be separated by sale or transfer.

The age at which a baby was weaned was of great concern,
although certainly the options were limited among poorer
women for whom extended nursing meant one less hungry
mouth at the table. It was also commonly believed that a nursing mother would not become pregnant, so that delayed weaning was probably practiced by some as a rough form of birth
control. Among those who saw infancy as a natural state reflec-
tive of original sin, however, it was important to get the baby
on its own as quickly as possible. Observers frequently offered
the fact that Indian women nursed their babies until they were

three or four years old as evidence of Amerindian "savagery."

Generally speaking, the importance of early infant regulation in weaning, toilet training, and self-reliance was widely acknowledged, if not practiced, by Anglo-Americans. Whether their rationale was religious or scientific, their goal physical or moral health, parents had a pragmatic sense of the risky state of infancy and worked to make their babies hardy and independent. Indian permissiveness toward late toilet training and the expression of sexuality through masturbation was criticized, but their habit of "hardening" infants with cold-water baths was much admired.

Self-styled professional advice on raising children was increasingly available to literate eighteenth-century parents, at first from ministers and then more commonly from doctors, as behavior became more closely linked to psychology than to morality. In 1749, Benjamin Franklin's widely distributed *Pennsylvania Gazette* carried a long, two-part article excerpted from a book by a London physician which outlined the proper care for infants based on the physician's work at the London Foundling Hospital. All of these professionals (they were uniformly men) recommended light clothing, cold baths, and exposure to fresh air, as well as the setting of regular schedules for feeding and sleeping, plain food after weaning, and careful supervision. We can only guess from the vehemence of their arguments that common practice was quite the opposite: babies must have been overdressed, rarely bathed, protected from fresh air, irregularly fed with inappropriate food, and either left unattended or badly cared for by older siblings or servants.

The evidence we have suggests that the treatment of most infants was unaffected by professional advice. The daily lives of the vast majority of men and women allowed little time for the nurturance of babies, and their incomes hardly stretched to cover special equipment of use only during such a brief period of life. The material lives of babies, therefore, changed little during the eighteenth century. The youngest child in the poorest household probably had no bed of its own, sleeping with its parents as many cases of "overlaying" attest. (Overlaying re-

ferred to babies who were suffocated when the mother acciden-
tally rolled on top of the child during the night.) More fortunate
babies were provided with their own sleeping arrangements,
either improvised or "purposely made." The cradle, made of
wicker or wood, usually had a hood to protect the baby from
drafts, holes or knobs for ropes that could be laced across the
baby and its bedding to keep it from kicking the covers off or
falling out, and rockers that could be manipulated by any
nearby foot to put the baby to sleep while leaving the hands
free for other tasks. The cradle had the additional advantage of
mobility: it could be placed near the fire for warmth during the
day, and under the curtains of the parents' bed at night.

Warmth was further insured by the way in which infants
were clothed. Fancy dresses and lace caps were special finery,
simple versions of which formed the daily wear of older babies.
Very small infants were wrapped in layers of fabric bands and
cloths, called swaddling, and wore as many as three caps on
their heads. This not only kept the baby warm, but was felt to
speed up the development of straight limbs, while tight cap-
ping of the head was to help close the "soft spot" in the new-
born's skull. There was no question that a heavily wrapped baby
was more convenient as well. It could be handled like a stick of
wood, even by a young and inexperienced sibling, without danger of its wriggling away. While doctors began to campaign
against such treatment after the mid–eighteenth century, its
continued use by new immigrants lasted well into the nineteenth century.

A creeping baby or toddler was potentially more of a chal-
lenge. European custom dictated that at this age children be
put into heavy corsets with bone or metal stays to keep them
straight and placed in a standing stool to prevent crawling. With
the addition of wheels, a standing stool became a walker, which
allowed the one-year-old an opportunity to get around on its
own. That a child given this mobility and left unattended—as
many were—might walk into the fire or down the steps and
permanently injure or kill itself was regarded as a sad but un-
avoidable hazard of life. It is likely that poor, rural, and immigrant children were kept in this sort of bondage right through

the eighteenth century, but by the time of the Revolution, the children of wealthier, better-educated parents were given both more freedom and more attention. Letters written by visitors record the first efforts of a toddler "shuffling across the room" under the amused eyes of her mother, and a two- and a three-year-old who were "fighting on the carpet during the whole visit."

The upper boundaries of infancy were not clearly marked in the eighteenth century. In one sense, children were seen as "infants" until they were deemed ready to contribute meaningfully to the family economy, usually at around the age of six or seven at the beginning of the century, and at eight or even older by the 1790s. In another sense, as soon as they could walk on their own, talk—however imperfectly—and give some indication of reason, understanding, and self-control, they crossed a boundary into the larger world of humanity. Even then, before about 1750, they did not enter a realm of childhood where they were recognized as needing special time for growth and development. Instead, they entered, girls and boys alike, into the subordinate domestic world of women and servants, a world of dependency that girls would never leave. Boys who were not yet competent to join the masculine work force in field or shop were expected to reside there as well: they wore skirts and leading strings (ribbons symbolic of submission that hung down the back), slept with their sisters and the servants, and remained under the control of their mothers. By and large, it was only during this brief period of five or six years that anything resembling childhood as we know it occurred in colonial America.

It is impossible, of course, to know how the vast majority of children were raised within their homes, for their stories only surfaced when there was trouble and the court had to be brought in or if their parents were literate and interested enough to record the events of everyday life in letters or journals. We know that parents were expected to keep young children busy, give them adequate training—practical, intellectual, and moral—and avoid permanently damaging, abusive treatment. In poor homes and on subsistence farms, even very young children were expected to perform useful tasks. It is likely that, in general, young children were among the least-attended members of the household, expected to fend for themselves as infants could not, but having little economic value to the family production unit.

The range of ways in which children were raised by more affluent and better-educated parents is known in more detail. Those who regarded the essence of children as sinful and saw the need to bring them to salvation as quickly as possible, generally identified as evangelicals, could be found at all times, in all parts of the colonies, and among all of the Protestant denominations. Their concept of the family as the authoritarian base for work and morality led to the most explicit statements on the need for strict control and constant supervision of children. Evangelicals were fond of laying down rules and prophesying the awful torments of Hell for the most harmless of youthful transgressions against the Divine Order of family life. They placed great emphasis on breaking the child's will as early as possible. If they truly practiced what they preached, their children must have led cheerless lives indeed. Food, clothing, sleep, and play were consciously restricted, and the atmosphere aimed at was one of constant sobriety and quiet. As one mother explained, "There was no such thing as loud playing or talking allowed of; rising out of their places, or going out of the room, was not permitted except for good cause; and running into the yard, garden, or street, without leave, was always deemed a capital offence." To achieve these ends, all manner of punishments were suggested, although it is no surprise that evangelicals most frequently advocated the use of the rod. Other disciplinary procedures included shaming the child, withholding love, and even starvation, advised by one father who, as late as the 1820s, withheld food and water from his fifteen-month-old son for several days because the child would not come to him when he put out his arms.

Whatever the effect on long-term personality, even such harsh measures did not necessarily keep evangelical children from doing what came naturally. The famous preacher of the mid–eighteenth century Great Awakening, George Whitfield, confessed that, despite such an upbringing, he had, among other "sins," masturbated, lied, read romances, and indulged in "filthy talk and foolish jesting." He had even stolen money from his mother to buy sweets, attend plays, and indulge in card playing.

It is not to the evangelicals that we can look for the invention of childhood during the eighteenth century. The place of "care-free" youth was in households that have come to be considered "typically American." The parents in these homes were often deeply religious, but their religious beliefs were set within the new context of the scientific, rational, and worldly goals of eighteenth-century thinkers who followed in Locke's footsteps. Many were upwardly mobile, working hard to create family fortunes so that their children would have the best in terms of education and culture, providing expanded opportunities in career and marriage choices. They frequently had country homes to which they hoped to retire on fortunes made as city merchants, and to which they fled or sent their families during the summer months to escape the heat and disease of the city. The number of such families was small, perhaps, but they had increasing influence as they rose in wealth and prominence throughout the eighteenth century. To a great extent, it was their secular ideas and economic hopes that were reflected in the Constitution and the new republic.

"Modern" parents read and accepted advice books suggesting that children were not filled with original sin, and that maturation was a natural process for the human animal. They were free in their expressions of love and devotion to their children, bought them presents, and recognized that when children played, they were not indulging their baser instincts, wasting time, or preparing for a life of idleness. Mrs. Tench Francis's description of a winter day, written in a letter to her absent husband in the mid-1760s, may not sound particularly unusual to us. "Johnny is just come up to me all over snow and Mad with a long story of a frolick he has had with Jeremy and somebody throwing snowballs," she wrote. Expressions of this kind are rare for the eighteenth century, however, and give us only a tantalizing glimpse of a family life we recognize and understand.

Pressure in these more liberal families for their children to be "good" revolved around achievement and caring social behavior rather than religious morality. Discipline, therefore, less frequently involved physical punishment, and more often employed appeals to love and reason. Since competition and a desire to succeed were considered positive aspects of basic human nature in the upwardly mobile family, emphasis was placed on the carrot, rather than the stick. In 1783, Timothy Pickering advised parents that it was "doubtless far better to apply to the *natural ambition* than to the *fears* of a child: the latter will only make hardened rogues of the bold, and confound the tender hearted: while nothing is more animating than just applause."

On the very upper fringes of American society, children lived yet very different lives, not merely because of the wealth of their parents, but because of their attitudes as well. These seem, at first, modern in their permissiveness and lack of direction, but they actually spring from an older European tradition. Among the gentry, children were apt to be at once indulged and ignored—treated as amusing little pets when present, but left to the daily care of servants or slaves during the crucial years between three and seven. Since they were not yet old enough to be trained in culture and the social graces, their parents paid little attention to either the older notion that young children had souls to save, or the more modern concept that they had minds to train. Memoirs of a Virginia woman, Eliza Custis, written in the early nineteenth century, reflect back on the mid-1770s when, at the age of three or four, she was encouraged to stand on a table, singing songs "which I did not understand" for her father and his gentlemen friends. As the men rolled "in their chairs with laughter" and even "the servants in the passage [joined] their mirth," the mother, "who could not help laughing, used to retire and leave me to the gentlemen."

Families at the very lowest end of the economic scale had little in the way of time or resources to spend on children, however beloved. Time was money, and with both mothers and fathers involved in the economic struggle of daily life, young children were not only left to fend for themselves, but also—often by the age of three or four—expected to care for those younger than they. Most households lacked extra hands, and on isolated rural farms there was no recourse to neighbors who, in any event, would have been busy with their own concerns. The many cases of accidental childhood deaths reported in sensational manner by Benjamin Franklin in the *Pennsylvania Gazette* throughout the eighteenth century clearly involved situations where children left alone were trampled by animals, burned at open fireplaces, or scalded by tipped pots of boiling liquid at unprotected hearths. The reports were both rural and urban: the two "young" children frozen to death in January 1754 who "had been sent out in the evening to bring home some sheep, but lost their way in the woods and were not found till the next day"; the Boston child whose mother "left it alone while she stepped out about some business" and was burned so badly that it died the next day; or, most symptomatic of all, the report in 1734 that on "Monday last a young child fell into a tub of water in Chestnut Street and was unhappily drowned before anybody perceived it." None of this presupposes a lack of love or affection, merely a scale of priorities in which the needs of children were ranked low, and their rearing subordinated to other, more pressing tasks.

So far, we have considered only the lives of small children whose parents met certain minimum standards for care and sufficiency. But what of those who had no family, or whose parents failed to provide for them adequately? For most of the colonial period, there were virtually no alternatives to inclusion in some family group, and community responsibility toward homeless children consisted only in making sure that they were placed in established households. The problem lay in finding a home to accept children who were too young to contribute fully to the domestic economy. Even kin were reluctant to take young orphans unless they had substantial financial resources to bring with them, and in most parts of colonial America, the children most likely to be thrown into dependence on the com-

munity were those from the bottom layer of society: the illegitimate children of destitute mothers and orphans of transient
paupers or newly arrived immigrants who had no family ties or
neighborhood associations.

The solution adopted by most communities was based on a
system used in England since the early sixteenth century. A
host family was guaranteed a return on its investment by the
expedient of receiving the child as a "bound" servant; that is,
the community in effect traded the child and its services to a
household head for the complete time of its minority. The
money expended on a young and unproductive "extra mouth"
would be recouped many times over by the value of its labor in
the years ahead. It was still something of a gamble. The child
might die and deprive the family of its anticipated profit, and
since the risk of childhood death was largest among infants and
toddlers and the wait longer before they made themselves useful, these very young children were the hardest to place.
Throughout the century, local governments frequently had to
offer supplementary support to prospective masters for the
early years. Since the community obviously wanted to keep the
payment as low as possible, a truly pernicious system of auction
to "the lowest bidder" developed, where the child was sold to
the householder who would accept the smallest fee. Accepting
the smallest fee usually meant accepting the lowest standards
of food, clothing, housing, and attention.

Again, this sale of children does not indicate insensitivity on
the part of the community, but reflects the realities of everyday
life in colonial America. A few indentures, as these contracts
were called, attempted to guarantee that dependent children
would receive the rudiments of reading, writing, and arithmetic and that when they were old enough, they would be taught
a craft or skill. For example, George Petsworth, when not quite
two years old, was bound out in Virginia in 1716 to serve until
he was of age. In return, his master was to "oblige himself [and]
his heirs, [to provide] 3 years schooling . . . that he may read well
in any part of the bible [and] to instruct and learn him . . . that
he may be able after his indented time to get his own living and
to allow him sufficient meat, drink, washing and apparel." This

indenture was enlightened for its time. Most orphans were merely bound out as "servants," a designation entitling them to nothing beyond mere maintenance, the assurance of hard work, and a guarantee that they would never acquire the skills necessary to improve their lot in life.

In the years after the Revolution, however, the idea that America was a land of opportunity became important as a cornerstone of the new nation, one of the things that distinguished it from the corrupt and stagnant social system in Europe. By the 1790s, several states from all regions passed laws prohibiting the binding out of young orphans as "mere" servants, requiring that they be provided the building blocks for future success that George Petsworth had been lucky to be offered near the beginning of the century.

Very young children who were not orphans were also bound out, not by the community, but by parents, particularly single mothers, who had no other way to support them. In Boston, New York, and Philadelphia they might be turned over voluntarily to the Guardians of the Poor, who made the necessary contacts, arrangements, and contractual agreements. In other cases, the parents conducted the business themselves and the borderline between indenturing the child and selling it was a very narrow one. Pennsylvania attempted to eliminate out-and-out child-selling by 1750, at least as it applied to immigrants who used their children to finance the family's passage to the New World. "People who arrive without the funds to pay their way and who have children under the age of five, cannot settle their debts by selling them. They must give away these children for nothing to be brought up by strangers, and in return these children must stay in service until they are twenty-one years old," wrote an observer of German immigration through the port of Philadelphia at midcentury.

It was, generally speaking, colonial policy to keep poor families together, providing them with "outdoor relief"—donations of money, food, or wood—to tide them over particularly difficult periods. Communities, however, possessed the right, based on English legal precedent, to remove children forcibly from parents who were deemed "unfit," either because of persistent poverty that caused them to be a continuing charge on public funds, or for moral inadequacy. In fact, poverty and immorality were usually seen as two parts of the same issue. A Virginia law in 1748 stated the interrelationship succinctly:

> To prevent the evil consequences attending the neglect or inability of poor people to bring up their children in an honest and orderly course of life where . . . it shall appear to the court that he, she or they neglect . . . instruction in the principles of Christianity . . . it shall be lawful for the churchwardens of the parish . . . by order of their county court, to bind every such child . . . in the same manner . . . as the law directs for poor orphan children.

Although most frequently applied to mothers with "bastard children," such laws could also affect two-parent households, and the large number of cases referring not only to interracial babies but also to German, Dutch, and Irish families give us a clue to some of the prejudices that operated. While we cannot measure the extent of resentment among those whose children were taken, at least one group of German immigrants went to court in New York in 1720 to protest that their children had been taken "without and against their consent . . . by which means they were deprived of the comfort of their children's company and education, as well as the assistance and support they might in a small time have reasonably expected from them."

The understanding that parents had a right to profit from the labor of their children was not unique to German immigrants. Eighteenth-century colonial parents in general had no qualms concerning child labor and never viewed it as a social evil to be eradicated. In a world where children made up half of the population, the importance of their economic contribution was just one more of the given facts of life. Pragmatism was bolstered by morality: "Idle hands are the Devil's playthings" went the old adage, and the point was driven home in an article, "American Manufactures," written by "a plain, but real Friend to America" as late as 1787: "[At what age are we] fit to go to work?—Surely the time of youth is a very proper period to serve our apprenticeship . . . we seldom see a person fond of labour in old age, who has lived an idle life when young."

Boys were "breeched" between six and seven years old, leaving the skirts of the female world behind, and assuming the clothing worn by males in the public arena of workaday life. The change was more than symbolic. Breeching not only marked the transfer of supervision and control over boys from mothers to fathers, but for most, sons of small farmers, it signaled entry into the full-time labor force as well. As the only workers their fathers could afford, they kept the same hours as adults, although it was recognized that their strength and ability were not up to the same tasks. The common expectation was that they could only do about half a man's work until they were twelve to sixteen, just as it was usually assumed that, during those years, they only needed about half as much food as a full-grown hand. Where farms were larger and the owners had access to extra labor, the work was more highly specialized, so that on the largest plantations in the South, where the work was done by gangs of slaves, black boys did not join the crew used for the very heaviest labor until they were in their "prime," that is, close to twenty.

The sons of craftsmen also began to work at about the age of six, frequently "helping" in their father's shops. While they, too, worked a full day, they were not allowed to participate in the skilled aspects of the manufacturing process—who could afford the risk of ruining a valuable piece of furniture lumber or wasting a good beaver skin?—but swept the floor, sorted spare parts, loaded and unloaded wagons, ran errands, and tended the shop. Poor people, both farmers and artisans, who could not afford to feed or clothe their own sons as less than full producers sent them to live with other families as "boys of all work," laboring in other men's fields, other men's shops. Often, too, in rural villages, craftsmen's sons worked as "extra" hands on local farms during the busy planting and harvesting seasons. For boys on the far edges of the frontier or in the most remote rural areas of the settled colonies, as well as those from poor laboring families in the towns and cities, this "go-fer" status, as we call it today, embraced the beginning and end of their training. In reality, it also marked the limits of their adult lives: subsistence farming of their own land, or labor on the fields and in the shops of others.

Girls underwent no symbolic transformation of their status equivalent to breeching in boys, nor did their lives change in any such dramatic way. They kept on doing what they had done since they were old enough to walk, only they gradually took on more domestic work and heavier responsibility for adequate performance. In a way, they were a step ahead of their brothers, since the tasks they had been performing in the buttery, at the hearth, over the cook pot, with spindle or spinning wheel, by the cradle or in the kitchen garden, had already been learned by the age of six. Except in the case of direst poverty, girls were likely to remain within the home, working with their mothers until they were married and their workplace was transferred along with their residence from their fathers' households to those of their husbands. If their parents could not afford their upkeep, they, like their brothers, were sent to live with others, usually as "servants." The outlook for such girls was equally bleak, limited to the bottom of the economic scale, and with greatly reduced chances for marriage. On the other hand, if they did marry, their eventual lot in life became dependent on the abilities of their husbands, and an up-and-coming spouse might dramatically improve a young woman's place in society.

Although it was acknowledged as perfectly proper, and indeed even moral, for children to begin work at six, parents who could afford it tended to equate work with training for the future, rather than with immediate economic gain. The primary obligation and duty of an eighteenth-century father was to educate his children so that they were set on the path of economic independence. The term "education" in this context covered a whole range of learning experiences, and it was only after about 1750 that it came to be more identified with schooling in academics. Basic literacy—a reading knowledge of the ABCs and a few simple biblical texts—was the responsibility of the family, and took place within a domestic setting, under the care of women. Writing was considered a separate, and probably unnecessary, pedagogical skill. Where there were enough households clustered together, as in the towns and villages of

New England and the Middle Colonies or on the larger southern plantations, a woman might be hired to run a "dame school" where she instructed both the boys and girls of several families at once. In much of colonial America, the scattered settlement pattern of farm and frontier precluded these communal classes, and mothers taught their own children as part of their domestic duties. Obviously, this system immediately limited the horizons of the large number of children whose mothers were themselves illiterate, whose families could not afford to pay the fee, however small, for the services of an outside teacher, or who lived in areas where the neighborhood could not attract a teacher.

Beyond rudimentary book learning, fathers took responsibility for finding serious on-the-job training for their ten- to twelve-year-old sons: apprenticeships to teach the skills of a lifelong occupation. This kind of education was common for boys from almost all social strata except the landed gentry, at least until midcentury. It applied to many of the younger sons of farmers whose land would not stretch enough to provide an inheritance for everyone in the next generation. It applied to the sons of successful merchants who bound them out to serve time on long ocean voyages where they learned to understand the business from the "waterline up," and where they made contacts in distant ports beneficial to their own later ventures. And it applied to the sons of artisans and craftsmen in every trade, at every level. Although fathers frequently trained their sons in their own skills, sparsely settled rural districts and small towns could not support too many craftsmen following the same occupation, so it was sometimes necessary to apprentice a child either away from home or into a different line of work.

The choice of a career or "calling," as the Puritans styled it, was the father's decision, but there is ample evidence that caring parents tried to take the individual temperament, abilities, and wishes of their children into account. As early as 1701, Cotton Mather stressed that every Christian should have an occupation that was "Allowable . . . yea Agreeable . . . and that he Entered into it with a suitable Disposition." In his autobiography, Benjamin Franklin painted a delightful picture of his father, who "took me to walk with him, and see Joiners, Brick-layers, Turners, Braziers, &. at their Work, that he might observe my Inclination, and endeavour to fix it on some Trade or other."

Throughout the century, in all parts of the colonies, fathers who died before their sons were old enough to be educated directed the executors of their wills that their sons be put out "at suitable age . . . to Trades or business *in agreement with* their desires [emphasis added]," as one German craftsman put it at about the time of the Revolution. Poor people whose estates could not purchase costly indentures pleaded with their executors that "the Children are to be put out to Good People but not as servants." Parents or guardians watched anxiously to make sure that the promised training actually took place, resorting to court action for breach of contract if it did not. Although in the European tradition apprenticeship was expected to last seven years or until maturity, jobs were abundant in much of the New World, and such agreements frequently ran only four years, cut even shorter by agreement or default if opportunity beckoned.

A much more significant difference between the Old World and New World concept of apprentice training was imbedded in the language of eighteenth-century American indentures and wills. Over and over again, along with stipulations concerning complete induction into "the art and mystery" of masonry, or hatmaking, or silversmithing, and the eventual presentation of "a new suit of clothes," or "his own tools," or "forty shillings" on completion of the apprenticeship, went the requirement that provision be made for "sufficient schooling" or "to attend school for one whole year," or, even more specifically, "to be kept in school to age fourteen at the latest and then put apprentice." The assumption that even common boys headed for lives as "mere mechanicks" needed book learning as part of their educational preparations was audacious, demanding a virtual revolution in the whole notion of schooling—who should have it, what they should learn, and how it would serve society as a whole.

Academic education in "grammar" or "Latin" schools based

on English models had existed in colonial America, especially in New England, well before the eighteenth century. An alternative to apprenticeship, these institutions prepared boys for the universities and eventual careers as ministers, teachers, and lawyers. They did not provide a general education in any of the subjects needed for practical success in life outside the church, classroom, or courthouse. Boys who entered grammar schools were apt to be the most promising brothers of those who were serving apprenticeships in more industrial pursuits, or from families where the fathers themselves were ministers, teachers, or lawyers.

Certainly they worked as hard, or at least as long, at their tasks as those who were bound to craftsmen. Classes were generally held six days a week, from seven in the morning to five in the evening, spring, summer, and fall, and from eight to four during the shorter days of winter, with an hour or two for lunch during midday. Although not "indentured" to the schoolmaster, the student was under his complete governance, although fathers might—and frequently did—interfere with what they felt was overly harsh treatment of their sons. The punishment for both academic and behavioral lapses was usually physical, since then, as now, there was a widespread suspicion that teachers who were "soft" and failed to use the rod would also fail to instill either respect or knowledge in their pupils. Some teachers, no doubt, indulged in what we would call "psychology." One New England master located the troublemaker in his classroom and beat that boy whenever the others failed to behave. We can only hope that this teacher's knowledge of Latin was superior to his understanding of human nature. As one would suspect, the other boys began to misbehave just to get their classmate in trouble, and the boy, in turn, began to beat up his fellow students in order to escape punishment himself. Perhaps, in an odd way, the master achieved his goal: he did indeed instill a sense of responsibility in the former troublemaker, or at least moved his disturbances from schoolroom to yard.

Academics were also seen as a necessary part of education for boys who were in training to become gentlemen—an actual occupational designation in the eighteenth century—but since there was "a deal of Difference to be observed in the Education of a Gentleman, and a mere Scholar," as one teacher remarked, the grammar school as described was not sufficient. Upper-class boys began learning their jobs as soon as they were breeched, merchant sons accompanied their fathers to the wharves and warehouses, and the boys of southern plantation owners traveled for days at a time with their fathers to the homes of other wealthy landowners, or to the taverns, churches, and county courts where the business of farm and government was mixed with the pleasures of social interaction. They received as much classical education as their fathers thought necessary, often with a private tutor, occasionally attending university, in England or the colonies, as much for the social as the pedagogical experience. They also received schooling in a variety of social graces from English, French, and Italian literature to music, dancing, and swordplay. Card playing, gambling, drinking, and racing they picked up on their own from their fathers and their peers. Traditionally, before the Revolution, their training was topped off with a final polish acquired by a tour of Europe, or at least of England, accompanied by a tutor or another adult male companion.

Throughout the eighteenth century, the real key to opportunity for advancement in income and status came to be seen as academic education. One father put it well, writing to his son, who was failing to take advantage of his schooling, that "many Children capable of learning, are condemn'd to the necessity of Labouring hard, for want of ability in their Parent to give them an education." The response to this widely shared belief in schooling as a magic potion for getting ahead was an explosion of plans, projects, and experiments in education, culminating in the nineteenth century in a unique "American system of public schools" that were free, compulsory, and universal. In the end, it changed the everyday life of all American children, demanding of them only one sort of work—book learning—and enclosing them tightly in a world of childhood, rigidly separated from the world of adults. While the eighteenth century groped only vaguely in this direction, a broad spectrum of educational experiences touched a far greater number and variety of children than ever before in western history.

Most were only lightly touched. In rural areas, children were dependent on the availability of a teacher willing and able to carry education beyond the ABC level learned at home. Moreover, while parents might recognize the importance of literacy to future opportunities, real work came first, and farm boys were free to attend school only a few weeks or, at best, a few months a year, during the intervals of planting and harvesting. In towns and cities, schooling was also what we might term occasional, although there was a ready supply of teachers, and the seasonal nature of work was less pronounced. There is evidence that some town schools offered night classes for the convenience of apprentices who had to work during the day, and occasionally for craftsmen's daughters and servant girls as well. One innovative feature of these common schools, as they came to be called, was that they were often open to girls, either along with boys, or in separate classes where the domestic skills of knitting and sewing were taught in addition to the elementary subjects learned by their brothers. There was a tuition charge for every child, either by the week, the "quarter," or sometimes by the subject, so that the breadth of the schooling received depended on the depth of the parental pocketbook. As the century progressed and the value of schooling was more generally accepted, wealthy men offered scholarships so that "deserving poor" boys might attend local schools; even colonials of very modest means who died without heirs left a portion of their meager estates for the "education of the local poor." In some places there were special-interest philanthropies as well, including charity schools entirely devoted to particular groups of disadvantaged children such as blacks, Indians, Germans, or Lutherans.

The academic charge to these schools was that they teach pupils "to read perfectly, to write a legible hand, and figure to the rule of three," an arithmetic device for finding an unknown number when three known ones are given. Although we cannot know how well they succeeded in terms of perfect reading, except to note that the method employed encouraged sounding out by letter and moving the lips—not recommended by today's speed-reading professionals—the diaries and account books left by adults whose education took place in common schools do not testify to outstanding teacher success.

Another agenda lay behind purely academic goals: an expectation that, along with the three R's, schoolchildren would be inculcated with social values. Most important were "the first Principles of Virtue and Piety," taught through the use of textbooks whose reading and spelling lessons were heavily biblical and moral in content. In addition to these lessons in Christian morality, ladled out in huge doses throughout the century, children headed even for such "mean" careers as shopkeepers, artisans, and traders received intensely practical training in social manners, since American educators believed, with some justification, that today's shopkeeper might be tomorrow's great merchant. The many books on conduct ignored the "overly genteel" or "foppish" manners of the upper-class drawing room, however, to focus on basic rules for behavior in the home, in school, in church, and on the streets. Consider this excerpt from Christopher Dock's book, *100 Necessary Rules For the Proper Behaviour of Children,* published in 1764 and intended for an audience of children of German background: "When you wash your face and hands do not scatter water about in the room . . . do not wolf down your food . . . or overfill your mouth . . . do not run wildly nor [urinate] in the streets . . . use the handkerchief when spitting or blowing the nose." Americans, it seems, were extremely sensitive to the criticisms of genteel European travelers who found them noisy, rude, coarse, and unmannerly, and while defensively denying that "foreign manners" were appropriate to the New World since "the refinement of manners in every country should keep pace exactly with the increase of its wealth [and the greatest evil in America is] an improvement of taste and manners which its wealth cannot support." It was urged that teachers who were hired for the common schools "possess good breeding and agreeable manners."

Beginning during the Revolution, the importance of educating the citizenry for its part in republican government became a favorite theme of both politicians and educators. The *New England Primer,* published throughout the eighteenth century with a picture of King George as a frontispiece, removed his crown and relabeled him "John Hancock," "Samuel Adams," or "George Washington" after 1776. In 1777, Pennsylvania required its schoolmasters and officers of academies and colleges to swear an oath of allegiance to the United States, and other states followed suit. By 1779, Thomas Jefferson had formulated an elaborate plan for a system of public schools in Virginia to prepare the "best and the brightest" for careers in public service. In the years following the war, schemes of general education proliferated, with rationales stressing the advantages to the nation of an educated public and placing patriotic indoctrination of children on a par with teaching them basic academics, morality, and manners. The most famous and influential of the educational writers was Noah Webster (1758–1843), author of *An American Dictionary of the English Language.* Himself an example of the New American, Webster argued tirelessly that a good education should instill patriotism, and produced numerous textbooks which were designed to "implant science, virtue and the principle of liberty to alter the European pattern and achieve American goals." He saw the two basic principles of the republic as providing the right to an education and a chance to earn upward mobility. Of course, his insistence on the necessity of using good American books instead of English imports did nothing to hurt sales of his own works.

As the numbers and influence of upwardly mobile colonial families grew continuously throughout the eighteenth century, the market for schooling expanded as well. Educational entrepreneurs flourished, advertising their services in local newspapers and appealing to the snobbery of a prospective clientele by emphasizing recent arrival from London, cultural hub of the world to Americans. More importantly, a new type of educational institution developed, flexible enough to send its graduates on to the university for further polish, or directly into the more advanced levels of the social and business world. Known as academies, these schools made their appearance in the cities, large towns, and more heavily populated parts of the colonies after the middle of the century. They accepted both day students and boarders, so that their benefits were available to families who lived outside the urban areas, and they occupied roughly the position in the educational hierarchy that middle schools and high schools do today.

Based on a model proposed by Benjamin Franklin to the Philadelphia Common Council in 1750, there were literally hundreds of these institutions chartered by the end of the century. Although the actual curriculum varied from academy to academy, most attempted to combine the courses of the Latin schools with those of the private teachers. Franklin recognized that this was overambitious: "As to their STUDIES," he wrote, "it would be well if they could be taught *every Thing* that is useful, and *every Thing* that is ornamental: But Art is long, and their Time is short. [They should learn] those Things that are likely to be *most useful* and *most ornamental.*" He then went on to outline, in several closely packed pages, a list of subjects that it would have taken several lifetimes to master. The Phillips Academy at Andover, Massachusetts, proposed to offer, in 1778, what was probably a more realistic curriculum, and one that became fairly standard for these kinds of schools: "the English, Latin, and Greek languages, Writing, Arithmetic, Music, and the Art of Speaking; also practical Geometry, Logic, and any other of the liberal Arts and Sciences, or Languages, as opportunity and ability may hereafter admit."

The expectation of a certain degree of cultural polish for substantial urban and rural men of business had its repercussions in the world of women, since the sloppy education of a child, whether male or female, reflected on the social standing of the family. A refined young girl had to learn the arts and skills of gentility as well as those of domesticity to preside creditably in the parlor or at the dining table of her ambitious husband. Upward mobility from generation to generation often meant that mothers lacked the necessary skills—Abigail Adams was a terrible speller—to prepare their daughters for the more sophisticated lives they would lead. Private schooling began to be available for girls by the 1730s to give them a good grounding in the elements of reading, writing, arithmetic, and English literature. This was usually regarded as "sufficient literacy," and they did not proceed to the classics, which were thought to be not only unnecessary for women, but also downright pernicious to their femininity. Instead, they received further career instruction for their roles as wives. A recurring advertisement in the Philadelphia newspapers offered children of both sexes writing, arithmetic, and "the true grounds of English spelling" while the schoolmaster's wife provided the girls with additional instruction in penmanship, French, singing, and "playing on the spinet," and his sister "lately arrived from London" specialized in dancing and "all sorts of needlework."

Sixty years later, private schools for girls had proliferated all along the Eastern Seaboard from Boston to Charleston. Like the Quaker-run Westtown, or the Moravian seminary in Bethlehem, they were based on the models for boys' academies, sometimes operating separately, sometimes as divisions of their brother institutions. Many of these were boarding schools that attracted girls from all over the United States and the West Indies, indicating how seriously parents regarded the proper education of their daughters for their occupations as wives and mothers. After all, sending a girl away from the shelter of home was not an action to be undertaken lightly.

Although the goals of literacy, morality, manners, and patriotism formed the basis of the education given to both sexes, the subjects for girls continued to stress particularly feminine accomplishments, and the ideals of the new republic were expressed in the mottoes and decorations they stitched into their compulsory samplers rather than in poems, essays, and valedictory speeches. One small indication only remains to us of possible dissatisfaction with the female status quo. In 1800, a young Maryland girl carefully embroidered on her sampler, "Patty Polk did this and she hated every stitch she did in it. She loves to read much more." Patty's rebellion extended only so far: she *did* work the sampler regardless of her feelings, and we can only speculate about the attitudes of the mother or teacher who encouraged her to put these sentiments in so permanent a form.

While adolescence as a necessary stage in human develop-

ment may not have been recognized or condoned in the eighteenth century, it clearly existed all the same. Boys and girls in
their mid to late teens pushed against both family and society,
and society and family pushed back. Parents coped in a variety
of ways: there was loss of privilege, such as being locked in one's
room or having one's allowance withheld; there was lecturing
and nagging; there was guilt. In the case of truly incorrigible
sons, there was disownment: "Because my son has renounced . . .
my Authority as a Parent . . . I consider myself as possessing no
legal authority over him." Mostly, however, parents appear to
have tried to come to terms with the adolescent drive for independence while continuing to maintain at least some modicum
of control. When Andrew Shelburne from New Hampshire attempted to run away to sea in 1779, his father got wind of the
scheme and, instead of trying to prevent him, helped his son to
choose a ship on which his uncles were also serving. On the
other hand, some parents found it remarkably hard to let go.
Henry Drinker, Jr., stayed out until "10 minutes after 10
o'clock" one fine summer night in 1794, and his mother complained to her diary that she had "wait[ed] up for him—not a
little uneasy. When young men go courting so far from home,
they should make their visits shorter, and not walk two miles in
a dark night alone; the risk of meeting some mischievous persons, or of taking cold at this season of the year, should have
some weight with them." Henry was twenty-four at the time.

Community fear of adolescent rebellion had its roots in the
very real problem of unsupervised teenagers. Such young people were particularly visible in the urban centers of colonial
America, both because these busy places acted as magnets for
rural runaways and because they were the dumping spot for the
thousands of unattached young people who arrived from
Europe during the century and whose lack of contacts or skills
kept them from finding any work beyond that as occasional
laborers. Adolescents hung about on street corners or in taverns
and frightened more respectable citizens in much the way that
urban gangs do today. In rural areas where there were not the
same opportunities for gathering in anonymity, teenagers still
found ways to "get into vile company [and] rabble up and down

in the evening [and] in the dark and silent night, when they should be in bed, when they are let alone to take their sinful courses." They met in fields and in barns—the boys to drink "until they vomited," the girls to read and discuss what must have been gynecological texts, referred to by one disapproving adult as "bawdy" books. Sexual misbehavior was a frequent offense, judging by court records of the time, although practical jokes were popular as well. Some were harmless enough—dismantling a hay wagon in the dead of night and reassembling it, precariously balanced, on the top of someone's roof—but others had a more sinister cast, such as lacing a neighbor's cook pot with enough tobacco to make the whole family very ill indeed.

Nor were the teenagers of more sheltered backgrounds averse to such hijinks. Young men off to college at about the age of fourteen and out from under parental authority, perhaps for the first time, were almost legendary in their failure to conform to adult standards of behavior: in a report to the president on the student body at Harvard College in 1725, Judge Sewall sorrowfully acknowledged that many of them "stole, lied, swore, picked locks, drank and were idle." By the time of the Revolution, our tradition of college rowdyism was well established, described nostalgically by a graduate of Princeton (then the College of New Jersey), who found that it did not "seem disagreeable to think over the Mischiefs often practiced by wanton Boy's." He included among such "Exercises and Diversions . . . Knocking at Doors and going off without entering; Strewing the Entries in the night with greasy Feathers; Ringing [the bell] at late Hours of the Night   Picking from the neighborhood now and then a plump fat Hen or Turkey for the private entertainment of the Club . . . Parading bad Women . . . ogling Women with the telescope" and the hazing of "timorous Boys and new comers." Although frowned upon by adult members of the establishment, such behavior, frequently destructive and sometimes actually criminal, on the part of college students was rarely brought before the courts but was punished directly by the school or referred back to the parents.

How to deal with mischievous or criminal behavior on the part of less privileged adolescents was another matter. Young

people who were on their own in the world were handled by
the public magistrates and, generally speaking, received the
same treatment as adults who committed like offenses. This is
not surprising in a society that distinguished people by condition rather than age. In line with the English common law, a
child of seven who was examined and found able to distinguish
between good and evil in an action was subject to the full wrath
of the law, including the death penalty for capital transgressions. Fourteen-year-olds were assumed to know the difference,
and while younger children might frequently be bound out as
a way of getting them under family governance and off the
hands of the community, for older youths fines, whippings, jail-
ing, and the death penalty were the common deterrents to a life
of crime.

On the other hand, teenagers who were still under parental
control were largely left to family management. The courts
were willing to back parents up: one particularly draconian
seventeenth-century Massachusetts law, still on the books
throughout the eighteenth century, specified the death penalty
for incorrigible adolescents who would not heed or obey either
their mother's or father's "voice and chastisement." The catch
was that the parents themselves had to bring their offspring into
court, and there is not a single example of the use of the statute.
Not only were parents likely to recoil from the extremity of this
particular law, but in general they seemed unwilling to wash
their dirty linen in public. Although we know that teenagers,
particularly boys, ran away from home with great regularity—
Benjamin Franklin is only the most famous example—parents
did not use the newspapers to advertise for their return in the
way they did to recover runaway servants. In many upper-class
families, at least, there was even a tendency to take a rather
tolerant view of youthful indiscretion, and to feel "that youth
must be suffer'd awhile to take their sway, and sow their wild
oats," as a disapproving New England minister described it.

In the 1760s and 1770s, the growing tendency of young men
to seek independence from their families became identified
with the struggle of the youthful colonies to break their ties of
dependence on the mother country. Thomas Paine, principal

pamphleteer of the Revolution, made the comparison explicit when he wrote: "The title which [Great Britain] assumed, of parent country, led to, and pointed out the propriety, wisdom and advantage of a separation. . . . Nothing hurts the affections both of parents and children so much, as living too closely connected, and keeping up the distinction too long . . . though [the children] may conceive themselves the subjects of their advice, will not suppose them the objects of their government." The link between personal and political liberty was more than rhetorical. Andrew Eliot, secretary of the Harvard Corporation, saw philosophy as a goad to action as he wrote, "Their declamations and forensic disputes breathe the Spirit of Liberty . . . which may hereafter fill the Country with Patriots." As a matter of fact, it was great numbers of "liberated" teenagers who filled the regiments and manned the ships of the Continental forces, although these were unlikely to be Harvard boys, who were far more apt to serve as officers or to purchase substitutes for their service in the ranks. It was rural or city youngsters of modest background like Andrew Shelburne who were caught up in the general sense of excitement and high adventure, or who saw the military as an early path to personal emancipation from parental control. Some chose independence at an age we would still consider childhood, rather than adolescence. Israel Trask, for example, was only ten when he left his parents' home in Massachusetts to serve as cook and messenger for the army. Two years later, that term of service over, he went aboard a privateering ship, making ten voyages. He was captured three times, impressed into British service once, exchanged twice, and finally escaped from a prison ship in Nova Scotia to make his way back to Massachusetts. By the time the war was over, Israel was still only eighteen, but had acted (and been treated) as an adult for almost half of his life.

The new nation, with its desire for economic independence and its vast new frontier lands ready for exploitation, made self-sufficiency a real option for teenagers, although rarely for one as young as Israel Trask. At the end of the seventeenth century, young men had to accept dependent status until they received their parental inheritance, married, and became householders. By the 1790s, those with a knowledge of accounting, surveying, bridge- or road-building, or a host of other skills at a premium in the changing world could leave childhood behind and become autonomous individuals.

Part II

THE WORKADAY WORLD

MAKING LAND AND

REAPING THE REWARDS

JOSIAH BARTLETT had been away from his farm for the better part of a year. An important man in his home colony of New Hampshire—admittedly a large frog in a rather small pond—he had been sent to Philadelphia as a delegate to the Continental Congress in September 1775. Within a month he had tired of "The Living in So Grand a City without the pleasure of a Free County air," and although he asked the New Hampshire convention to send someone to relieve him, when no one was forthcoming, he remained to do his duty. He made his real priorities clear, however, in a letter written home to his wife less than two weeks before the pronouncement of the Declaration of Independence. Having disposed briefly of the weather and the state of the war, Bartlett turned to more important matters: "I am sorry to hear frost has Done Damage with you," he wrote. "[I] hope it has not Killed all the Beans &c the Corn will Commonly Grow again. How is the flax in General like to be; what are like to be the Crops of hay with you; how is the winter & Sumer Grain like to be &c: Please to write me what is like to be the Success of the farming Business this year." Only after these crucial concerns were addressed did he add, almost as an afterthought: "I have been for about a week on a Committee of one member from Each Colony to form a Confederation or Charter of firm & Everlasting Union of all the United Colonies: It is a matter of the greatest Consequence & requires the greatest Care in forming it."

Like many of his associates in Philadelphia that year, Bartlett was first and foremost a farmer and, as such, a particularly appropriate representative of the emerging nation. Nine out of every ten Americans at the time of the Revolution lived in a rural landscape of fields, woods, and gardens, and most of these earned their livelihoods primarily from the crops and animals they produced. Whatever they were called—husbandmen at the beginning of the century, farmers at the end; yeomen in the North, planters in the South—the basic fact of everyday life in the eighteenth century remained the same. Frontiersmen, plantation owners, slaves, indentured servants, and day laborers spent most of their waking hours "scratching" the soil, planting seeds, weeding fields and gardens, and harvesting crops. In addition, they tended and fed livestock and sheared, milked, and slaughtered them. Finally, the products of all this industry were prepared for consumption, storage, or sale. The seasons of the year ruled the endless cycle of tasks—so many days or weeks of planting, cultivating, and harvesting; so many of clearing trees, stumps, and rocks where necessary; of digging and cleaning ditches; of threshing and winnowing grain. The routine varied, of course, according to the climate in which the farmer lived, the kinds of crops he grew, and the number of livestock he kept. It was broken by hunting and fishing, by market or court days, and by visits to nearby town taverns or neighboring plantations.

Farmers' wives, daughters, and female servants were no less governed by the seasons, responding to the need to "put up" vegetables and fruit as they ripened, to preserve meat at slaughtering time, and, in most places, to help in the fields under the pressure of the harvest. They also had their own traditional outdoor work: tending gardens and poultry, milking cows, and carrying water. Superimposed on these chores were the daily and weekly indoor tasks associated with the woman's role as housekeeper—preparing meals, making and mending clothes, caring for children, cleaning, and washing, to name but a few. Because of these daily routines that were carried out regardless of the season, farm women were far less likely to be able to escape, even for a brief time, to woods, town, or neighbor. Slave women in the South performed the seemingly inhuman feat of combining the work of both sexes: the full-time, traditional field labor of men, and the regular female domestic jobs within their own family circles.

In these very broad outlines of farm life, its seasonality and chores, we can see little that is specifically American, nor much that would distinguish the farmer's life and that of his wife in 1800 from those of their great-great-grandparents of one hundred years earlier or, for that matter, from those of their great-great-grandchildren one hundred years later. They merely followed the patterns that generally apply to anyone whose life is tied to nature and the living products of its bounty.

Eighteenth-century men of learning, however, imbued with the spirit of the Age of Reason, were less interested in the necessities imposed on farming by nature than they were in a potential revolution in crop production that they felt could be achieved by applying "usefull Knowledge" to the technology and methods of agriculture. They saw the farmers of their own day as old-fashioned, close-minded traditionalists. Samuel Deane, author of *The New England Farmer,* wrote in 1790: "Farmers do many things for which they can assign no other reason than custom. They usually give themselves little or no trouble in thinking, or in examining their methods of agriculture, which have been handed down from father to son from time immemorial."

Deane and his fellow critics of American husbandry could not have been more wrong. They were scientific theorists, and looked to English agriculture as a model for their rural "industrial revolution." Where New World farmers differed in practice and performance from the British example, they were scorned as wasteful and slovenly. From north to south, foreign visitors condemned land and livestock management, low yields, the use of primitive tools, and resistance to technological innovations. What they took for ignorance and refusal to change represented, in fact, almost two centuries of constant adaptation to the special environmental and social conditions of the New World. Pioneer farmers in colonial America were more than frontiersmen of the wilderness: they stood on an agricultural frontier of strange land, unfathomable weather, and previously unknown plants and animals. In addition, the long-established relationships of man to land that adhered in rural Europe were turned upside down in a country where land was cheap, but labor expensive. "As to labour and labourers—what a difference!" bemoaned one colonial farmer. "When we hire any of these people we rather pray and entreat them. You must give them what they ask. . . . They must be at your table and feed . . . on the best you have." By the end of the eighteenth century, American farmers had long since departed from the traditional crops and ways of life of their Old World counterparts and had created patterns of culture and agriculture tailored to the specific conditions of the widely varying regions of the huge continent.

They did not, of course, throw away any scraps of rural folk wisdom they had brought with them that might be serviceable in their strange, often unfriendly, and always unpredictable new environment. American husbandmen, for example, continued to rely on an Old World lore of farming based on astrology: cabbages were planted during the old moon, meadows hayed during the new, and grain harvested during the wane; pigs and sheep were never slaughtered in the wane of the moon lest their meat be dry and tough. New World crops that were not part of the European experience acquired traditions of their own. Corn, for example, was planted with the waxing moon, often at night, in groups of four kernels to a hill. "One for the blackbird, one for the crow, / One for the cutworm, and one to grow," went the colonial folk rhyme.

The New World yeoman or planter faced many areas of unpredictability concerning matters of soil composition and its suitability for particular crops, pest control, plant disease, and erosion. For these, he relied not only on traditional wisdom and astrological lore but also on practical experience. The look of the weather, the feel of the soil, information from friendly Indians regarding local conditions, and careful experimentation in crop rotation and fertilization all entered into his calculations. In the eighteenth century, migrating farmers from Europe, Africa, or established settlements in the older colonies made use at first of the agricultural standards that they brought with them from their previous homes. They were particularly dependent on analyzing the growing properties of soil through an examination of its color and the kinds of trees it supported. Conventional wisdom dictated that black soil was best, especially when it was porous and light and emitted "a fresh pleasant scent on being dug or ploughed up, especially after rain"; dark gray and reddish were next best, while ash-colored soils—light or dark— were least productive. Many held to the Baconian notion that the really best soil could be found wherever "rainbows touch the earth." Occasionally, however, the ecology of the colonist's homeland gave him a different perspective: the Dutch were willing to accept sandy, gravelly, and marshy soils rejected by English settlers, since they fell into familiar Netherlandish categories, and Dutch farmers knew they would produce excellent crops if properly "dyked and cultivated."

The type and fertility of the soil was but one variable on a continent whose sheer size extended over a thousand miles from north to south. Even where the New World lay in the same zones of latitude as the European homelands, the climate was different—more extreme and larger-than-life. It was colder in winter, hotter in summer, dryer in some places, far more humid in others. The occurrence of earthquakes and floods and the spectacular nature of the thunderstorms often suggested supernatural involvement—whether of divine or satanic origin was a question to be debated. Regionally unique patterns of weather and climate meant that even a native-born American moving a relatively short distance from home had to cope with "a different climate and a different world," as one New Englander transplanted to the Pennsylvania frontier at the end of the century put it. The changes might be subtle, affecting only the length or timing of the growing season, but they were of vital concern to those who were planning to move and of a great curiosity even to those who were permanently settled but whose daily lives depended on the seasons. Josiah Bartlett had noted with interest in 1776 that although the fruit trees had finished blooming and the "Cherries [were] of Some Bigness," the Philadelphians were complaining of the "Backwardness of the Spring." At home in New Hampshire, he knew, the cherry

and peach flowers were at their height and the apples only just
beginning to blossom.

The further the settlers moved south out of latitudes that
bore at least some relationship to the climate of their Old World
homes, the less they could rely on inherited lore for understanding the nature of their environment and the more they were
forced to adopt new ways of living that they often found highly
uncongenial. While promotional literature extolled the Deep
South as "a new garden of Eden," actual residents had a different tale to tell. "I herewith wish to have everybody warned that
he should not hanker to come into this country, for diseases
here have too much sway, and people have died in masses,"
warned an immigrant to South Carolina in 1737. A planter who
had lived in Georgia for over eight years described summer
living in excruciating detail: "I find the heat very oppressive,
and gives one, for two or three hours in the afternoon, a languor
which I never experienced in England even in the hottest days;
the only way to be tolerably at ease, is to keep one's self perfectly quiet, to sit still in rooms that admit much air but no sun,
and to be cautious in diet: this season lasts through July, August,
and most of September." On the other hand, extreme swings of
occasional cold weather were no more welcome. Hot water
bottles split and froze to "solid lumps of ice" in the bed even
when covered with good English blankets, live eels froze to the
bottom of the kitchen water bucket, and an orchard of orange
trees was destroyed along with an olive tree "of such prodigious
size, that I thought it proof against all weathers."

Nor was southern soil in the coastal regions highly regarded by
those who actually lived or traveled there extensively. For the
brief period between 1763 and 1783 when East Florida formed
a part of British colonial America, we get an almost surrealistic
glimpse of the Anglo agriculturist trying to make something of
this exotic environment. He knew that there was a livelihood to
be made and profits to be gained from these strange territories,
for the Spanish drove successful herds of livestock in the area,
and left behind in St. Augustine thriving orchards of "oranges,
Lemmons, Pome Citrons, limes, figs, and peaches," in addition
to "apricots, guavas, plantains, pomegranates, shadocks and ber-

5.1 Patrick Campbell included this engraving of a newly cleared frontier farm in his *Travels in the Interior Inhabited Parts of North America*, published in Edinburgh in 1793. Although the buildings on the property, particularly the one on the left, are probably unrealistically elaborate, the fences and the large areas of land with the stumps left after the trees were cut represent American practice in first "making land" (pp. 57, 151). *(John Carter Brown Library at Brown University)*

5.2 Although this watercolor was painted by Eliza Susan Quincy in the 1820s, the two buildings at the left show the placing of eighteenth-century farmhouses in New England when the homestead was occupied by a family over a long period of time. The house on the right is the birthplace of John Adams; the one on the left is the home into which he moved with Abigail Smith Adams after their marriage and in which their son, John Quincy Adams, was born (p. 158). *(Massachusetts Historical Society)*

5.3 Stages in the production of Virginia tobacco from William Tatham, *An Historical and Practical Essay on the Culture of Tobacco*, London, 1800 (p. 162). *(Library Company of Philadelphia)*

5.4 As farms in the upper Chesapeake diversified their crops, male slaves moved into more skilled, mechanized jobs, but female slaves remained at the hoe in the tobacco field, under the watchful eye of the overseer, as Benjamin Henry Latrobe noted when he "sketched [this scene] from life near Fredericsburg, [Maryland]" in 1798 (p. 167). *(Maryland Historical Society)*

6.1 A wide variety of craftsmen, such as coopers, draymen, ship-wrights, and common laborers, worked along the Philadelphia waterfront in 1800, when William Birch engraved this view of the Arch Street Ferry. Most of those pictured here enjoyed little in the way of job stability, but walked along the waterfront each morning in search of a day's employment (p. 182). *(Library Company of Philadelphia)*

6.2 The "Little Navigator" stood in front of James Fales's shop in Newport, Rhode Island, to call attention to his abilities as a maker of nautical instruments in the early nineteenth century. The polychromed wood figure was valuable enough for Fales to take it with him when he moved his shop to New Bedford, Massachusetts (pp. 183–184). *(New Bedford Whaling Museum)*

6.3 Obvious pride in his business and the quality of his merchandise led Elijah Boardman of New Milford, Connecticut, to have his portrait painted in 1789, standing at his desk with his shelves of costly textiles beyond. His elegant clothes were probably made of fabrics from his own stock, and his attitude is reminiscent of the many eighteenth-century merchants who posed with their account books on the table in front of them, their ships visible through a window behind. The elevation of "mere tradesmen" to positions of status and influence was just getting under way by the last decade of the century (p. 183). (*The Metropolitan Museum of Art*)

6.4 Industrial production was no less commercial for taking place in a rural setting. This sketch of a sawmill near Fort Anne, New York, in 1777 appears bucolic at first glance, but the quantity of processed lumber pouring out of the mill and the stacks of finished product at the left of the picture belie that impression. Imagination must supply the noise and pollution attendant on such a process (pp. 187–188). *(Haverford College Library)*

gamots." Yet despite this evidence, Anglo-Americans deemed the soil unworthy as nothing but flat, sandy expanses, marsh after marsh, swamp after swamp, and the rest pine barrens, "such as no person would move to, from the worst of our colonies, in order to cultivate them." Most small yeomen seemed to agree. Incoming settlers chose the difficult overland journey to the hardwood lands of the southern backcountry over a sea voyage to acres of scrub pine and sand, even when offered large subsidies by Florida land speculators whose own homes were more comfortably situated in Carolina or Georgia or England itself.

As late as the Revolution, mature farm communities existed only in a narrow ribbon about one hundred miles wide from Maine to Georgia, and the majority of American farmers lived to some extent in a frontier situation. Pioneer farming differed sharply from agriculture in those places where the challenges of new environments had already been met and their problems, if not solved, at least recognized and managed. The particulars of setting up a farm in the wilderness varied, of course, from region to region, yet the very nature of being on a frontier created common patterns of everyday life that pioneers shared across space and time, despite many differences in detail. For one thing, getting there was never easy since the trip had to be made after the harvest of the previous season was over and before planting time arrived in the new home. This meant traveling during fall or early winter, enduring frost and snow that chilled the bone and froze the flesh. Early in the century men alone went West. Young men from New England villages moved together, "hiving out" to form new farming communities that bore the surnames and social patterns of their old homes. Individual southerners, accompanied by one or more slaves, moved to set up new plantations. By the mid-1700s, clusters of established settlements, occasional isolated homesteads, and roads—however poorly marked and often impassable—made it more feasible for the whole family to migrate at once. Still, pioneer farming was not for the fainthearted. Abandoned sites were constant reminders of imminent danger and potential failure. The threat might be as implicit as a small farm burned by Indians or as graphic as the entry in a journal from

1748: "[August] 24th. Found a dead man on the Road who had killed himself by Drinking too much Whiskey: the Place being very stony we cou'd not dig a Grave; he smelling very strong we covered him with Stones and Wood and went on our Journey. . . ."

After the Revolution, the door to the West opened more widely and the nineteenth-century pattern of groups of farm seekers moving west, their wagons filled with wives and children and piled high with household goods, began to take shape. They often received the hospitality of those already established as they looked for lands in the neighborhood on which to settle or as they passed through to a predetermined destination. Travelers frequently complained of the quarters they were offered: "[On] to Mr. Elliot's; where ourselves, our servants, several wagoners, his wife, and eight children, and a young daughter, all undressed and went to bed on the floor together in a miserable log-house," wrote one passerby in 1784, rather ungratefully we might think, since the alternative was a blanket on the open ground in the wet autumn night. How Mr. Elliot felt about his uninvited visitors is not recorded.

Mrs. Mary Dewees, who left Philadelphia in 1787 with a group of immigrants headed for Kentucky, was certainly used to a better life. In a letter to a friend, she described a "little hut" she stayed in for two days as "not half so good as the little building at the upper end of your garden." She remained remarkably cheerful all across the mountains in a wagon, despite "the horrid roads and the stoniest land in the world," noticing "Nature . . . dress'd Beautiful, beyond expression," and enjoying the company of other families who overtook them on the trail since it was "more Agreeable travelling than by ourselves." Mrs. Dewees slept in the wagon with her sister and the children through wind and rain, prepared meals over a campfire, and was relieved after a week of such overland travel to transfer to the flatboat resembling "Noah's Ark not a little," which was to carry them down the Ohio River. The boat was forty feet long, "our room 16 by 12 with a Comfortable fire place; our Bed room partitioned off with blankets: We are clear of fleas, which I assure you is a great relief, for we were almost devoured when on Shore."

Fleas were a nuisance, but the eighteenth-century frontier farmer faced greater danger to his person and his crop from a variety of other creatures. Many of these perils were indigenous to the new environment: wolves that fed on sheep; foxes among the poultry; squirrels, crows, blackbirds, and caterpillars in the corn; grasshoppers on grain, grass, and turnips; and the "little despicable insect" that grew inside the pod, feeding on "pease" and making it impossible to transfer this staple of the English farm diet to New England, Pennsylvania, or New Jersey. While such predators were no joke, John May reported somewhat tongue-in-cheek on a farmer on the western frontier of Pennsylvania who figured into his expected corn crop the one bushel in ten that would go to the squirrels.

Confrontation rather than accommodation was the usual response of settlers, where possible: a South Carolina Act of 1703 promised ten shillings to "whatsoever white person by himselfe or slave shall destroy and kill wolfe, tyger [panther] or beare," and five shillings "for every wild catt." By the mid-1750s, when large areas in North Carolina had become open range—a forerunner of the nineteenth-century Wild West—cattle ticks had taken such a toll of the stock that a law was passed requiring the segregation of sick animals and the immediate burning of their carcasses. Even more extensive remedies included burning over the whole range to get rid of persistent parasites, pointing out to reluctant "cowboys" that this measure would improve the grass crops as well.

Introducing European livestock and crops like peas into the New World provided fresh worlds to conquer for pests already resident in the ecosystem. Wheat—the favored grain of England and much of Western Europe—arrived with the first seventeenth-century settlers, but was highly vulnerable to attack by both indigenous and transported enemies. The "blast" or "blight," now known as blackstem rust, made its appearance in New England by the 1660s and practically wiped out viable wheat growing there by the early eighteenth century. It was spread unintentionally by the barberry bush, which was also imported to produce berries for jams and jellies, but which proved to be an alternate host for the parasitic fungus that caused the problem. Eighteenth-century farmers lacked the scientific expertise to identify the true cause of blast, which was not, in fact, discovered until 1870, but they pragmatically noted the relationship of barberries to wheat destruction. Beginning in 1726, New England towns passed laws requiring the removal of barberry bushes under threat of a fine in the "Sum of Ten Pounds Lawful money," a considerable penalty for the time.

When direct action against threats to the crop failed, as it frequently did, colonial farmers adapted what they grew to the realities of New World farming—often with far-reaching effects on the whole economy of eighteenth-century America as well as on the everyday patterns of life of those who were immediately affected. Some New Englanders, aware that a fast-maturing crop could be harvested before the rust had a chance to develop, switched to winter wheat, but most gave up wheat production entirely. They relied more and more heavily on maize, Indian corn as it was sometimes called, and added more fields of less-popular European grains such as rye and barley. During the second half of the century, farmers began to turn to the potato, first as a garden vegetable grown with the beets and carrots and kept only as "a rarity to eat with roast meat," but after the Revolution as a field-grown major crop. A continued taste for wheat bread created social distinctions in the rural Northeast, since only the more affluent could afford bread made from imported grain; the standard bread of farm families became a mixed loaf known as "rye and Injun." The real winners were Pennsylvania and Maryland, which became the eighteenth-century "breadbasket" by growing wheat as a staple crop to supply the fast-growing markets of America, the West Indies, and Europe.

Feed for animals presented different problems. The wild, indigenous grass of the new continent was useless as fodder since it died back in cold weather, and early seventeenth-century settlers found that their cattle were unable to survive the winter. Yet, even as they worried about how to generate a satisfactory hay crop, the problem had already begun to solve itself. English grass seed was introduced in the fodder and bedding of the first livestock to be sent across. It adapted and thrived, meeting up in the south with guinea and Bermuda grass naturalizing from seed in the bedding of imported slaves. All of these grasses, along with other extra-continental varieties, did so well that they outstripped the pioneers themselves. Timothy, Herd's grass, Kentucky bluegrass, red-top, Indian bluegrass, goose-grass, and a host of other "naturalized citizens" were waiting to welcome eighteenth-century settlers and their cattle, and were, in fact, mistaken as indigenous when the frontier caught up with them.

Other Old World opportunistic immigrants at times seemed a "primeval curse." Constant vigilance and a dreary, continual round of weeding became the everyday lot of all farm workers as they fought to keep the overexuberant stowaways in check: stinkweed, which caused abortion in livestock; Saint John's wort, which discouraged cattle from eating hay; couch grass, which strangled sprouting Indian corn; and plantain, nicknamed "Englishman's foot" by the Indians, because it moved so quickly in the path of the pioneers.

European weeds created problems for Amerindian farmers, but the English planter himself posed a terminal threat to their very way of life. While contact with European trappers had changed Indian culture in ways both acknowledged and unrecognized, continuity, even in altered form, became virtually impossible with the establishment of permanent colonial farms and rural communities. Pennsylvania Indians, for example, who converted to Christianity lived apart in separate communities, but acculturated in many material ways. They built cabins that were furnished with European cooking utensils, beds, tables, and benches, adopted European dress, and emphasized the cultivation of European-style gardens. A few Indian leaders encouraged giving up the old ways entirely. John Heckewelder described an old chief, "Captain White Eyes," an ally of the Americans at the time of the Revolution, who urged his people "to adopt the ways of living by agriculture and finally become civilized . . . he told them to take the example of the Christian Indians, who by their industry, had everything they could wish

for, and never suffered from want." This was an overly rosy
view of the opportunities for Indian farmers, who were always
at risk of attack by white neighbors who distinguished their
enemies by race rather than culture and saw all Indians as
threats to be eradicated.

On the other hand, throughout the whole of the eighteenth
century, white farmers creating new settlements beyond the
edges of established colonial territories also faced the possibility
of extinction by the indigenous population that "inexplicably"
refused to disappear or adapt. The actuality or rumor of a burnt
and smoking farmstead or village was always just over the hori-
zon. In fact, however, as with the other environmental dangers
of the New World, Anglo-American frontier farmers had as
much to fear from the troubles they brought with them from
the Old World as from those that were native to the New.
European controversies with the French and Spanish were
transferred to the colonial setting. Slave uprisings threatened
individual masters and whole neighborhoods alike; and colonials even turned on one another. Boundary disputes between
New York and Massachusetts during the 1750s, for example,
pitted farmer against farmer so that "our Houses have been
torn down about our Ears, burnt before our Eyes, our Fences
thrown Down, our Corn Fields laid waste . . ." Symbolically,
many of the attackers donned the disguise of Indians. Finally,
after the Revolution, soldiers sent to protect the pioneers often
remained to vandalize: ". . . I and another brother toper
[drinker] . . . rambled [out] ready for mischief, we pulled down
[a garden fence] and let the cows, horses and sheep into the
garden to destroy the contents."

Given the problematic nature of survival, much less success,
in frontier farming, we can only marvel at the continuing
stream of those who were eager to try. Many who set off had
already bought land from the proprietor of the colony in which
they planned to settle or from one of the numerous land speculators who controlled much of the new territory. Toward the
end of the century, the grant was often part of a government
payoff for having served in the Revolutionary army. Still many

others merely squatted, setting up homesteads without title and hoping for the best.

Although some frontier farmers were experienced agriculturists and most knew something about farming, many were truly babes in the woods. In 1775, for example, Nicholas Cresswell noted in his journal while traveling the Pennsylvania frontier: "At Captain Stephenson's. Instructed his people [how] to make a stack of wheat." In almost all cases, however, whether professional or neophyte, new settlers faced the gigantic task of "making land," as they called it, out of wilderness, and everyday life during the first season involved clearing trees to make fields for the crops that would follow. The trees could either be cut down, with the intention to "grub out" the roots later, or girdled, Indian-fashion, by removing a large strip of bark all around so that they died in place. The crops were then sown among the resulting stumps or skeletons.

Each method had advantages and drawbacks. In general, felling the forest in the beginning took far too long and cost too much in initial labor without any payout in edible crops. On the plus side, if the trees were oaks, pines, cypress, or cedar, they were convertible into immediate cash crops like lumber or potash. They could also be used in house and fence building or as fuel, although much of the timber that was cut was thought to be merely in the way and was burned. English observers who came from an agricultural tradition where timber was scarce and every tree precious saw the scene of huge blazing bonfires as "truly savage."

Girdling, on the other hand, readied a field for hand-tool cultivation almost instantly, since the lifeless carcasses did not interfere with the sun needed by the crops. However, this alternative did not provide lumber for building or fuel, and as they decayed where they stood, the trees became hazards for years. As one settler described: "[They] fall over fences and demolish them, and not infrequently men and boys have been killed." Both girdling and cutting left obstacles in the field that prevented the efficient use of plow technology, and made it necessary to continue the use of hand tools long since superseded in Europe and in mature American settlements.

Under these circumstances, the best an individual settler could hope to prepare was one to three acres by planting time, hardly enough to feed a family. While hogs and cattle could, to some degree, feed themselves in the forests of the southern colonies, meat was rarely tasted unless the settler had brought barreled pork with him, an unnecessary encumbrance and expense. Although game and fish were available, time could scarcely be spared to obtain them. Farm women who accompanied their menfolk to the frontier or who arrived when the homestead was barely set up lacked both time and tools to quickly reestablish their economic roles in clothing and dairy production or in the preservation of garden and orchard crops. It was years before frontier farmers could achieve the mix of home production and cash crops that re-created the patterns of daily life in the older settlements.

The paradox of "making land" in the wilderness was that extreme isolation was juxtaposed with an inability to be self-sufficient. Of the isolation, there can be no doubt: it was the principal feature of life on the frontier noted by eighteenth-century travelers. Sometimes isolation was intentional, as in the South, where people "plant[ed] themselves at a distance, for the sake of having an uncultivated country around them for their cattle to range in." In many cases, it was the result of being the first settler in newly opened territory.

The loneliness of solitude was movingly described by John Reynolds at the end of the century when, at the age of fifteen, he was left to tend a barely started farm alone, while his father left for several months to collect the rest of the family. "I had not a book, not a scrap of printed paper. I had one letter from my uncle Edward to my father . . . that I oft-times read. Each day I cut a notch on the door cheek, and on Sabbath one of double size. Thus I kept tally of the days and weeks, and often counted the notches to pass the time which hung so heavy. Every night the wolves howled around my cabin, and the owls hooted—discordant noises, well fitted to nurture melancholy." Even after the family had arrived and the neighborhood began to fill up, the cow continued to suffer, according to young John. "Having no company she would not stay with us. We found her [a long distance away at a neighboring farm]. We could not drive nor lead her home. After we had got her part of the way she broke from us and ran back." Eventually, the only solution was to sell her to the neighbor.

However alone they may have felt, frontier farmers were more dependent on the larger society and the marketplace than even the most determined Virginia tobacco growers with their eyes turned to the going price of tobacco in London. Without a place to buy supplies, they might well be reduced to eating grass "to allay the cravings of hunger," as were a group of new settlers in Sandy River, Maine. For weeks they had waited anxiously for the return of a party that had set out on foot for Augusta, forty miles away, to buy corn and carry it in baskets on their backs to another town to be milled and then home "to keep their families." Without cash in hand, newcomers were also at a disadvantage since credit was hard to come by for strangers in recently settled areas where people did not know each other by face and family. The intricate network of favors granted and obligations incurred that was an integral part of eighteenth-century rural life in old communities took decades, if not generations, to establish. "Shabby clothes," a "suspicious countenance," or failure to provide bona fides in the form of a letter of introduction from someone well known in the locale were enough to leave the newcomer without shelter for himself or stabling for his horse, much less an advance on supplies until "the crop came in."

Pioneers, therefore, often concentrated first on extracting cash from what the wilderness had to offer. They sometimes killed two birds with one stone, using the timber cleared to make a field as fuel for a quick boiling of maple sugar, or leaching the ashes of burnt wood to turn them into potash, salable to export merchants and soap or glass manufacturers. These were regarded as stopgap measures, however, or perhaps as a sideline on an already-established farm. Unlike the fur traders and lumbermen who made lifelong careers of living off the bounties of nature, the pioneer farmer was less interested in exploiting the wilderness than he was in taming it. He could not regard himself as truly settled until he could reap a crop that he himself had sown. It was the harvesting of that first crop that marked his transition from wanderer to settler, from frontiersman to farmer.

On every farm, in every region, at any time in colonial America, that first crop was "maize," as the Indians called it—"that which sustains life." Foreigners and newcomers often referred to it as "Indian corn," but for most Americans it was known as just plain "corn," the basic grain of the country, in the way that the English used the term to apply to wheat and the Scots to oats. It had saved the lives of the Pilgrims in Plymouth, and paid the rent in Jamestown. In 1700, Francis Daniel Pastorius wrote from Germantown, Pennsylvania, that "one cannot, the first year, plant either wheat or rye in such new land, but only Indian . . . corn. . . ." It grew in the rich, fertile fields of the western frontier where the girdled trees still stood close, and with the addition of a few fish heads or a little "pondmuck" for fertilizer, it even grew in sandy, unpromising soil along the coast.

There is, in fact, no possible way to overemphasize the importance of corn in the daily lives of eighteenth-century Americans. It linked seventeenth-century New England Puritans to nineteenth-century black slaves in Georgia, backcountry Appalachian settlers to New Jersey Quakers, New York tenant farmers to wealthy Virginia plantation owners, Indian warriors to Pennsylvania German pacifists. Ears of corn formed the central motif of the seal of Kent County, Delaware, in 1683, and decorated the tops of the columns of the national Capitol in 1803. As frontier settlements matured into stable, long-established farm communities, farmers continued to grow this uniquely American crop even when they turned their primary attention to profitmaking staples like wheat or tobacco, to livestock production for wool, meat, or dairy products, or to the diversified growing of grains, fruits, vegetables, poultry, cattle, hogs, and sheep.

Although eighteenth-century colonial mythology continued to insist on a picture of the Indians as uncivilized, nomadic savages, the ubiquitous rows of ripening corn stood as silent tributes to Native American agricultural ability. Over the centuries before the arrival of European settlers, Central American Indians had developed a rather unpretentious indigenous grass into a highly nourishing grain that came in dozens of varieties, six colors, and more than twenty shades. Basically, the colonists focused on only two of these options: yellow for feeding the livestock and white for human consumption, although the occasional red "sport" ear found by a young man during a husking bee entitled him to a kiss from the girl of his choice.

As the backbone of American agriculture, corn had innumerable advantages and very few drawbacks. Along with its ability to thrive in new ground with minimum preparation, this native plant was highly resistant to the insects and diseases that made growing European grains so tricky. Nor was it perishable. Stored seed germinated even after ten years, and the food value of dried corn was retained virtually forever. Furthermore, it was a most obliging plant: in the northern colonies, where the growing season was short, it matured in ten weeks; in the tropics, where the pace was more leisurely, it required four to five months. It produced three times the yield per acre of wheat, and did it with only one-third the seed, prompting a Swedish traveler in the 1740s to dub it "a lazy man's crop." Finally, the timing of the harvest was not nearly so critical as it was for other crops. It could be picked and used for different purposes during many different stages of its growing cycle, and it could be stored just as it came from the field, to be husked, shelled, and its silage "tramped" during the less-hectic winter season. Its principal drawback was that it rapidly depleted the soil, and a field that had grown corn for three years had to be either rotated out of production to allow its nutrients to recover, or heavily fertilized.

Since the method of corn production changed little during the eighteenth century or from one region to another, generations of American farm families shared a common experience. Planting, cultivation, and harvesting of the crop involved all members of the family. Sticks for planting, hoes for weeding and cultivating, hands for pulling, and even knives for harvesting were tools that could be managed by anyone, regardless of age or sex. In addition, corn, while it was growing, was highly vulnerable to predators, particularly rats, mice, and crows, who seemed to prefer it to all other crops. The only available solution to the problem was the one long used by the Indians: the corn patches were "patrolled" by women, children, and the elderly by day, and by the menfolk at night. The patrols were scattered throughout the crop, on the ground or in roughly constructed platforms in the trees, where, as one historian has described, they "shouted, waved their arms, threw rocks and clods of dirt, beat on pans, and whistled to frighten away birds and animals." "Shoy hoys," or scarecrows, were tried, as were swinging shingles or pewter plates. Most popular with young boys by the late eighteenth century was the chance to fire their fathers' rifles filled with scatter shot. This not only helped to frighten away pests, but helped the future colonist improve his aim, and occasionally put extra game on the table.

Almost everyone grew his own corn, so domestic market prices were apt to be low, and the overseas market was weak because it never suited the taste or the culture of Europeans. Still, in an indirect form, corn was an important component of the market economy. Having been used as food for livestock, it arrived at market in the form of pork, milk, eggs, chickens, and beef. As liquor, it was particularly important to western farmers in their search for a cash crop, since it was the one corn product whose profits were not lost in the high costs of transportation. A single pack animal could carry six times more value in whiskey than it could in grain. Small wonder that when the newly created Federal government imposed a tax on liquor in the 1790s, there were uprisings all along the frontier from New England to Kentucky.

At home on the farm, there was no end to the uses of this most versatile of grain crops. In addition to providing fodder for the animals, the stalk served as garden fences, snow breaks, and caulk for the holes in the barn. Corn husks were often used as paper substitutes, and in 1802, a patent was issued on a process for making paper from them. Cornmeal fermented in water provided a cleaning agent to remove the odor from used barrels so that they might be recycled. Shucks could be used as mattress stuffing, chair padding, and insoles for worn-out shoes. When braided or woven, they were made into horse collars, chair backs and seats, baskets and hats. Most useful of all were the cobs, which appeared as everything from kindling and torches to mouse- and knothole plugs, fishing corks, jug and bottle stoppers, temporary tool handles, and even as sanitary supplies in the "necessary," as the outhouse was called.

Primarily, of course, corn was food: the most important source of human nutrition in colonial America. It was eaten, in some form or other, every day, perhaps at every meal, by the overwhelming number of colonists who were rural and not rich. Since it could be picked at several stages of its development, it served as both vegetable and grain. Young, or green, it was roasted or boiled on the cob, pickled in brine, and stewed with beans and bits of meat for a dish the Indians called "succotash." Dried and ground, it was made into porridge, fried, and baked. The same recipes appeared under different names in every region of the New World: "Hasty pudding is here called mush," Josiah Bartlett wrote to his wife in New Hampshire from Philadelphia. Had he traveled more widely he might have also heard it called "samp," "supawn," "loblolly," or "hominy grits." The baked variety was presented as "hoecake," "johnnycake," "journeycake," "pone," or "dodgers." "Parched" and powdered, it served much the same function for Indian hunters or frontiersmen that freeze-dried food serves for backpackers today, and "popped" corn was, perhaps, the only treat or snack food most eighteenth-century Americans ever tasted. The one thing corn lacked was enough gluten to make a successful loaf of leavened bread; thus, it was mixed with everything from rye to pumpkin in an attempt to satisfy the craving of European immigrants and their descendants, for whom "risen" bread seemed to be a cultural necessity.

As frontier areas matured into settled colonial communities, corn remained a basic fact of everyday farm life, but it ceased to dominate rural activity and culture. No other common denominator took its place. Instead, during the eighteenth century, each region developed its own special eye-catching qualities, noticed by visitors from abroad and by those who ventured from one colony to another. These differences extended to almost every aspect of everyday farm life right down to the simple physical appearance of stone fences and cow barns in New England, worm fences and open cowpens in the South. In time, even casual observers could distinguish northerners from southerners and each from frontier settlers by the clothes they wore, the food they ate, the pastimes in which they indulged, and the accents in which they spoke. By the end of the century, regional differences in farm life extended far below the surface of material life to embrace the goals and moral values of their inhabitants.

By 1700, four generations of transplanted English yeomen had built ethical traditions in New England based on small holdings, mediocre soil, and a short growing season. The farmer was no genteel overseer. His hands bore the calluses and ingrained grime of daily labor as he worked his own land alongside members of his family, with transients or youngsters from neighboring farms hired on at the busy season. While some New Englanders rented a bit of extra pasture or a cornfield from a neighbor, few were entirely landless. The difference between rich farmers and their poorer neighbors was one of degree rather than kind; the way to real wealth came from being a merchant or a professional, not a farmer.

Wealth was not the vision that drove the eighteenth-century New Englander to his plow before sunrise, nor his wife to her butter churn. It was an ideal of self-sufficiency that envisioned a life lived entirely off the production of the household, assisted when necessary by mutual exchanges of goods and services among close neighbors who were, for the most part, kin as well as friends. Many romantic verbal pictures were painted of such rural existence, particularly by an admiring naturalized citizen, S. Jean de Crevecoeur, in his collection of *Letters From an American Farmer.* In a typical vignette, he tells of a farmer who is unable to plow his fields because of sickness or accident: "In due time we invite a dozen neighbors, who will come with their teams and finish it all in one day. At dinner we give them the best victuals our farm affords; . . . pies, puddings, fowls . . . nothing is spared that can evince our gratitude." In the evening, he continues, the young folks arrive to "partake of the general dance."

In real life, however, self-sufficiency was elusive—virtually impossible for most New England farmers, particularly as the eighteenth century wore on. There were so many items that had come to be considered necessary for even a "barely decent" way of life—coffee, tea, sugar, ceramics—that could not be produced at home or even in the neighborhood and had to be purchased for cash. Many New Englanders became farmer-artisans, acquiring the skills to make goods like shoes, cloth, or pottery in the off-season that could be sold for money. The preferred way to obtain cash, however, was to convert farm raw materials into marketable goods. Depending on where they lived, New England farmers processed and sold maple syrup, maple sugar, cider, brandy, liquor, and cured and barreled beef and pork. Since much New England land was better adapted to grazing than to plowing, cattle and sheep were particularly important. Cattle not only produced meat, but also dairy goods. New England butter, while judged poor in taste, was plenty good enough for the slaves in the West Indies for whom it was intended, since it could be kept for up to three years if preserved in a saltpeter-salt-sugar solution instead of just brine. By the end of the century, the people of Goshen, Connecticut, were annually exporting up to four hundred thousand pounds of cheese deemed as good as that of Cheshire in England. This business made them, in the opinion of one traveler, "more wealthy than any other collection of farmers in New England." Sheep became more important throughout the eighteenth century, particularly in places like Nantucket and Martha's Vineyard, where the Gulf Stream moderated the bitter winter of the North, while the farmers around Narragansett, Rhode Island, used their land to develop a special breed of saddle horses—small, hardy, and fleet of foot.

Two other rural occupations that began the eighteenth century as part-time, off-season money producers for farmers in New England had become, by the close of the period, large, well-organized businesses in their own right. One of these was the lumber industry, which, by 1750, employed full-time log-

gers in Maine and New Hampshire to ship firewood and building timber south to Boston. The prices were good, some even
said exorbitant, and the market was year-round since it took ten
cords of wood a year to supply cooking and heating fuel for a
single house. It was almost impossible to work at lumbering and
farming at the same time, since, as one contemporary observer
noted, "The best season for sawing logs is in the spring, when
rivers are high: this is also the time for ploughing and planting.
He who works in the sawmill at that time must [therefore] buy
his bread and clothing, and the hay for his cattle." While the
individual farmer-artisan continued to apply the lumber from
his own woodlot to a variety of woodworking crafts such as the
making of bowls, barrels, or shingles for a cash return, it was the
large-scale lumber industry that supplied most of the needs for
urban construction and shipbuilding.

Fish, however, became the major export from New England
during the eighteenth century. The farmer-fisherman had
become the fisherman-farmer by the time of the Revolution, as
more than one in ten New Englanders earned his living primarily from the sea. Independence in fishing began on a community model: both the locally built sloops from Cape Cod and the
processing of their catch were worker-owned and -operated
enterprises. Certainly the daily life of fishermen was no easier
than that of full-time farmers. Separated from their families for
weeks or even months, their back-breaking technology embraced nothing more sophisticated than lines cast out and
drawn in hand-over-hand, hoisting fish that weighed well over
forty pounds. Self-sufficiency became less possible for fishermen
during the century as larger boats meant longer trips, so that
the season overlapped with farming season. Large merchants
took over the business and organized the annual catch, which
was cured, sorted, packed, and shipped abroad.

As a special breed of fishermen, whalers were even more
dependent on the market economy. They were gone from their
farms for years at a time, and returned with products—whale
oil and spermaceti—that were not basic necessities of life, but
were used in the rapidly growing worldwide market for consumer goods in finishing leather, making soap, and producing

high-quality candles. As the consumer market grew after 1750, the whaling fleet kept pace, sending out as many as two hundred and fifty ships a year by 1770. Nantucket and New Bedford grew prosperous on their strange catch, as Provincetown did on fish, or Goshen on cheese, but these were local opportunities and developments. For the most part, New England farmers scrounged around, doing a little of this and a little of that, sending most of their sons off in search of better opportunities and richer land. No single product so pervaded the whole region that the daily bread of the poor tenant or the fortune of the rich yeoman was measured by its market price.

How different were the dreams and realities of planters in the South where, by 1700, tobacco had become the currency of the old colonies of the Chesapeake, and rice was well on its way to similar preeminence in the more recently settled lands of South Carolina. King James I may have railed against the "stincking weed of America," but even in the face of imminent starvation, the earliest settlers in Virginia tended tobacco in every conceivable spot, including the public pathways. When South Carolina was established in 1670, its lands were bought primarily by so-called "Barbadian adventurers," who had a history of industrial planting in the sugar business behind them, and who searched diligently for a cash crop that would allow them to repeat their success on the mainland. During the eighteenth century, they settled on rice and then indigo, reproducing their life-style so accurately that English documents continued to refer to "Carolina in ye West Indies."

Successive generations of white planters who established permanent homes and families in the southern colonies built on the concepts of land as capital, crops as cash, and agriculture as a business leading to wealth and power. As in any modern business, a very few succeeded wildly, many enjoyed modest prosperity, and many more failed to achieve even a small share of the economic prize. It was the tiny number of successful agricultural entrepreneurs, however, who shaped the dreams, although never the reality, of the everyday lives of the majority of southern farmers. It was the great planters who came to control their neighbors economically and politically, who represented the South to most northerners who had never been there, and who wrote their region into the Constitution with far-reaching effects on the events of the next century.

The most frequently articulated goal for the successful planter was to live the life of a gentleman, but this was not in any way synonymous with a life of indolence or ease, requiring the active management of huge plantations of up to twenty thousand acres, mass-producing tobacco or rice for sale on the international market. The owner never ran the machinery— hoe, scythe, or flail—but worked hard planning, overseeing, and financing the business. He engaged in a rational and systematic search for the best and most salable products, devoting time and energy to research and development. He set the standards for the methods of production: when and how to plant, tend, harvest, and prepare for markets, down to the technical requirements of his particular staple; the exact moment for "topping" the tobacco plants, whether or not to flood the rice fields. When he organized the production of food, clothing, and shoes, the tools and implements of everyday life on the plantation, it was not in search of independence or self-sufficiency, but because it was cheaper to produce these things at home than it was to buy them. When the business grew large enough, it was he who dispersed its manufacture, creating several smaller, self-contained units with separate overseers and workers either grouped close together or scattered across a county or even a colony. He took responsibility for arranging transportation, dealing with customers, and obtaining the financial credit necessary to the operation of any large business. When the weather was bad and the crop failed, or when the crop was too good and the market was glutted, he faced the headaches of an inadequate "cash flow" and a rising tide of debt to the London or Scottish merchants and bankers who were his creditors.

If his were the headaches, so too were the rewards. Although at the beginning of the century, the ideal of becoming part of the English gentry was already fast fixed as the goal of southern planters, the best of them were described by one continental visitor as living only "in a less sordid manner" than those around them, with a greater variety of food, and larger, more comfortable dwellings. By the time of the Revolution, the top of the class could take pride in the description of an English visitor who wrote: "[Southern] Planters live more like country gentlemen of fortune than any other settlers in America . . . many of their houses would make no slight figure in the English counties . . . furniture, wines, dress, etc . . . in the midst of a profusion of rural sports and diversions, and in a climate that seems to create rather than check pleasures, [they are] just such planters, as foxhunters in England make farmers." The relatively recent acquisition of their possessions was evident in the reminiscences of a native Virginian, looking back and commenting, "In 1740, I don't remember to have seen such a thing as a turkey Carpet in the Country except a small thing in a bed chamber. Now nothing are so common as Turkey or Wilton Carpetts, the whole Furniture of the Roomes Elegant and every Appearance of Opulence."

Along with the crystal, china, and silver plate, fine clothes in the London fashion, handsome carriages and well-bred racehorses came the other advantages of success: the exercise of political power, the genteel education of sons and daughters by private tutors, grand tours of Europe and summer escapes to American spas in the mountains or to the seaside resorts in the North. Most notably, however, success permitted utter indulgence in the famous "southern hospitality," where dozens of guests complete with retinues of slaves were housed, fed, and entertained at the host's expense. Richard Lee, for example, not only held several summer "fish feasts" and "barbecues" along the banks of the river each year, but also threw occasional "bashes" at Lee Hall during the winter, like the opulent fourday ball attended by seventy guests in January 1774 that became legendary in the annals of plantation social life.

Central to the success of all these schemes was the ability of the great plantation to make a profit and this, in turn, rested on the availability of a large, dependable, cheap labor force. Initially, this problem was primarily addressed in the Chesapeake by the use of indentured servants or transported criminals from the jails and city streets of London or the depressed agricultural regions of Britain. For many reasons such white servants proved not to be much of a bargain; they were often unable or unwilling to do the jobs the new agriculture required, and they usually left when their indentures were over (sometimes even before) to make their own way in the world, having imbibed the dream of the planter's life along with their training in tobacco culture. Moreover, the cost of their upkeep was not entirely within the master's control. As Englishmen, even unfree Englishmen, they had a claim to the English servant's "customary rights to food of reasonable amount and quality, adequate clothes and shelter, and a certain amount of rest and leisure."

It was the enslavement of blacks that permitted the full development of southern agribusiness whether tobacco or wheat, rice or indigo. Entrenched as a legal system in the Chesapeake by 1700, black slavery provided the majority of field workers on major tobacco plantations. South Carolina planters, familiar with the West Indian system of absentee ownership, black slavery, and staple agriculture, employed only slaves from the very beginning: in the rice-growing backcountry, these workers comprised virtually the total population. After a series of black uprisings in the 1730s, the racial imbalance was seen as potentially explosive, and a law was passed requiring that one white man be present for every ten blacks on any plantation.

The crucial necessity of slave labor for the profitable operation of southern cash farming seemed to be proven by the example of Georgia. Founded in 1732 by a group of Trustees who prohibited slavery in the colony in order to make it a haven for poor Englishmen, Georgia's settlers, including several groups of hardworking German immigrants, found that they could not compete with slaveholders in neighboring colonies. They left their newly established homesteads in a steady stream, eventually causing the failure of the enterprise, its takeover by the Royal Government, and a change in its laws. Most southerners came to equate their ability to make money with their right to hold slaves, and in 1780, Virginia veterans of the Revolution successfully demanded that the legislature reward their service with a slave as well as the three hundred acres needed to start a tobacco plantation, cattle ranch, or wheat farm.

Over the course of the eighteenth century, the increasing reliance on black slaves as agricultural workers set the South apart as a distinct region, despite the diversified ways of everyday farm life from Maryland to Georgia, from seacoast to mountains. Slavery, however, was far more than an efficient system for getting the crops in and turning a profit. Social status as well as economic success depended on the ownership of both land and slaves so that, as contemporary observers at midcentury put it, a man could scarcely "appear in polite company" or marry his children off "in reputation" if he owned no slaves. Moreover, since agricultural labor was the way of life for the overwhelming number of black men, women, and children, white southerners were loathe to see their families "slaving" in the fields, and physical labor came to lack the dignity it was accorded in the North. Perhaps only an infinitesimal number of southern planters could actually achieve the ideal of total freedom from physical labor—including that of dressing themselves—but anyone with a shred of pride would, at least, keep his womenfolk away from the hoe or the plow.

Between the great plantation owner and the poorest tobacco grower lay many layers of inequality that marked the everyday lives of farmers in the Chesapeake. They were all dependent on tobacco, since it was the currency of their region, but those without the land or capital needed to invest in large-scale production were less and less able to compete. Small landowners with perhaps a few slaves or servants eked out a living from year to year, while as many as one-third of the farmers had no property of their own at all, but lived as tenants on holdings rented from others, either for cash or "a share of the crop." William Holte, who arrived in Maryland around 1700, was such a tenant farmer. When he died, ten years after arriving in the New World, he owned £4 of property: a blanket, two iron pots, some old furniture, two cows with calves, and two small hogs. In addition, there was a crop of 1,750 pounds of tobacco worth another £5, barely enough to cover his rent, taxes, clothing, and the repayment of several loans he had incurred in compiling even this small number of possessions.

Such poor farmers followed the same routine as their wealthy neighbors and shared their vision of the ideal life as well, but they did the physical work themselves alongside a single slave or perhaps a son. During the 1730s, in the face of increased competition, both Maryland and Virginia passed laws requiring the inspection of tobacco in the hogshead for the purpose of grading it and insuring quality control. The methods of small producers often resulted in crops of poorer quality, perhaps so poor they were labeled "trash" by the inspectors and were refused shipment entirely. In these cases, the crop was burned at the warehouse, as the hoped-for profits of fifteen months of unremitting labor went "up in smoke." After midcentury, the smaller tobacco growers in the eastern counties were almost completely squeezed out, moving west to the Piedmont to start the cycle all over again, or turning to the staple production of wheat and cattle which could find a ready market in the West Indies.

What was true for southern white folk was true for blacks as well. Their everyday lives varied over the course of the century, and from place to place, less voluntarily but no less widely. The single slave who worked alongside a poor master and his family shared his owner's tasks and skills in clearing, preparing soil, tending fields, and harvesting crops. He shared the cooked hominy, vegetables, and meat that made up the usual one-pot meal, although frequently he was allotted the less-nourishing "Hoppin' John," composed only of grits and peas. If his master was a little further up on the social scale and kept indentured servants as well as slaves, his lot was probably worse. In Georgia, for example, during the 1740s it was reckoned that it cost £9 per year to keep a male white servant, compared to only £3.46 for a black slave. The difference was accounted in both clothes and food. Servants were clothed after the style of their masters in character of garments, if not in quality, while slaves, at least in warm weather, merely wore loose, untailored garments of lin-sey-woolsey and went barefoot. The real difference came in food allowances: servants received seven times as much food as slaves, on average, and their alcohol ration, in the form of beer, was valued in cash at almost as much as the entire food *and* clothing ration of their black coworkers.

As tobacco became less profitable throughout the century, large plantations in the Chesapeake began to diversify their crops, and the daily lives of the slaves who worked them changed dramatically. More and more came to live in large groups of ten or more, in quarters distant from the master's house, and most, both male and female, became members of "gangs . . . toiling under the harsh commands of the overseer," as they planted, hoed, pulled, and "follow[ed] each other's tail the day long," as one Scottish visitor noted. Very few southern planters invested in plows or carts, since they were unwilling to turn over the land and labor necessary to provide fodder for the draft animals used to operate these conveniences. Toward the end of the century, as more Chesapeake farmers adopted the technological advantages long established on northern farms, male slaves were used for the more skilled jobs of plowing, mowing, harrowing, and carting, but black women continued their old familiar routines of hand hoeing and weeding, as well as grubbing stumps from the swamps in the wintertime, breaking new ground which could not be handled with the plow, cleaning stables, and spreading manure.

Along with all these changes came longer, more stringent days and seasons as well. Only three holidays—Christmas, Easter, and Whitsuntide—were recognized; Saturday became a full workday; and while field workers often had Sunday to themselves if no emergency like the danger of rain to the wheat harvest or the need for housing the tobacco arose, house servants had their usual tasks in the kitchen and at the table, often made more demanding by the presence of large numbers of guests. Night work was also increased, so that by 1789 many jobs were routinely done by firelight: "each had a task of stripping [tobacco] allotted wch takes them up some hours, or else they have such a quantity of Indian corn to husk, and if they neglect it, are tied up in the morning, and receive a number of lashes. . . ." In order to streamline business practices, planters began to plan on a year-round basis, so that valuable labor was not "wasted" during the winter months but was turned to jobs like the improvement of roads and carriage drives, or the cutting and carting of timber.

Everyday life on the great plantations of the lower South must have seemed highly exotic to anyone used to traditional English farm practice. Through most of the period the majority of the inhabitants were black—as many as 90 percent in some areas where the climate was regarded as particularly dangerous for white residents. "I observed, whilst at Georgia great Quantity's of Choice good Land for Rice," wrote Samuel Eveleigh in 1735, while on a fact-finding trip to the new colony, "And am positive that that Commodity can't . . . be produced by white people. Because the Work is too laborious, the heat very intent, and the Whites can't work in the wett at that Season of the year as Negrs do to weed the Rice." While technological improvements had reduced the task of weeding by the 1750s, they did little to minimize the threat of the ecology to the health of blacks, since added to the natural problem of a "wett" environment were the diseases brought on by the standing water in the man-made irrigation ditches.

Absentee owners entrusted most of the operation to huge gangs of slave laborers, overseen by black crew masters, and since rice was grown in Africa but not in England, it is likely that the annual routines developed from African traditions: spring planting was done by pressing a hole with the heel and covering the seeds with the foot; in summer, slaves hoed together in a row in unison to work songs; in October, the grain was winnowed in baskets of African design. Skills in fishing and boating were also brought by black captives from Africa, and a group of so-called "fishing Negroes" replaced local Indians during the eighteenth century on the waterways of South Carolina. The variety of nets they used and their ability to cast those nets, as well as the flat- and round-bottomed boats from which they worked, were a blend of West African water technologies. In their brightly painted canoes or *pettiaugers,* it was black slaves who provided basic transportation of goods and passengers in that half-drowned land to the rhythm and tune of African rowing songs. The possibility that a life on the water also offered an opportunity for freedom did not escape either black slaves or their white masters, and a white woman was allowed to hold the ferry franchise across the Ashley River in 1741 only on the condition that she "find and provide two able and sufficient persons to Row in the Boat with one white man who shall constantly attend the Said Ferry as well by night as by day."

African and West Indian backgrounds meant that blacks were far more prepared for livestock management, southern-style, than were their white owners or other European observers of the eighteenth-century scene. Here was an area in which the ecology, settlement patterns, and needs of the market all came together to create agricultural practices wholly foreign to the English philosophy and pragmatic experience of what made efficient, economic, and even "moral" farm procedure. While northerners were accused of sloppy and inadequate care of their livestock, southerners seemed positively perverse in their failure to stable, feed, or fence their animals: hogs ran free in the forests; and cattle and horses ranged far and wide on grassy, scrubby, or lightly wooded lands.

What agricultural traditionalists and reformers failed to see, of course, was that it was not "a want of attention" but the choice of a different cultural pattern that made the colonial South the forerunner of that most distinctive of all American rural scenes, the nineteenth-century Wild West. A warm climate, available-year-round natural food, and, most of all, vast spaces made open-range herding after the fashion of early Spanish settlers or Gambian cattlemen both practical and profitable. Cowpens were set up in the remote part of the range, where black slaves, called "cowboys," rounded up the cattle for branding, tended new calves, and guarded the grazing herd by night. Five hundred to one thousand cattle might be cared for by "a single [negro] man used to a Cowpen and of a good Character." Innumerable regulations regarding branding and proof of ownership make it clear that the occupation of cattle rustler began in tandem with that of cowboy.

Of course, neither cowboys nor rustlers were representative of everyday life in the eighteenth-century South. Nor, for that matter, were great planters of tobacco, rice, or wheat, nor even the small planters or tenant farmers who made up the majority of the white population in the eastern, Tidewater regions. By the time of the Revolution, the hilly Piedmont area and, to the west of that, the valleys of the Appalachians were rapidly being settled by tens of thousands of frontier families who poured down from Pennsylvania and points north all the way to Georgia. They had little in common with the stereotypical "southerner" of the East except for their acceptance of black slavery, nor did they reflect the old hopes and dreams of the New England ideal. In fact, they often had little in common with each other except a hunger for land, a desire to be left alone by government officials, and catch-as-catch-can lives shaped by the conditions of frontier existence. Referred to by one contemporary as a "mixd Medley from all Countries, and the off Scouring of America," they included new immigrants and "born" colonials; Scots-Irish, German, Swiss, English, Scottish, and Welsh ethnic groups; most Protestant denominations and a large number of the unchurched.

A similar mixture of backgrounds, goals, and ideals makes it hard for us to generalize about everyday rural life in the Middle Colonies. Since these rich lands were not heavily settled until the eighteenth century, farmers there never experienced the decades of isolation that led, both in the North and the South, to the formation of peculiarly regional patterns of life, either real or ideal. Furthermore, from the very beginning, middle colonists were always closely related to commercial outlets in Philadelphia and New York City. Long before the Revolution, these two ports, growing along with their farming hinterlands, had surpassed all other coastal cities in population and trade. While small communities of non-English immigrants, particularly those from Holland or Germany, sometimes clung to older patterns of culture derived from their ethnic and religious backgrounds, they also joined their Anglo neighbors in a pragmatic focus on promoting the welfare of their families and their pocketbooks. The issue was not subsistence, or even self-sufficiency, but cash on the barrel head, as the old saying went. By 1755, Thomas Willing, a successful Philadelphia merchant, wrote to one of his business contacts in Barbados that he could "never barter for the Country produce because the Farmer and Miller will have money on delivery & frequently before they deliver their articles."

In many ways, the farmers of the Middle Colonies had the best of both worlds. Like southern planters, the fertility of their soil and the extent of their lands allowed them to develop agriculture as a highly profitable industry. On the other hand, conditions were not so radically different from those of Europe that they required concentration on exotic crops or abandonment of the rural culture and values of the Old World. Rather, the geography and climate encouraged the exploitation of diversified staple crops that were part of the settlers' heritage, and provided both food for their families and marketable goods for the other mainland colonies, the islands, and Europe. Their seasons were similar to those of New England, only better, the winters shorter, the summers warmer. Where it required one hundred twenty-five acres to provide modestly for a family of five in New England, ninety acres supported the same number of people more generously in the Middle Colonies. To the north, farmers could expect to reap ten to fifteen bushels of wheat per acre: Pennsylvania farmers could average twenty to thirty bushels, and if Long Island yeomen were conscientious about manuring their fields, they could achieve forty to fifty bushels.

The importance of wheat on the world market made it the primary staple of the Middle Colonies, where the farmer could expect that "the first crop of wheat will fully pay him for all the expense he has been at, in clearing up, sowing, and fencing his land; and at the same time, increases the value of land, eight or ten times the original cost," according to a contemporary observer. The vision of such profits made agricultural innovators of many eighteenth-century farmers in Pennsylvania, although throughout the entire century the basic tools for earning a living on the frontier continued to be knives and axes, sickles and scythes, hoes and flails. Yet even among these simple tools, American "improvements" were in evidence by the time of the Revolution. For example, a new style of axe, its weight perfectly balanced between the blade and poll (flat edge), its handle of the length and curve exactly fitted to the height and swing of the axeman, could fell three times as many trees in the same time as a European axe. Other inventions or innovations like the seed drill, the grain cradle, and new plow and wagon designs were dreamed up in Pennsylvania workshops, to be exploited by entrepreneurial farmers. Although at midcentury most farmers still "sowed grains successively on the same land without manuring until it was exhausted and left it fallow," within a few decades they were experimenting with the use of artificial fertilizer, particularly gypsum and lime, so that it was reported in 1775 that between the Susquehanna and Schuylkill rivers, "every farmer has a Limkiln burnt for the dressing of his Land."

Although the eighteenth-century plow was essentially part of traditional wood technology, Middle Colony farmers were more likely to use them than were New Englanders, reinforcing their vulnerable cutting edges with bits or strips of iron. While harvesting remained a slow process, even after the development of the grain cradle, which cut and gathered the grain simultaneously, threshing was "mechanized" by horses plodding their heavy, slow path around and around, treading out the wheat from the chaff, long before farmers to the north gave up relying on the flail wielded by manpower alone. For hauling and transportation there were two-wheeled carts convertible to sleds in winter, and heavy four-wheeled wagons requiring teams of horses to pull them, forerunners of the covered wagons that became the mobile homes and moving vans of the nineteenth-century pioneers. Called "Conestoga wagons" after the township in which they were developed, they were matched by heavy draft horses specially bred in the same region and known by the same name. In New England, on the other hand, four-wheeled vehicles were practically unknown before the Revolution, nor were draft horses common. It was Old World oxen that provided muscle power on northern farms, where draft animals existed at all.

The need for animal power as part of the farm economy suggests the crucial shortage of labor that plagued many successful farmers in the Middle Colonies. Like their southern neighbors, their farms were large enough to require more hands than the typical family could provide; like those to the north, the crops that were most suited to their environment did not recommend the use of slaves as the solution to their labor problems. While successful planters in the South came to rely more and more on slavery and less and less on indenture throughout the eighteenth century, agricultural entrepreneurs in New York, Pennsylvania, and, to some extent, New Jersey developed a complex and widespread system of tenancy.

To be a tenant was, by definition, to live and work on some-one else's land and to pay for the privilege in cash, goods, or services. Beyond that, there were as many different ways of tenancy as there were landless people. For some, it was a poor and meagre life with little hope for future improvement, scarcely a step up from indenture, and even less secure. Often designated "inmates," these unfortunates either shared the owner's house or lived in shacks on the property. They were often required to do other work besides their chores on the farm, particularly if the farmer had some skill in a craft like weaving and saw it as a means to a second income. In this case, the tenant might also be a weaver and his wife and children spinners, as well as laborers in the field and servants in the owner's house. Where wheat was the staple crop, there were many months when there was little to do in the fields, and the cottagers were expected to spend most of their time in such craft production. Although, theoretically, the tenant had the freedom to improve his own lot as well as that of his employer, the year-round obligations of two occupations often left him with little time to "bury his own turnips, attend to business in town, or plow his flax patch."

Still other tenants were sole possessors of their farms, living in the main house and holding long-term leases good for one, two, or even three "lives." These properties were often like the "pretty farms" Peter Kalm noticed as he sailed up the Hudson in the summer of 1749, with hundreds of acres of field, wood, garden, and orchard; handsome Georgian houses with the latest in domestic technology and consumer style; and good barns and stables. Tenants on such properties paid rents that varied from "four live fat hens and a day's riding [work for the owner]" to substantial payments in wheat or cash, and were almost indistinguishable in life-style from prosperous owners. The tenant

elite on Claverack and Livingston manors in New York, for
example, even had their own exclusive social club where they
"clung together, wining, dining, and playing."

Between those for whom tenancy represented the end of the
line for themselves and their children and those who lived lives
of plenty on their rented farms were the great majority of
middle colonists for whom tenancy was seen as a way station,
a rung on the ladder to fulfillment of the American dream of
land ownership. Many were very poor: they had only their
muscles as assets, lacking the two to five hundred pounds of
capital needed to invest in a place of their own. There were
those recently released from their indentures with only a few
coins and a set of new clothes. There were German "redemptioners" who had sold themselves and their families for a term
of years to pay for their passage to the New World and were
using the time to acquire the cash, language, and skills on which
they could build a future. There were the sons of farmers who
owned enough to support themselves, but not to provide for the
next generation.

Early in the century, the outlook for these beginners was
optimistic. Landlords desperate to have their property improved often supplied their tenants with start-up capital, farm
implements, animals, mills, and markets. By the end of the
century, however, things were far less rosy as the price of land
in the settled part of the new nation rose beyond the hopes of
even the most determined, unless they moved to the frontier
and began the cycle all over again. Many declined the hardship
and the risks, turning away from generations of rural background and farming experience to learn new skills and seek
their livelihoods in the streets of the burgeoning cities and
rapidly developing towns.

6 "TINKER, TAILOR . . . MERCHANT CHIEF"

J ACK of all trades," wrote Adam Smith in *The Wealth of Nations* in 1776, "will never be rich." As this first great British enunciator of the "dismal science" of economics saw it, the "maxim of every prudent householder [should be] never to attempt to make at home what it will cost him more to make [or process for himself] than to buy . . . in every improved society, the farmer is generally nothing but a farmer; the manufacturer, nothing but a manufacturer." Eighteenth-century Americans, however, seemed unwilling to be improved. Their stated ideal was self-sufficiency rather than increased economic sophistication, and colonists often expressed pride in their ability to turn their hands to almost any task. One New Jersey farmer/tavernkeeper boasted shortly after the Revolution: "I am a mower, a shoemaker, farrier, wheelwright, farmer, gardener, and when it can't be helped, a soldier. I make my bread, brew my beer, kill my pigs; I grind my axes and knives; I built those stalls and that ohod there; I am barber, leech and doctor." It is almost impossible to envision the daily life of one who engaged in all of these pursuits; we can only assume that he had adopted an editorial "I." What he really meant was that he had become prosperous enough to have acquired a significant homestead and regarded the work of his womenfolk, tenants, indentured servants, and slaves as his own.

In point of fact, craft specialization was as much a feature of working life in the New World as it was in the Old. Large southern plantations had a real need for trained craftsmen on the premises, since they were frequently too isolated to call on outside professionals. Construction work could only be done by resident craftsmen, and while the household and personal goods used by the master and his family usually came from the international fashion centers, necessities for the slaves could be made more cheaply on the plantation. Slave owners often hired traveling craftsmen to teach their skills to the slaves and to supervise their work until they were able to produce on their own. On the largest plantations, there were enough slaves and enough work for full-time specialists like Jefferson's slave John Hemings (son of house slave Sally Hemings and a white carpenter, John Nelson), who was able to execute, on his own, such intricacies as "chines [Chinese] ralings" and "Parlour cornices." George Washington listed among his slaves waiting men, cooks, stablemen, stockkeepers, carpenters, smiths, a gardener, a carter, and a wagoner, as well as three coopers and a miller who worked at a nearby gristmill.

In somewhat smaller establishments, where a single individual could not be kept fully employed at a single craft, capable blacks were trained to do several kinds of work, the real prototype of the American handyman. The "Negro fellow name BOB," who ran away from his owner near Williamsburg in 1767, was described in the *Virginia Gazette* advertisement for his return as "an extraordinary sawer, a tolerable carpenter and currier, pretends to make shoes, and is a very good sailor." Poor southern farmers who lacked capital to purchase even the simple equipment needed to produce cloth, make candles, or process dairy products, and who lacked spare labor for home industry beyond tilling the soil, had only the options of buying goods, renting an artisan-slave from a wealthier neighbor or, most commonly, doing without.

On northern farms, a son or hired hand with the tools and skills of the carpenter's craft was invaluable in the building, maintenance, and repair of house, barn, and other outbuildings. Another son, trained as a cooper, could supply barrels for the storage and shipment of raw and processed foodstuffs. While many, perhaps most, would have preferred to be "nothing but" farmers, in Adam Smith's phrase, this became less and less possible during the eighteenth century for all but those with the largest commercial spreads. In settled rural areas of New England and the Middle Colonies, by the time of the Revolution, hope of acquiring enough land to support a family on farming alone had receded further into the distance, and one observer noted that "Many thousands rather than go farther back into the country where lands are cheap or undertake the arduous task of clearing new lands, turn to manufacturing and live upon a small farm." This "union of manufacturers and farming," as Thomas Copper explained in 1795, was not necessarily inefficient, since it was "very convenient on the grain farms, where parts of almost every day and a great part of every year can be spared from the business of the farm and employed in some mechanical, handycraft, or manufacturing business."

Every rural town or village, no matter how small, supported some specialized craftsmen who manufactured goods "wrought for sale" as their "only or principal livelihood," wrote the anonymous author of *American Husbandry* in 1775. Artisans in new settlements were often called upon to produce goods for which they had no training beyond a general understanding of the tools and the material: house carpenters, for example, might be set to making boats or coffins; shoemakers asked to supply leather bags or breeches; weavers required to do their own dying or fulling. We should not suppose, however, that any untrained amateur could tan a piece of leather adequately, build a loom and weave an acceptable length of cloth, or knock together a chest of drawers out in the barn in his spare time. Mastery of these skills and the countless others that produced the artifacts of everyday life required thorough training with an expert, followed by considerable practice. We can get a sense of the folly of trying to "do it yourself" by considering the experience of a young boy and his father who attempted to build a small cabin on the western frontier at the end of the eighteenth century. Having erected simple log walls, the pair turned their attention to clapboards for the roof. "I had seen staves [boards] split with a frow [wedge]," John Reynolds wrote in his memoirs many years later, "and we had bought one in Franklin. With much labor . . . we cut down a tree . . . mangled off a cut (for neither of us had ever chopped). When we split the piece, we found it was useless as it had a twist [in it]. . . . We were now at our wits' end . . . [and in addition] our hands were blistered. . . . The next morning my father . . . obtained [an experienced] man to make us some clapboards and help to cover our cabin."

From their inception, therefore, most rural neighborhoods included at least one carpenter, joiner, sawyer, and cooper in woodworking; a weaver and a tailor for clothing production; a tanner, currier, and cordwainer or shoemaker for fabricating leather objects; and a blacksmith for metalwork. Where stone was the local building material, a mason was sure to appear on the tax list. With only an apprentice, the rural craftsman provided the neighborhood with common goods from furniture to shoes to farm equipment in exchange for cash or for "goods in kind" from his customer's field, pasture, or dairy. Sometimes he transformed material provided by the customer himself: wove cloth of yarn spun by the women of the farm from the wool of the family flock; made chairs or tables from wood cut in the customer's own woodlot; produced shoes or leather breeches from cow, deer, or sheepskin tanned on the farm. Sometimes he paid cash for the raw material and sold the manufactured goods to other local residents.

Like their farming neighbors, rural artisans were part of an economy seen, by one historian, as an "orchestra conducted by nature." Some tasks could not be done in the cold of winter, others had to be put off during harvesttime, and still others waited on raw materials that were only produced seasonally. As the days grew shorter, shop hours kept pace, since few craftsmen could afford enough artificial light to continue work when the sun went down. To the best of their ability, however, colonial craftsmen tried to keep their shops as efficient as possible and to regularize their schedules and methods of production for the best return on their investment in time, tools, and materials.

It is pleasant to imagine a simple woodworker, for example, carefully matching his lumber, joining a chest together without resort to nails or glue, and applying all of his thoughts and energies to carving beautiful designs on the finished piece, per-

haps whistling in contentment as he stands back to view his
handiwork. Many, no doubt, possessed the skills to produce such
"masterpieces," but the time required was not worth it unless
the customer was willing to pay extra for the quality—and few
were. To put his training to best use in earning enough money
to support himself and his family, the furniture maker, therefore, employed as many shortcuts and economies as possible.
He used standard patterns, nails and glue where they did not
show, and paint to cover mismatched lumber; simplification
allowed less skilled workers to do most of the job while the
master attended to finishing details. Although much colonial
furniture was "bespoke" (made to order), it was not unusual for
the craftsman to assemble it from a collection of parts more or
less mass-produced ahead of time.

Basic goods like pottery, agricultural tools, nails, and stockings that could not be locally produced had to be imported,
often from other rural areas. Useful but nonessential articles,
like the leather fire buckets ordered from Philadelphia by the
North Carolina Moravian community at a dollar apiece in 1773,
or pure luxury items, such as spermaceti candles, satin gowns,
and silver tea services sought by rural gentry trying to keep up
with the fashions of the "civilized world," were imported from
more sophisticated manufacturing centers. Steady local demand for an item often encouraged a craftsman to settle in an
area, so that population increase and greater common prosperity brought not only greater numbers of essential artisans to a
neighborhood, but a greater variety of specialized workshops as
well. In the rather typical Chesapeake county of Talbot, settled
in the seventeenth century, cabinetmakers, goldsmiths, and
fullers appeared by the 1750s, coach- and watchmakers after
1775. Towns in need of particular services occasionally advertised in the newspapers; for example, "Middletown, the Metropolis of Connecticut," in 1758 stated that "The trade of a
Currier is very much wanted [and a good artisan] may get a
pritty Estate in a few Years."

In the hundreds of growing towns in New England and the
Middle Colonies during the second half of the eighteenth century, transportation and merchandising networks made it possi-

ble for artisans to serve markets that extended all the way to the urban centers of Boston, New York, and Philadelphia. One successful enterprise was apt to attract others, so that many towns became known as centers for particular products: the weavers of Germantown, Pennsylvania, turned out 70,000 pairs of "Germantown" stockings per year by the time of the Revolution; and "Lynn shoes" from Lynn, Massachusetts, topped the 80,000 mark by 1767. Other towns experienced a more diversified form of industrial development, none perhaps more successfully than Norwich, Connecticut, where, by the Revolution, there were good-sized workshops producing, among other things, paper, stockings, chocolate (5,000 pounds a year!), earthenware, ironware, brassware, guns, wire, shingle-nails, clocks, and watches, all for a continental market. Of course, a large number of specialists required an equally large number of support craftsmen to supply them with the necessities which they had neither the time nor the skill to make for themselves.

The largest towns and cities not only employed the greatest variety of craftsmen and specialists, but also developed service industries peculiar only to urban society. Adam Smith mentioned "porters" as one such occupation, but there were many other less obvious examples. Bakers were scarcely needed in rural communities where everyone had a hearth, most with ovens recessed into their walls, and grain—if only corn or rye— was readily available. Large numbers of city folk, on the other hand, lacked the ready cash to purchase flour in bulk, the space to store it, or the ovens in which to bake it. There were over one hundred bakers in Philadelphia by 1790, providing ready-made bread, or baking the loaves prepared by thrifty housewives who found it cheaper to employ their services than to use expensive fuel in home baking. Some bakers specialized in "fast food," offering meat pies and other pastries, cakes, and biscuits hawked from baskets or carts in the streets, and still others were specialized sugar bakers, icers, or confectioners merging the baker's skill with that of the candy maker.

A partial list of the "mechanical" arts offered in colonial cities provides a glimpse into the complexity of the everyday work of eighteenth-century urban people (see table, p. 181). All who

URBAN CRAFTS IN EIGHTEENTH-CENTURY AMERICA

SERVICE CRAFTS	INDUSTRIAL CRAFTS	MARITIME COMMERCE
Retail baker, butcher, confectioner, chocolate grinder, tailor, breechesmaker, seamstress, tobacconist, snuffmaker *Building* bricklayer, brickmaker, carpenter, housewright, wharfbuilder, glazier, oiner, mason, stonecutter, paver, plasterer, painter *Travel and transport* blacksmith, farrier, smith, carter, drayman, innkeeper, tavernkeeper, porter *Other services* barber, laborer, scavenger, watchman, perukemaker (wigs), sawyer, woodcorder	*Textile trades* dyer, silkdyer, feltmaker, hatter, bonnetmaker, weaver, stocking weaver *Leather trades* glover, saddler, harnessmaker, whipmaker, shoemaker, heelmaker, cordwainer, skinner, tanner, currier, leatherdresser *Food and drink processing* brewer, maltster, distiller, sugarboiler, miller, bolter *Shipbuilding crafts* blockmaker, caulker, mastmaker, ropemaker, rigger, sailmaker, shipwright, boatbuilder, ship joiner *Metal* brassfounder, brazier, clockmaker, instrumentmaker, locksmith, watchmaker, goldsmith, jeweler, looking glass maker, gunsmith, pewterer, tinworker, tinker, coppersmith, silversmith, wheelwright *Furniture and other woodworkers* cabinetmaker, chairmaker, upholsterer, coachmaker, carver, lastmaker, saddle tree maker, turner *Miscellaneous* chinamaker, china mender, combmaker, brushmaker, printer, engraver, limner, potter, soapboiler, tallow chandler, staymaker	*Mariners* sea captain, pilot, seaman, sailor, flatman, shallopman, cooper

Source: Adapted from Gary Nash, *The Urban Crucible, Social Change, Political Consciousness, and the Origins of the American Revolution,* "Table 1. Occupational Structure of Philadelphia and Boston, 1685–1775," pp. 387–390.

engaged in these occupations shared in the uncertainties of life, from unseasonal weather to bad economic times to the effects of war or ravages of epidemic disease. Some crafts enjoyed greater stability; they were more valuable in money and prestige either because they required longer to learn and more skill to pursue, or more capital investment in tools and material. Successful silversmiths, goldsmiths, instrument makers, and printers not only mingled with the "better sort" but also might hope someday to rise to eminence in politics or social life. Elias Boudinot, a fifth-generation Huguenot silversmith who lived on a comfortable estate in New Jersey, maintained business connections at the top level in both New York and Philadelphia, and served as president of the Continental Congress, a member of the House of Representatives, and director of the United States Mint, a job for which his early training no doubt helped him qualify. At the other end of the scale, in America as in Europe, shoemakers, tailors, weavers, and mariners always seemed to be at the bottom of the barrel, along with female artisans such as milliners, seamstresses, and spinners. It was here that one also found the large number of urban workmen, designated merely as "labourers," who had no particular skills to sell and counted on the strength of their muscles to gain them occasional work by the day along the docks or at one of the many construction sites that proliferated in rapidly growing cities.

Between these two extremes lay the careers of most other craftsmen. A bricklayer who possessed ability and an entrepreneurial spirit—and on whom fortune smiled—might become the owner of a flourishing business, employ several workers, own his own home, and watch his children rise in the world. A slight change of fortune, however, might suddenly thrust him into a situation like that of an unemployed bricklayer named Landrum, whose wife, Lydia, and daughter, Mary Ann, arrived at the Philadelphia poorhouse in December 1800, "in a state of starvation and nakedness and brought in a Cart, the Mother being so extremely Numb with cold that she was entirely helpless."

The fragility of prosperity and of life itself was expressed in a popular sailor's song, "Spanking Jack," the title piece of a book printed on wrapping paper and cheap enough to be bought by the poorest artisans.

> But what of it all lads? shall we be down-hearted
> Because that mayhap we now take our last sup?
> Life's cable must one day or other be parted:
> And death in fast mooring, will bring us all up
> Yet 'tis always the way on't—one scarce finds a brother
> Fond as pitch, honest, hearty, and true to the core,
> But by battle or storm or some fell thing or another
> He's popped off the hooks, and we ne'er see him no more
> But grievings a folly
> Come let us be jolly;
> If we've troubles at sea boys, we've pleasures ashore.

The pleasures referred to were essentially alcoholic, and it is likely that many, if not most, workmen spent a large percentage of the working day, as well as their leisure time, "mildly glad with liquor," as one master craftsman put it. At 11 A.M., and again at several times during the afternoon, work ceased, small spreads of liquor, cheese, and sweets appeared, and an atmosphere of relaxation prevailed. The master, his journeymen, apprentices, customers, and friends who dropped by all participated in singing, joking, and card playing; passing around the bottle; and verbal banter. The process of work itself was helped along by this socializing between workers and masters. Many journeymen had apprentices read to them from newspapers or broadsides as they worked, or kept up a continual stream of discussion about their work or "hot" topics of interest in politics, religion, or local scandal. Singing while working was almost universal, and Benjamin Rush, a late-eighteenth-century doctor and gentleman, observed that indigo dyers were "peevish and low spirited," because they "did not even hum a tune" while they labored.

For most of the eighteenth century, urban shops remained small enough to maintain these superficial personal relationships despite an increasing call for goods to supply the rapidly expanding population. Even the most prosperous masters rarely employed more than five to ten workers, and demand was met by the start-up of new shops usually clustered together along a single street or within a single neighborhood. When one shop received an order too big to be filled on time, the extra work was "jobbed" out to a neighboring craftsman, or some of his journeymen were borrowed for the emergency. Sometimes the only work done on an item by the craftsman from whom it was ordered was his "mark," indicating, spuriously, that it had been made in his shop.

The continuation of these traditions of community (between one shop and another) and family (between master and worker within each shop) hid the ways in which the real lives of artisans were actually changing over the course of the century. At the top of the craft market, masters of successful urban workshops began to outgrow their positions as co-workers. They did less and less of the actual hand labor, perhaps no more than exercising quality control over the goods that were produced, or putting the finishing touches on a high-scale piece ordered by a favored customer. As one historian ironically noted, "The average colonial American . . . craftsman loved his craft so well that he could hardly wait to get out of it and into some less arduous, more lucrative line of work."

As he spent less time in the workplace, becoming instead a salesman and merchandiser of his goods and investing his capital on rental properties or merchant ventures, the master artisan became more socially respectable, a sober member of the growing middle class. He spent more time in the coffeehouse, less in the tavern; offered his services to community and church councils; and joined with other masters in trying to regulate pay and increase profits. His wife, who had once worked in the shop as well, was withdrawn to live the increasingly restricted role of housewife—tending the children, managing household servants, and engaging in the social world of tea drinking, visiting, and shopping for the consumer goods that were an essential part of middle-class life.

No such upward ladder presented itself to journeymen and laborers in urban trades and crafts. Before 1750, craft shops, like farmsteads, maintained some of the social responsibilities of

the old domestic household. A worker, as part of his or her
master's family, was entitled to a certain amount of security: a
roof over his or her head and a minimum guarantee of food and
clothing. Even transients were often "taken on" by the month
or year, receiving not only wages but "found," that is, meals and
occasionally lodging. This provided them with a kind of hedge
against inactivity, injury, illness, and inflation. After midcentury, however, the wage system began to supplant even this
remnant of paternal obligation. Workers found that their personal freedom had increased at the expense of their economic
viability, as most employers took them only by the day, paying
them higher wages but without the guarantees. By the time of
the Revolution, perhaps one-third of all free men in the cities
had incomes below the poverty line. Even with marginal work
done by their wives and children to help supplement family
resources, they were frequently reduced to accepting public
aid in the form of flour or firewood, or to spending some time
in the almshouses which had become fixtures of the urban
scene.

It required full-time employment—rarely achieved—by both
husband and wife, and a year with no unforeseen disasters, for
independent artisans in the lower crafts and unskilled laborers
to cover the essentials of rent, firewood, food, and clothes for a
family of five. Only the very best years allowed the payment of
taxes and medical bills; the purchase of candles or soap; and
diets consisting of more than bread, meat, potatoes, turnips,
milk, and beer. Bad years trimmed the "fat" from even this lean
life style; more grain in the diet, doubling or tripling up in
houses, and families shivering throughout the winter without
adequate clothes or fuel. Small wonder that near the end of the
century Dr. Rush noted in his textbook, *Medical Inquiries and
Observations Upon the Diseases of the Mind,* that "mechanics"
were particularly prone to what he called "hypochondria," suffering from delusions that they were dead or damned to hell,
or that they had become animals or plants. "Many," the book
went on, acquired an "indisposition to rise out of bed, and a
disposition to lie in it for days, and even weeks."

Women who were heads of their households and supported

themselves and their families by sewing, washing, cooking, or spinning faced still worse hardships. Many relied solely on prostitution and others augmented insufficient incomes in this way as well. The fabulously wealthy merchant Stephen Girard, whose wife was institutionalized for insanity, callously noted that he attended to his sexual needs through "the acquaintance of a young Quakeress, tailoress by trade, with whom I amuse my self at very little expense and when I have time." The earliest attempts at urban industrialization in America involved the desire of potential textile manufacturers to cash in on the pool of impoverished female labor, lower welfare taxes, and compete profitably with English cloth imports, all at the same time. By midcentury, Boston, New York, and Philadelphia had each experimented with erecting workshops where hundreds of poor women and children labored, spinning linen on company-owned wheels. All failed, largely because even very poor women could not bring themselves to toil for so little money in such an unfamiliar and uncongenial environment.

At the end of the century, Philadelphia succeeded briefly in bringing the Industrial Revolution to the American city through textile manufacture as the "Friends of American Manufactures" allowed female spinners to continue working at home while setting up a new factory to employ men on both mechanized weaving equipment and hand looms. On market days during the winter and spring, one of the superintendents handed out flax to "hundreds of urban women who apply and bring recommendations of their honesty and sobriety." The spinners were paid when they returned with finished yarn of the expected quality and quantity. In addition, four English spinning jennies were set up to provide cotton thread for the men who rented the looms located in the basement. In the grand Federal Procession of July 4, 1788, a thirty-foot carriage decorated with cotton was drawn through the streets of Philadelphia with workers atop, operating the new carding engine, a spinning jenny with eighty spindles, an oversized hand loom with a fly shuttle, and a cotton printing machine. Behind this "wonder" marched the male weavers, both factory workers and independent craftsmen. Significantly, the two to three hundred female hand spinners did not march: they had already faced the fact that the new machinery both cut the demand for their product and undercut their price by 25 percent. Within two years, the factory, with all of its machinery and £1,000 worth of material and finished goods, had burned to the ground in a suspicious fire, commonly thought to have been set by a conspiracy of these militant and perhaps desperate urban wheelspinners.

Despite the Philadelphia experiment, large-scale factory operations in an urban setting were not really feasible in the eighteenth century, since cities were built on waterways chosen for their navigable qualities rather than for the power they could generate. The early American textile industry, instead, was established on the rural landscape or in smaller towns where there was an ample water source and less competition for its use. Although the story of factories and their workers is usually set in the nineteenth century, one well-known historian of technology has insisted that "the real beginning of the American Industrial Revolution coincided remarkably with the American Revolution." His definition of "industrial" covers more than the traditional concept of a large factory and includes small craftsmen who were thinking in new ways—experimenting with different technologies or producing new and unusual products. At midcentury, Peter Kalm, the Swedish traveler, reported on a Pennsylvania papermaker who made paper "that would not burn" from mountain flax, a kind of stone with "easily separable soft fibres" (asbestos), and on a man who had developed a way to make candles from spermaceti, the fat taken from the brain and head of a whale. Fabric makers developed "linsey-woolsey," particularly suited to American needs, by combining the two technologies of wool and linen production, while Pennsylvania gunsmiths came up with the way to manufacture a new kind of rifle, much more accurate than anything seen before and most useful in hunting small game or picking off lone Indian raiders along the frontier.

There were many industries, also located on the rural landscape, that made use of large, power-driven machinery and whose workers already lived lives that we have come to associate with "industrialization." We miss their significance, perhaps, because their smaller, earlier cousins had for so long been "a part of the world's peaceful, natural heritage." By the end of the century, commercial water-driven mills, up to six stories high and turning out over three thousand pounds of superfine white flour per hour for shipment all over the world, became nearly as common in wheat-farming regions as tiny local water wheels producing only a few pounds of coarse, brown, whole-wheat meal for neighboring farmers. Sawmills and the lumber camps that housed their "uncivilized" workers moved further into the wilderness as local forests were depleted. They marked their passage from Maine to Carolina with polluted drinking water and fish kills resulting from the dumping of tons of sawdust, by-product of improved technology like gang saws that could turn out as much as 15,000 board feet annually. Iron "plantations" were scattered in the deep backwoods from Kennebunk, Maine, to Buffingtons, South Carolina, with their greatest concentration in the Middle Colonies. Foreshadowing most clearly the industrial developments of the future, the work and life-style were nearly unbearable, so that one owner advised another to take on a certain skilled worker as the best he would find, although he admitted that the man was "a little disordered in the head."

Other manufacturing enterprises began to take on the appearance of industrial organization, if not mechanization, during the eighteenth century. Fisheries and shipbuilding were the largest, although paper mills, saltworks, and glass "houses" also contributed small but significant profits to the world of American manufacture. Some important industries were organized, supplied, and capitalized by merchants as extensions or adjuncts of their import businesses. The 140 distilleries that operated in the port cities by the time of the Revolution were all owned by merchants who imported molasses from Barbados or elsewhere and turned it into rum that was less expensive than the West Indian product and far cheaper than imported brandy. It was also merchant-manufacturers who satisfied the voracious colonial sweet tooth, turning imported crude "muscovado sugar" into the refined white variety Americans preferred in ever-increasing quantities to flavor their imported chocolate, tea, and coffee. They produced over 23,000 hundredweight a year during the 1770s, which was only about three-quarters of what the market demanded; the rest was imported from England.

The percentage of American income spent on English sugar, as opposed to the locally refined product, was a faithful indicator of the overall amount of colonial income that went for the purchase of imported manufactures. Some things like inexpensive textiles or earthenware were cheaper to buy than to make; others were high-end luxury items like satins and fine china that were beyond the capabilities of American industry to reproduce. As colonial manufacture of inexpensive bread-and-butter items increased through the century, they competed with, and often took the place of, the English product; however, this decrease was more than balanced by an increase in the market for fancy goods. This did not satisfy British merchants, manufacturers, and politicians, who spent much of the century in a vain attempt to limit, if not eliminate, competition in the New World. The Proclamation Act of 1763, prohibiting expansion westward by the colonists, served commercial as well as political ends. As General Thomas Gage wrote to Lord Barrington in England on the eve of the Revolution: "[It would be] for our interest to keep the Settlers within reach of the Sea-coast as long as we can. . . . Cities flourish and increase by extensive Trade, Artisans and Mechanicks of all sorts are drawn thither, who Teach all sorts of Handicraft work before unknown in the Country, and they soon come to make for themselves what they used to import."

The British, of course, had no objection to the kind of tradesmen we think of as merchants and shopkeepers, particularly those who stocked English goods, and the importance of merchandising increased dramatically with the help of a century-long series of population explosions. Although the number of the poor grew throughout the century, the number of those with disposable income grew even more rapidly, so that it seemed, as a contemporary moralizer put it, that "all the world [is engaged in] an orgy of get and spend." What one person wants, another will soon supply, and whole layers of middlemen

were added to the colonial economic scene to fill the needs—
real or perceived—of a burgeoning consumer society. They
operated on every level of business, from hucksters, peddlers,
and mountebanks, through shopkeepers of general and specialty stores, to merchants great and small. Buying and selling
became the way of life for those who created great fortunes
therefrom as well as those who clung precariously to the bottom
rung of the economic ladder. Although we tend to use the terms
interchangeably, eighteenth-century colonists had specific definitions for the various sorts of businesspersons with whom they
dealt. "Merchants" were wholesalers who were active in trade
directly related to international markets; "shopkeepers" were
general retailers whose stock came from the merchants but
whose customers were local residents. There were also specialty designations: "grocers," for example, sold—usually at retail—imported foods like coffee, cocoa, wine, lemons, and pepper, while tobacconists, ironmongers, and chandlers featured
tobacco, ironware, and candles, although they might also carry
other small wares. "Huxters" purveyed their goods along city
streets in carts, while "peddlers" traveled the back roads from
farm to farm, or from one rural village to another, their wagons
stuffed with a variety of goods, from English pins and textiles
to colonial earthenware and iron cooking utensils. Most color-
ful, though least reliable, were the "mountebanks," who
hawked an assortment of questionable articles like quack medicines from astride a bench at country fairs, attracting customers
by means of stories, tricks, and juggling.

For many colonial Americans, "keeping shop" was a sideline
that grew naturally out of their positions as craftsmen. Just as
farmers became farmer-artisans supplementing their incomes
with household manufactures often produced by other members of the family or by servants, craftsmen became artisan-
shopkeepers, staffing the store with wives, children, or servants.
Those too poor to own shops had their wives act as hucksters,
like the "fish wives" of Philadelphia, who sold their husbands'
daily catch on the pavement just beyond the market stalls of the
more prosperous bakers and butchers. While some sold only
their own goods, like John Wilkinson, brushmaker, who adver-

tised in *Poor Richard's Almanac* in 1737 that he was "opposite
to the Post Office, Philadelphia [and] still continues to buy hogs'
bristles, and make and sell all sorts of brushes . . . at reasonable
Rates," others supplemented their offerings with related articles or special stocks obtained from general merchandisers.

Rural artisans were particularly likely to take on shops, since
they were centrally located in their communities and had to
make up for the inevitable slack times that came with having
such a small number of regular customers. True to the semibar-
ter nature of backcountry life, they usually offered to "take
country goods in trade," that is, whatever surplus the farmer
had to trade in exchange for such articles as "Irish Linen, Brown
sheeting, White ditto, shoes, men's saddles, snuff, writing paper,
Nails, Locks, iron potts, and Dutch ovens," all mentioned in the
accounts of a Piscataway, Maryland, shopkeeper, along with
"green hams, teas, spices, dyes and drugs, furniture, silver, pewter, glass, and ceramics." A storekeeper in nearby Chesterton
"stocked" convict labor along with the rest of the merchandise.
Where there was a prosperous gristmill, the operator was most
likely to serve as the proprietor of a small country store, not
only exchanging goods for grain, but also becoming the farmer's
eye to the world, as his mill/shop became the place to exchange
news as well as goods. At crossroads in the backcountry South,
the shop was part of an establishment that doubled as an inn or
tavern.

Shopkeeping, like craftsmanship, was unlikely to provide a
sole means of livelihood on the frontier or in very small villages,
but in more settled farm areas and particularly in growing
towns and urban centers, there were many who supported
themselves entirely on their ability to buy and sell. Widows in
large cities, especially those whose husbands had left them a
little capital or a dwelling in a convenient part of town near the
market or the wharves, sometimes did very well for themselves.
Their ads appeared in colonial newspapers, noting that they
stocked seeds—particularly for the garden crops that women
grew—dry goods, and notions, along with household items like
soap, dishes, and spices. Occasionally they also carried ready-to-
wear garments, indicating that some of them may have been

milliners or seamstresses—artisans in their own right. Other urban shopkeepers sold expensive and purely decorative items, catering to a growing upper class heavily involved in conspicuous consumption, or, as they called it, "exterior emulation." The usefulness of status objects in climbing the social ladder was explained by a French traveler in the waning years of the century: "The rich man loves to shew the stranger his splendid furniture, his fine English glass, and exquisite china. But when the stranger has once [admired them], he is dismissed for some other newcomer, who has not yet seen the magnificence of the house nor tasted the old madeira that has been twice or thrice to the East Indies."

The retail business was a risky affair for urban shopkeepers who tried to keep up with the consumer revolution. Changes in style and taste in Europe, quickly communicated to America, could leave them with a large investment in obsolete stock. A downturn in the economy, even if brief, persuaded steady customers to put off purchases of luxury goods until things looked up again. Too many ships arriving laden with expensive china glutted the market and drove the price below what would earn a profit. Competition was also brisk in the smaller towns, and customers were sophisticated enough to shop carefully for price, quality, and credit. Advertising techniques varied from free samples to special service to printed fliers and newspaper notices. Partners in one Virginia store distributed handbills and posted them in public places, but they also recognized that this was but the first step in good marketing strategy. It was necessary to make the store and its merchandise as attractive as possible: one of them wrote to the other that he should be sure "to *Display* the Dry Goods which is a matter very *essential to promote the Sales* as every Article is to be *in view*," and recommended that in case the rum lost its color, they should keep a "small keg of colouring . . . for the purpose of giving the Spirits an additional tinge which will add much to the Sale."

Credit was the rock on which many small businesses foundered. Ezekial Brown opened a store in Concord, Massachusetts, in the early 1770s, and mortgaged his property to obtain the capital needed to purchase stock. Trade was brisk. Brown had a prime location near the center of town, he was friends with the residents, and his shop became a social center where "men traded gossip with their goods over plentiful glasses of rum." The shop expanded, and Brown bought more merchandise, this time on credit from his suppliers, while himself extending credit to his farm customers until the harvest came in. Although he probably followed the practice of the time in offering discounts of up to 10 percent for cash or thirty-day payment and charging interest of 6 percent on those debts carried longer, he was caught in a bind. Sagging economic times in Concord before the Revolution, fierce competition from other shopkeepers and local artisans, and failure of his customers to pay up led to the attachment of all his property and landed Brown in the debtor's jail in Boston.

The Boston merchants, Frazier and Geyer, who called in Ezekial Brown's loan were, undoubtedly, in something of a bind themselves. Although international affairs, particularly those relating to Great Britain, ultimately affected all colonials, it was the merchants who suffered the consequences most quickly and directly. For many, their whole stock in trade depended on maintaining a relationship with the market in England, where they sold American goods like tobacco in exchange for the English manufactures that were the lifeblood of colonial existence. Even those who were engaged in coastwise trade with other mainland colonies or who dealt primarily with the West Indies or with southern Europe depended on the British Navy for the protection of their ships and on Britain's relationship with other countries to keep their markets open. War with France or Spain oould olooo off carofully cultivated contacts or sources of revenue vital to the continuation of their businesses.

While dissatisfaction with their treatment at the hands of the English government put northern merchants at the forefront of opposition to provocative actions by Parliament like the Stamp Act or the Sugar Act, their reliance on the mother country turned many of them into Tories when the push of regulation became the shove of Revolution. Southern planter-merchants, on the other hand, generally saw patriotism as more gain than loss. The merchandise in which they dealt was basically their own staple tobacco crop and their everyday lives were tied to the rhythm of its production. After midcentury, their control over its international trade had slipped away to foreign merchant houses, set up right on colonial wharves along colonial rivers and in colonial port towns. Rich southerners had come to see themselves as "slaves" in this new economic system: "The [foreign] merchants generally purchase the tobacco in the country," one British observer wrote, "by sending persons to open stores for them . . . in which they lay in a great assortment of British commodities and manufactures, to these . . . the planters resort, and supply themselves with what they want, and as they are a very luxurious set of people, they buy too much on credit; the consequence of which is, their getting in debt to the London merchants, who take mortgages on their plantations, ruinous enough, with the usury of 8%."

Many northern urban merchants were, of course, also in thrall to English creditors, but their problems were less part of a regional commitment to a particular life-style than they were to personal business practices or an unlucky gamble on a particular market or cargo. Individual northern merchants might ruin themselves through "exterior emulation," but, in general, their business and domestic lives were far less intimately connected. By the second half of the century, they had often separated their working space from their living accommodations, the countinghouse still located on or next to their wharves, their homes in more desirable residential districts far from the "riffraff" who frequented the docks, and their summer homes well out in the country where they could play at being gentleman farmers. Success was not only dependent on overseas contacts but on inland ones as well, from whom flour, furs, lumber, and other regional products were obtained for the export part of their businesses. The hours spent in coffeehouses, where overseas news and commercial information were available, or engaged in social "politics" with Royal officials were not merely recreation but a necessary part of the everyday method of doing business.

The comfortable merchant in Philadelphia, New York, or Boston walking city streets from office to wharf was well aware of his need to maintain intimate connections with inland traders and shopkeepers, but probably gave little thought to the daily lives of the thousands of transportation workers who made the system work. Before the Revolution, most were watermen with vessels and skills adapted to the cargo they hauled and the waters over which they carried it. Black "canoe men" rowed up the Savannah River to collect skins, while Scots-Irish settlers guided double canoes down Tidewater streams, hogsheads of tobacco athwart the gunwales. Freighters and double-masted shallops sailed down the Hudson River or through Delaware Bay, run by professionals from the surrounding Anglo and German farm country. They brought their loads of grain and bread weekly to the cities, returning home with cash and imported goods for their rural customers.

The coming of the Revolution disrupted these established transport systems, since the British blockade of the coast made it far too dangerous to rely on the water. Primary responsibility for moving goods around came to rest on a miserably inadequate network of roads and on men who were drawn from farm labor to supplement an insufficient number of professional wagoners. This created labor shortages in the fields while it increased the demand for the hay and feed grains needed to "fuel" the draft horses who pulled the wagons. In respect to everyday life, however, it broadened the horizons of many who might have remained "down on the farm." They came to share with others involved in the carrying trades long periods of absence from their families, lessons in how to cope with life in the big cities where their journeys led them, and reliance on each other in doing jobs that isolated them from the more settled folks through whose lands they passed.

The most extreme version of the traveling life, unique in its isolation from others and its dependence on comrades rather than family, was that of the oceangoing mariners. These men lived in a world of their own, with daily routines and seasonal cycles far more closely related to centuries of cosmopolitan sailing traditions than to the everyday lives of eighteenth-century colonial Americans. Days were divided by watches, not by sunrise and sunset: while active laboring time—ten to fourteen hours a day—was about the same as that of farmers or craftsmen, half of the sailor's working "day" took place in the wee hours of the night. The rhythm of life was marked not by the seasons, but by the length of the voyages: several weeks to the West Indies, several months to Europe and the Mediterranean, sometimes several years to Africa or the East Indies. Each voyage was fraught with its own particular dangers. The fearful storms of the North Atlantic brought forth the mate's cry in the night, "up every soul nimbly, for God's sake, or we all perish," and a terrible toll in lives lost overboard, or in limbs and bodies crushed and broken, as the crew frantically worked to cut away rigging, pump out the invading sea, and save their little world from instant annihilation. The long and grueling trips to the East Indies, boring in their lack of ports of call and frequent days of becalming, carried always the threat of dreaded scurvy as the fresh fruit ran out.

Most disliked of all was the trip to Africa to collect slaves. It was considered with reason a very unhealthy place, where the deadly diseases of malaria, yellow fever, and dysentery were common, and strange fevers struck whole crews, leading to a common seaman's warning to "Beware and take care / Of the Bight of Benin; / For one that comes out, / There are forty go in." It is likely that as many sailors died as the slaves they transported, sometimes more. Furthermore, the length of these trips—already seemingly endless—was often extended by months of agonizing waiting on unfriendly shores while the captain tried to collect a full cargo.

Ashore in the colonies, the seaman stood out in the crowd. His very body proclaimed his occupation: he walked with a rolling gait, "[swinging his] Corps like a Pendulum," his skin was wrinkled, "metal-colored," and leathery beyond that of the most hardened outdoor worker on land, and his hands were often scarred and disfigured in particular ways; in addition, many wore tattoos on their forearms of some popular design such as the Jerusalem Cross. Renting a bed in an inn or boardinghouse in some port of call, the merchant/sailor hung around the wharves in the poorest, most disorderly section of the city, finding companionship with others of his kind. Sailors' ardent pursuit of the life they missed at sea—unlimited liquor, dancing, entertainment, sex, and, perhaps, just the freedom to move further than a few hundred feet in any direction—together with their tendency to roam in unruly groups that looked suspiciously like the dreaded "mobs" of eighteenth-century cities, made them far from popular. Indeed, as the Revolution approached, "Jack Tar" was a common figure among those who took to the streets.

Most sober, solid citizens avoided mariners whenever possible, just as they avoided the seamy part of town in which the "meaner sort" congregated. Merchants, of course, could afford no such luxury: these were their employees, this was the location of their business. Until or unless a merchant became rich enough to retire from the trade and put his capital into something less risky, like real estate or financial bonds and notes, he was bound to the uncertain world of the sea, on which he risked his pocketbook and life-style, if not his mortal existence.

For many northern colonials, the potential gain was worth the risk, and enterprising young men had only to look around them to see that the fortunes and status of the great families rested on international trade. The progression was pretty well defined by the end of the century. The beginner started with some merchandise, a little liquid capital, and a few pieces of furniture. If he prospered, he added a share in a vessel, a house to live in, a couple of rental properties, and some financial paper in the form of government bonds or bank stock. Eventually this could be parlayed into several ships, blocks of city property, land in the West, and even more capital investment. By the time success was assured, he would have acquired a country seat and some manufacturing investments such as a share of a distillery, a sugar refinery, or an ironworks. There were enough rags-to-riches stories around to whet the appetite: stories of men like Stephen Girard, for example, who arrived in Philadelphia in 1776, "a disreputable foreigner—blind in one eye, unable to speak polite English . . . and [already] in debt to businessmen in his native Bordeaux." Just six years later, he was worth £2,280, and by 1794 could claim assets of £55,211. Yet for every merchant like Girard or John Hancock of Boston, who "affected a fine raiment, had splendid equipages [carriages], built handsome houses, amassed rich furniture and plate and procured family portraits," there were at least six who acquired no more than a "modest competence," or who failed entirely and went bankrupt, migrated elsewhere, or went into other occupations.

Such uncertainty gave the wealthiest merchant something in common with the poorest unskilled laborer. The latter skirted the edge of starvation, homelessness, and the poorhouse; the former hovered on the brink of bankruptcy and debtor's prison, although the ordinary pauper was unlikely to arrive at his destination in the manner of a merchant named Soyer who, in 1784, "[ordered] up his coach to ride . . . so that he went at least in taste," a fellow merchant reported, adding sympathetically, "If there is any pleasure to going to gaol in that way I do not begrudge him it." The stress and anxiety that produced "hypochondria" in working folk was echoed in the depression expressed by businessmen when they confessed in letters that they were "Loaded with Ceare & Trouble," or lived a life of "care & anxiety," or even more dejectedly, "This is a hard harted Iron-Fisted & inhospitable world, and too many is caught in its snare."

Those unwilling to face the stress or the risks of a merchant's life, but who aspired to some sort of gentility, had to avoid career choices involving physical labor, which always marked those of the "lower sort." This limited their options severely, since there were not many eighteenth-century jobs that fell into what we would call the white-collar category: offices that employed more than a couple of clerks, factories with layers of management, large-scale engineering firms, widespread banking operations, and shops with significant sales forces all lay in the future. The choice for the sons of the upper class when there was not enough property to go around or for those of less-exalted status with a desire to rise in the world and enough money to acquire education lay in one of the professions. Careers in government, medicine, the law, the ministry, or teaching presented a great opportunity to exhibit the entrepreneurial spirit, since none of these fields demanded any specific credentials or licenses for entry. Success in the professions depended on background, contacts, and, most of all, on personal ability, both technical and self-promotional. There were, of course, expectations. For most denominations, ministers should have been ordained in one of the European establishments to whose American pulpit they aspired; lawyers and judges were most respected when they had studied and been called to the bar from one of the Inns of Court in London; doctors had ideally attended classes in Edinburgh, Scotland, or, near the end of the century, medical school at the University of Pennsylvania or Harvard; and teachers were most credible when they could point to graduation, or at least attendance, at Oxford, Cambridge, or one of the New World colleges. Yet none of the great Puritan ministers, like the Mathers or Jonathan Edwards, was ordained in Europe, and the first chief justice of the Supreme Court, John Jay, had studied at Columbia (then King's College) but had trained for the law only by "reading" for three years with a practicing lawyer.

The backgrounds, training, and social position of doctors were particularly varied during the eighteenth century. For centuries, whole phalanxes of different people had participated in health care provision, and many colonial Americans continued to rely on midwives, apothecaries, and barbers for medical advice and treatment. Even the blacksmith had a role to play: a child with a sty in its eye might be cured by a visit to the blacksmith shop where, drawing closer and closer to the steamy heat, curious to observe the work, the atmosphere broke the sty, and the blacksmith received the credit. This pragmatic approach was as good as any other in a place where doctors were so rare that towns advertised for resident "bonesetters, midwives and physicians," promising subsidies of land or money to those who agreed to live "among us Some years," and at a time when the best-trained practitioners relied on bloodletting and purging as their principal treatments. Still, they knew about infection, and the head of the Fort Pitt militia during Pontiac's uprising in 1763 ironically remarked: "Out of our regard to [the Indians] we gave them two Blankets and an Handkerchief out of the Small Pox hospital. I hope it will have the desired effect."

There was, perhaps, more common sense in the approach taken by Benjamin Franklin, a "philosopher" and "scientist" rather than a medical man, when he advocated diet to maintain health, rather than the use of medicine to restore it, once lost. Some of the suggestions he made in *Poor Richard's Almanac* in 1742 still have appeal in our diet- and exercise-conscious age, including, for example: "Eat and drink such an exact Quantity as the Constitution of thy Body allows of, in reference to the Services of the Mind"; "They that study much, ought not to eat so much as those that work hard"; "Excess indulgence in Meat and Drink, is also to be avoided"; "A greater Quantity of some things may be eaten than of others, some being of lighter Digestion than others"; "If thou art dull and heavy after meat, it's a sign thou hast exceeded the due Measure"; "Use . . . a little Exercise . . . before Meals, as to swing a Weight, or swing your Arms about with a small Weight in each Hand; to leap, or the like, for that stirs the Muscles of the Breast."

Then as now, however, it is likely that most Americans continued to eat as they pleased, and to rely on books like *Every Man his Own Doctor,* also offered by Franklin in the *Almanac.* Here, colonials could find information on physical problems that beset humanity in general and men in particular, but discussion of "female problems" or complaints was pointedly missing. For much of the eighteenth century, there was widespread cross-cultural belief in the idea that women were the proper managers of their own health and bodies. Among Amerindians, for example, it was generally accepted that the women's power to give birth and the men's power to hunt had to be kept separate. Since, according to one historian of the Chippewas, "the warriors feared they would become paralyzed or lose their hunting ability if they broke the taboo and entered the wigwam of an expectant mother," certain Indian women, the equivalent of midwives, took care of all matters associated with birth. Although European traditions seem to have contained no such mythological explanations for a division between medical issues of men and women, the separation was clear nonetheless. The position of the midwife was secure and respected: she was regarded as a professional to be paid for her ministrations, consulted during pregnancy, totally in charge in the delivery room and usually able to overrule husbands who tried to interfere. Moreover, she was a credible witness in court when some dispute arose over the nature of the birth or the death of a fetus or an infant.

So-called "man mid-wives," usually doctors, began to appear in the second half of the century, after William Shippen returned to Philadelphia from his medical training in London and Edinburgh in 1762 and set up the first systematic series of lectures on midwifery. His lectures not only included such subjects, illustrated, as pelvic anatomy, the pregnant uterus, and use of obstetrical instruments, but also demonstrations using mannequins or living poor patients who thereby received his services *gratis*. Although Shippen offered his lectures at first to both male physicians and female midwives, he soon limited his students to men. Toward the end of the century, it became more fashionable and considered medically "safer" and "easier" among upper- and middle-class urban women to have a male doctor in attendance at childbirth: among other things, they eased the process with opium and forceps. Use of a male physician was not necessarily the choice of women, however, as midwife Martha Ballard noted, with some satisfaction, when she delivered the Robbins' baby in Hallowell, Maine, in 1794: "Doctor Parker was called, but shee did not wish to see him when he Came & he returned home." Many male physicians lacked scientific understanding as well as practical experience. In describing the symptoms of pregnancy to his married daughter, Harriet, the eminent Dr. George DeBenneville never mentioned the cessation of menstruation, listing instead "coldness of the outward parts," that "the Belly waxeth very flat," that "the Veins of the eyes are clearly seen," and, finally, the appearance of a "small living creature" in urine that had been stored for thirteen days.

The overlap between amateur and professional medical practitioners extended across every level of society and every sort of treatment for every sort of illness. On southern plantations and northern farms alike, wives were the primary providers of medical services. Herbs and roots used by the Indians were among the most frequent medicines for both amateurs and professionals. Tobacco was a first line of defense: "It helps digestion, the Gout, and Tooth-ach, . . . feedeth the hungry, . . . purgeth the stomach, killeth nits and lice. . . ." The best doctors combined old European folk remedies and Indian therapies with the most up-to-date scientific techniques, like a prominent New Jersey physician at midcentury whose infallible "Cure for Pleurisy" included both bleeding the patient and administering a "Decoction of Rattlesnake Root mix't with Cinnamon powdered and an equal part of prepared Harts horn," forty grains every three hours. It is not surprising that when George Allen was taken sick on the frontier, he was afraid to take the "small brown powder" sent by the doctor, preferring to rely on the painkilling effects of laudanum, an opium derivative. He got well, while his friend Samuel Lightfoot, also "taken with ye Flux," drank the medicine and was buried a few days later.

Given the state of medical knowledge, prayer was really the most highly regarded of the healing arts. In fact, many New Englanders who were "Traders in the Art, Mystery and Business of an Apothecary and the Practice of Physick" used doctoring as a sideline to their real professions as ministers. This was partly due to their positions as the best-educated and most respected members of their community, since membership in the elite was often the major qualification for doctors before the Revolution. Joseph Pynchon was not only a member of a leading family in Springfield, Massachusetts, a politician, and an overseer of Harvard College; he also carried on a flourishing practice among the local elite, who swallowed his advice along with his famous "centipede soup," despite his lack of any formal training in medicine.

By the end of the century, although medical understanding had not improved significantly, its practice was becoming more professionalized. Larger urban centers, particularly Boston and Philadelphia, had dispensaries and hospitals, published standard fees for specific conditions, and attempted to establish requirements for training. As the number of doctors increased, those of midwives and apothecaries declined, although in rural areas and along the frontier older patterns continued well into the nineteenth century.

Lawyers had no required course of study or licensing procedure to follow, but they did have to be admitted to the bar in order to act in their clients' interests before the court. As early as 1700, a legal career required a degree of specialization and experience that largely ruled out dilettantes and part-time practitioners. Most attorneys derived their primary income from a regular and extensive practice, although their work was inextricably connected to politics. Those who acquired a surplus usually invested it in other enterprises like land speculation or merchant ventures, the real roads to eighteenth-century wealth.

The education needed to embark on a successful life as a lawyer could be obtained in a variety of ways: by attendance at the Inns of Court in London, through formal or informal apprenticeship with an established lawyer, a clerkship in government or the court, self-study, or prior experience in Europe. By the time of the Constitution, the emphasis was on the apprenticeship system, in which an enterprising young man "read" with a busy mentor and gradually took over the more routine parts of his paperwork, while observing his mentor's exploits in court. Just as the doctor's stock in trade included his mysterious bottles of medicine and bag of evil-looking instruments, a young lawyer's best capital was a large and judiciously selected library of books to which he could refer for the accumulated wisdom of his profession.

While the American legal system was part of the English structure before the Revolution, and closely modeled on it thereafter, the profession itself reflected the differences between Old and New World society. In England, there were sharp social distinctions between the various types of legal experts, and these were codified by the kind of work they did. In America, the divisions were far less rigidly related to inherited status. Justices of the peace, to be sure, were drawn from genteel backgrounds and served functions similar to those of their English counterparts, often exercising even greater power because of the autonomous, isolated nature of New World settlements. Judges in the colonial courts, on the other hand, ran a much wider gamut. While they might be learned men like Samuel Sewall of Massachusetts, or wealthy colonial gentlemen like William Allen of Pennsylvania, they were just as likely to be men of few pretensions and less knowledge, like the Vermont judge in 1784 who inquired of two lawyers in his court the nature of the document about which they were arguing. When told it was a demurrer, he responded, "I do not know what a demurrer is, but I know what Justice is, and this plaintiff is entitled to a judgment." Lawyers were not divided into specialties as they were in England, and as one Maryland practitioner explained in 1796: "No man can be called an able lawyer . . . unless he is a skillful attorney, an able special pleader, a good conveyancer and an accurate solicitor, and expert draftsman of bills, answers, and pleadings in equity; and also with the mode of opening, process, and entering judgments."

It got a young lawyer off to a good start to have come from an influential family where he received a good general education and a trip to London to study at the Inns of Court, but there were no barriers within the profession itself for those who made their own way in the world, especially if they were bright, personable, and diligent. If they were successful—made good business contacts, married well, and engaged in the open-ended world of colonial politics cleverly—they could expect to rise to the top of the social and economic heap. Many of the leaders of the young republic were drawn from just such legal careers: John Adams, from a respectable but mundane yeoman family; James Wilson, an educated but impecunious immigrant; and Alexander Hamilton, the illegitimate son of a ne'er-do-well West Indian drifter, to name just a few.

Over the course of the century, lawyers and judges came to form a relatively tight-knit group within their respective colonies. Rather like mariners, they spoke a particular occupational language and operated within a highly specialized world. Many of them were based in small, inland towns, but they had correspondents as well as casual legal partners in the large cities, and all of them, however wealthy or powerful, spent long weeks on the road traveling with the court as long as they were engaged in active practice. Most colonial justice was dispensed on the "circuit," that is, the legal apparatus—judges, lawyers, clerks, and all—moved from one county seat to another on a prescribed route and schedule. John Adams described this daily life vividly in his letters to Abigail in the 1760s before their marriage, as he followed the circuit from Plymouth to Falmouth to Boston: "Tomorrow Morning I embark for Plymouth," he wrote, "And What Company shall I find there? Why a Number of bauling Lawyers, drunken Squires, and impertinent and stingy Clients. . . . I believe I could furnish a cabinet of Letters upon these subjects . . . describing the Characters, Diversions, meals, Wit, Drollery, Jokes, Smutt, and Stories of the Guests at a Tavern in Plymouth where I lodge, when at Court."

Since the courts were the branch of government most likely to touch the lives of ordinary people, the judges, local magistrates, and lawyers that comprised them were among the most influential people in any community. They controlled the economic parameters of public and private life, from the affairs of the greatest merchants to those of the "wronged" woman seeking support for her bastard child. They settled local questions over the siting and maintenance of roads, bridges, ferries, wharves, warehouses, and mills, as well as appointing county officers. And they held the power of life and death, freedom, confinement, or corporal punishment over those accused of breaking the law.

Despite their power and expertise or, more likely, because of them, lawyers were regarded with a combination of suspicion and dislike by ordinary colonial Americans. Much of this attitude was part of the cultural baggage brought over from Europe, where it was often said that "the Devil was a lawyer from the Beginning." The ability of lawyers to argue either side of a case and, in fact, to do so occasionally in rural areas where only one qualified member of the bar could be found to appear in court led perhaps to the sardonic poem published by Benjamin Franklin in *Poor Richard's Almanac* in 1740:

> I know you Lawyers can, with ease
> Twist Words and Meanings as you please;

That language, by your Skill made pliant,
Will bend to favour every Client;
That 'tis the Fee directs the Sense
To make out either Side's pretense:
When you peruse the Clearest Case,
You see it with a double face;
For scepticism's your Profession;
You hold there's Doubt in all Expression.

Teachers suffered from a similar dislike of their way with words in the more than faintly anti-intellectual atmosphere of eighteenth-century America. Even in New England, where education was more highly regarded than anywhere else in the colonies, the attitude was far from favorable. At the town meeting of Westfield, Massachusetts, in 1711, for example, "it was voted that the select men shall provide a schoolmaster," but "it was also voted by the Town that they would not have a scolar for a schoolmaster." Later in the century, the Reverend Mr. Woodmason noted sadly that backcountry folk in the Carolinas did not "delight in historical Books . . . as do our Vulgar in England, for here the people despise Knowledge, instead of honouring a Learned Person, . . . they despise and ill treat them."

Scorn for teachers, however, was often well grounded. Many were themselves but partially educated young men who found the work a way of earning money in a more or less genteel way until they finished their own educations. They were highly mobile, seldom spending more than a term or two in the same school, and those who chose teaching as a vocation could be found advertising in one after another of the urban centers, as they sought permanent acceptance of their talents. The ones who did best, perhaps, were those who offered the more pragmatic skills, like Theophilus Grew, who advertised in Philadelphia in 1743 that he taught "Reading, Writing, Arithmetick vulgar and decimal, Merchants Accompts, Geometry, Algebra, Mensuration, Surveying, Gauging, Trigonometry, Dialling, Navigation and Astronomy; also the use of Globes, Maps, Sea-charts, Planispheres, scales, sliding Rules, and all manner of mathematical Instruments." Here was a curriculum that a budding young merchant might put to some use without wasting his time on unproductive forays into classical literature or esoteric philosophy.

A classical education really only served two purposes: it was regarded as an appropriate "ornament" for the sons of the gentry, and as career training for young men who intended to enter the ministry. By the middle of the century, however, higher education was sometimes actually a detriment to a church career. Beginning in the late 1730s, a religious revival, similar to movements of spiritual renewal taking place in Europe, had swept through the American colonies. So intense and powerful that it was known at the time as the "great and general awakening" and to later historians as the Great Awakening, its adherents often looked with suspicion on "rationalist" scientific explanations of God as some kind of "clockmaker" who had set the universe in motion and then left it to its own devices. In some cases, the Great Awakening represented a rebellion of common people who felt that "what Harvard and Yale graduates were teaching was too academic," and in others it was a reaction to ministers who, while being supported by their parishioners, lived lives that served more as moral warnings than examples. Lack of attention to their clerical duties, sexual peccadillos, and, most often, drunkenness were among the charges leveled at them, although few reached the extremes of one South Carolina clergyman, a man of "ill fame [who, while] in his cups, baptised a bear."

Established churches were violently split apart as "old sides" and "new lights" struggled for control, setting father against son, neighbor against neighbor, and just about everybody against the presiding minister. The argument between tradition and training on the one hand, and "enthusiasm" and "revival of the spirit" on the other, proved equally divisive within the congregations of English Congregationalists and Anglicans, Scots Presbyterians, German Lutherans, and Reformed Church members. There was nothing genteel or "Christian" about many of the confrontations that took place, as the battle in some churches became physical and ensuing riots spilled over into the streets, leaving parishioners and pastors alike cooling their heels in the local jails. In many communities, the breach took years to heal, while in others the rift became permanent as alternative establishments were built, competing for the hearts and minds of the devout.

Ministerial performance during the Great Awakening frequently reached high levels of emotion and entertainment. Itinerant preachers, akin perhaps to the television charismatics of today, roamed the countryside, speaking to enormous crowds and encouraging public conversion, so that one New Englander noted that "it must be owned that some of the crying or roaring Women among us have brought forth something that may be both seen and felt." On the other hand, among worldly, genteel churchgoers like Madame Gabriel Manigault of Charleston, traveling preachers were merely one of the available entertainments in town. She noted in her diary for one January at mid-century that, at various times, she "went to the Assembly . . . went to the Play . . . went to hear a Quaker [woman] Preacher . . . [and] went to hear Mr. Whitefield."

George Whitefield (1714–1770) was at once the most prestigious and persuasive of the Great Awakening preachers, as proved by his ability to sway no less a skeptic than Benjamin Franklin, who, while he "never doubted . . . the existence of the Deity," found that organized religion "serv'd principally to divide us, and make us unfriendly to one another." Attending one of Whitefield's sermons in Philadelphia, Franklin admitted that "I perceived he intended to finish with a collection, and I silently resolved he should get nothing from me. I had in my pocket a handful of copper money, three or four silver dollars, and five pistoles in gold. As he proceeded I began to soften, and concluded to give the coppers. Another stroke of his oratory made me asham'd of that, and determin'd me to give the silver; and he finish'd so admirably, that I empty'd my pocket wholly into the collector's dish, gold and all."

Despite the energy of the Great Awakening, there were many colonials, particularly in the backcountry, who "had never seen a minister or heard a sermon, scripture reading or prayer 'in their Days.'" Those who attempted to minister to them often took a good deal of abuse from the large number of colonists who neither admitted nor desired any church affiliation at all and were described by one frustrated clergyman as "Idle People without either Religion or Goodness . . . the lowest vilest Scum of Mankind." Nonbelievers thrived in settled communities as well, most noticeably in the back alleys and squalid lanes of the larger cities, where they frequently complained about the great variety of preachers fighting over them to save their souls.

Nor was a minister ensconced in the established pulpit of a settled community free from economic uncertainty. Most colonial congregations held on to the power of the purse even when they respected and revered the position and the words of the preacher. Sometimes they paid in produce, sometimes in cords of wood. Small fees might be collected for the performance of duties at marriage altar, baptismal font, or graveside. A residence with garden or small farm might constitute part of the salary, but the condition or potential of this property was not guaranteed. While salaries might be offered in terms of tithe (one-tenth of the congregant's income), there was no way of enforcing the obligation. Joseph Fish, who came to North Stonington, Connecticut, as a young minister in the 1730s, was painfully aware of this reality throughout his fifty-year tenure in that pulpit. He farmed, not only to provide food for his table, but also for a salable surplus from the sheep he sent to market in Boston, and he accepted supplementary income from two separate missionary societies in whose employ he taught neighboring Indians.

The minister's economic dependence on his congregation also put him at the mercy of the doctrinal swings that took place at the time of the Great Awakening and from time to time thereafter. While, theoretically, his tenure was secure once he had been "elected" or accepted in the pulpit, he was always in danger of being "starved out" in favor of someone whose views were more acceptable to his flock. While clergymen were socially acceptable, and their daughters were considered suitable partners for sons of the gentry, those of doctors and lawyers were preferred as having brighter prospects and greater dowries.

By the end of the century, other, more lucrative career choices were just beginning to open up for young men who looked to rise in respectability through the exercise of mental rather than physical ability. There was so much to be done in a new nation with enormous spaces to fill and a rising population to serve. New technologies would require men trained in engineering skills to design and supervise the building of lighthouses, bridges, canals, and roads that would link the continent together in a network of internal improvements. New institutions for capital creation and money management would be needed to provide financial backing for grandiose schemes and projects. Manufacturing establishments would require skilled business organizers and operators to oversee the changeover from hand production in the craft shop to mass production in the factory. New schemes had to be devised for retailing goods and making them available to a far-flung and growing population. While the majority of Americans would continue to earn their livings as farmers, craftsmen, shopkeepers, doctors, lawyers, ministers, and schoolteachers throughout the following century, some of their sons, trained at the end of the eighteenth century, would help to change the face of America and alter forever the daily lives of most of its inhabitants.

Part III

THE PUBLIC DOMAIN

7   COMMUNITY: NEIGHBORHOOD

T HE NOTION of community includes two quite different concepts: *neighborhood,* which has to do with geography; and *network,* which involves relationships. The former is maintained through transportation, the latter through communication. In today's world, there is very little difference: Neighborhood knows few limits for quick movement, from one nation to one world to one universe; network has the option of almost immediate contact, at least with someone's answering machine.

The everyday lives of colonial Americans were much more sharply restricted by the limitations of the eighteenth-century technologies of transportation and communication. While scientific experimentation and small-scale testing had begun to nibble at the edges of age-old methods of transportation, no revolutionary transformation took place before the coming of the railroads and the development of the steamboat in the nineteenth century. Minor improvements in the design of wagons, better breeding of horses, and the building of more roads and bridges, albeit not better ones, provided the only links between communities that were planting themselves ever more widely in space across the seemingly endless geography of the American continent.

Communication, for its part, was entirely limited by the availability of physical transportation. Although eighteenth-century experiments in electromagnetism laid the groundwork, it was not until the middle of the nineteenth century that the telegraph began to transport information by means of electrical impulse. Until then, the only way for people to exchange ideas or make contact with each other was to go in person or send a written message that had to be physically transported and delivered.

Since the lack of artificial lighting further limited travel to daylight hours, the area in which daily interaction could take place was scarcely more than a few miles in any direction, and the point at which "far away" began was nearer at hand. For those who lacked the time to travel or the skills of literacy with which to communicate, a move twenty miles across the mountains or into the "wilderness" of the frontier might mean leaving family and friends forever. A voyage on a merchant ship meant months, or even years, away from home and out of touch, without knowledge of the loss of a wife or parent, or the birth of a new baby. In our world of instant communication and continual contact, it seems a miracle of resolve and determination that networks of colonial Americans managed to stretch over great distances: newly arrived Europeans hooked up with long-emigrated brothers or sisters; Quakers remained united in religion, family, and business from London to the West Indies to Philadelphia to the Carolina backcountry; runaway slaves from plantations in Georgia were reunited with families living in New Jersey.

Since most colonial Americans were tied to local geographical neighborhoods far more tightly than to any distant network, the physical features of any particular place played a major part in shaping its community: no village was going to grow into an important town or city if it was tucked away inaccessibly behind steep, rocky mountains without the potential for developing either roads or water transport. On a broader scale, climate, soil, and general networks of rivers, bays, mountains, and valleys affected community patterns of interaction in much the same way they influenced family, farm, and working life. Rural neighborhoods, villages, towns, and cities grew quite differently from each other, depending on their geographical location in the New World.

None of the communities that grew out of the colonial American experience really replicated those of Europe, although, as usual, New England presented the most familiar facade. From the very beginning of colonialization early in the seventeenth century, families there were not merely encouraged, but mandated, to settle in towns just as individuals were required to settle in families. Farmers were expected to live together in villages, within eyeshot of a meetinghouse that doubled as chapel and town hall, within the earshot of the bells that summoned them to worship or to war, walking each morning to the fields that lay beyond the settlement. Necessary facilities clustered around a center: crafts shops and general stores; lawyers' and doctors' homes/offices; the local school; and, naturally, the tavern, which, in addition to its ordinary functions, was used as a public meeting hall in an emergency. There, visiting clergy "could always find comfortable lodging and a well-ordered bar." In the very center lay a small, muddy piece of "commons" where the militia drilled on Saturdays and the animals were brought each morning at the sound of the herdsman's horn, to be taken out to the more distant, common grazing grounds. Theoretically, a community not only worshipped together, its members sat together in town meeting where, although only the household heads could vote, everyone from the town eccentric to the women of the community might raise or discuss issues of local importance or more weighty matters that needed to be taken to the General Court of the colony.

The Old World ideal village of "community farmers" was never really viable in colonial America: the spaces were just too enormous. The township of Dedham, Massachusetts, for example, covered two hundred square miles, and although it first established the village of Dedham with a population of about one hundred people in one corner, within fifteen years another village was underway some ten miles away, and a few years later, yet another was built over twenty miles distant. These new towns, and the dozens of others that were created within other townships throughout New England, were too spread out by the eighteenth century to make commuter farming practical—the great part of the day would have been taken up with getting to and fro. Many farmers pulled down their barns and re-erected them on their distant holdings. By about 1720, they also built homesteads on their land, moving their families away from the old community and leaving the town center, in the words of a local minister, "[as] a place of the greatest retirement and the most profound silence except on the Sabbath."

Still, these New England farmers did not merely scatter and abandon the concept that the "social virtues" could only be practiced in towns. They continued to feel the need of a central place where children could attend schools, places of worship were readily available, and "wild and savage Behaviour [would be] put out of Countenance." "Outliers" continually petitioned their town meetings for the right to establish new towns closer to their holdings, or, failing that, to be allowed to set up more "convenient institutions," like meetinghouses or schools. As Samuel Kibby of Concord, Massachusetts, explained when he joined one of these petitions, he had trouble getting his five daughters to Sunday meeting so far away: he had only one horse and they had to take turns riding since "they were so heavy that only one could ride at once."

As land pressure became intense and New England families moved west and north, they continued to cluster their community functions in population centers. Public facilities such as the meetinghouse, schoolhouse, mill, and graveyard remained located alongside the private economic services of the tavern, shops, professions, and craft industries. It was still possible to conduct all business and see all one's neighbors in a single trip to town, if it took place on the right day of the week. Storekeepers like the Dwight family of Springfield, Massachusetts, found that customers were coming in from twenty different communities in a six-month period and expanded their business, creating branch stores in neighboring towns, not from a philosophical devotion to close-knit community, but because maximum profit lay in direct service to local places.

By the time of the Constitution, there were over 1,000 towns in New England. New Hampshire alone, although still considered part of the frontier, could boast 198 "inhabited towns," as well as any number that existed only on the plot plans of land developers. Twelve of the twenty-two urban communities in the United States (defined as having a population of over three thousand) could be found in eastern or southern New England, and the prominence of town building in the region was noticed by virtually every traveler, usually with approval. In 1780, a French visitor to western Connecticut wrote home that he had "never traveled three miles without meeting with a new settlement, either beginning to take form or already in cultivation." He went on to marvel at how quickly settlers were able to build "large, handsome, and convenient" dwellings, and then remarked, "I shall be asked, perhaps, how one man or one family can be so quickly lodged; I answer, that in America a man is never alone, never an isolated being. The neighbors, for they are everywhere to be found, make it a point of hospitality to aid the new farmer."

Outside of New England, from New York to Georgia, from the Atlantic across the Appalachians, neighborhoods were quite different and probably unique in Western experience. Commercial, political, and social functions of life were broadly dispersed across the landscape to serve farms and plantations which were in themselves far more widely distributed than they were in either Europe or the northeast colonies. Lack of familiar closely settled towns led to a stubborn myth—still sometimes repeated in history books—that colonial America was a land of mile after mile of roads that never arrived anyplace except at other roads, and that individualistic citizens lived on scattered farms in self-sufficient isolation without reference to neighborhood, village, or town. Contemporary travelers from abroad were quick to notice the absence of community centers and to point out that, as one German visitor put it in 1756, "[Pennsylvania farmers] live so far apart that many have to walk a quarter or a half-hour just to reach their nearest neighbor." Even native residents added to the myth. When Benjamin Franklin searched for the cause of the many deaths that had taken place at the hands of the Indians along the Pennsylvania frontier in 1755, he ignored the fact that town-settled New England had had its share of Native American attacks and explained that these latest raids were "a natural consequence of the loose manner of settling in these colonies, picking here and there a good piece of land and sitting down at such a distance from each other."

The Middle Colonies could, in fact, boast a fair number of good-sized, prosperous towns, but they lacked the hundreds of rural villages that in New England were dignified by the title of "town." County systems of government made local township control seem unnecessary and irrelevant, and there was no common religious experience to provide community glue. The multicultural, multireligious nature of most rural neighborhoods made it unlikely that a single church or meetinghouse would serve an entire population. The small town of Newtown, New York, which once flourished where the runways of La-Guardia Airport now stretch, never reached a population of as many as one thousand souls during the colonial period, yet, by the time of the Revolution, it included Presbyterian, Dutch Reformed, Anglican, and Quaker congregations. Even the smallest towns in Pennsylvania with predominantly German populations usually contained both a Lutheran and a German Reformed congregation. When the community was too small to support two buildings, an economy of scale was affected by erecting only one and calling it a "United church." The title referred strictly to the building and not the congregants, the service, or the ministers, who were frequently at each other's throats in the kind of quarrels that only close relatives or intimate neighbors can have. When a neighborhood included both an English and a German, Dutch, or Swedish population and each group lived clustered by itself, the church was not set in the town at all, but on a crossroads convenient to the greatest number of its members. For most of the eighteenth century many of the sects—Quakers, Mennonites, German Baptists— built no meetinghouses at all, but gathered in the homes of their participants on a rotating basis.

When Peter Kalm, the famous Swedish scientist, traveled up the Hudson River from New York City to Albany at midcentury, he noted with surprise how few settlements there were, "even very small ones," although the riverbanks were constantly dotted with farms. What most neighborhoods offered were unplanned hamlets, or even single public establishments standing alone such as a tavern beside the road or a mill beside a stream. Busy roads like the Lancaster Turnpike had a tavern every mile or so, and little settlements grew up around these operations; company stores might be located near a mine, forge, or furnace to serve the workers and their families; and one or two craftsmen, like blacksmiths or woodworkers, might set up shop to serve travelers who stopped at crossroads inns or taverns.

Population centers that grew successfully in the Middle Colonies during the eighteenth century were primarily county seats that became market towns for the extensive agricultural regions that surrounded them. Often their establishment was motivated more by politics than by the natural advantages of the site itself. Lancaster, Pennsylvania, for example, lay in rich farmlands but had nothing to recommend it as an important place to erect a town—lacking access to even a modest waterway—except that it was owned by Andrew Hamilton, prothonotary of the Supreme Court of Pennsylvania and an extremely influential man in Philadelphia. It was only after the site was chosen that the world, as it were, beat a path to its door and made it the center of commerce for the inland part of the commonwealth. By the time of the Revolution, a large number of transients doing business at the county seat, together with a small but "citified" population, supported a number of urban amenities. There were regular markets whose stalls were occupied by butchers rather than farmers; specialty shops like bakers and silversmiths; coffeehouses as well as taverns; libraries and dancing assemblies; and, occasionally, paved, though unlit, streets. These amenities continued to be promoted as a way to attract commerce. In 1771, county officials were particularly concerned that the streets of the town of Lancaster remain in good repair, not only for "the benefit of its inhabitants," but also to "the advantage of all who trade and resort there."

The further south one went, the more the nontraditional loose appearance of the neighborhood fooled outsiders into thinking that no community existed at all in this strange and exotic social landscape. As the Reverend Mr. Hugh Jones, an English minister newly arrived in his colonial parish, explained in 1724: "Neither the interest nor inclinations of the Virginians induce them to cohabit in towns; they are not forward in . . . the making of particular places, every plantation affording the owner the provision of a little market; wherefore they most commonly build upon some convenient . . . neck of land in their own plantation. . . ." Just about all tobacco planters and rice growers vied for places along the water in order to deal directly with merchant ship captains, arranging for the export of their own tobacco or rice crops and the import of the European consumer goods they so loved and desired. Less fortunate planters, unable to acquire river frontage, shipped their crops to the docks of their larger neighbors who, in effect, acted as community merchants or shopkeepers. It was these planter-merchants who became really rich.

Eyewitness accounts by travelers and descriptions by insiders themselves indicate that if one rode past and saw something that looked like a town, and if, in fact, one looked more closely and saw that it functioned like a town, it was probably a plantation. A German visitor who passed through Maryland and Virginia in the 1780s reported that, rather than build a single large house, plantation owners erected "small, badly kept cabins" to serve as "living-rooms, bed-chamber, guest-chambers, store-rooms, kitchens, quarters of the slaves, and who knows what else," giving the whole, from the road, "the appearance of a small village."

In addition to the distant physical resemblance to a town, there were many ways in which plantation life mirrored life in northern villages, although, as tutor Philip Fithian of Princeton remarked, "a Town where most of the Inhabitants are black." In size, some of the larger plantations could easily compete with eighteenth-century corporate communities: Thomas Jefferson's spread covered thirty-nine hundred acres criss-crossed by twenty miles of roads and was home to over two hundred people, including a wide variety of craftsmen. Planters further dispersed their slaves, building auxiliary quarters out near the furthest fields since, as in the case of New England farmers, it was not efficient to have them walk more than an hour to the day's job.

As quickly as the best locations were taken, southern planters of every economic status extended their domains into the spaces between the waterways of the Tidewater and, by the 1740s, into the Piedmont, beyond the falls of the river systems. This required a whole complex of roads to supplement the waterways now inaccessible to many of the settlers. In the back-country, many of these roads were scarcely more than Indian trails, but at some point they all met up with "main highways" that helped them keep in contact with deep-water ports. Although the distances were great in the Tidewater, the relative flatness of the land and the sandy, stone-free nature of the ground made it possible to move across the landscape with relative speed. According to one circuit-riding minister, one could ride "50 miles in a summer afternoon, and sometimes a hundred miles in a day," with the added benefit that there was "noe occasion for shoeing [the] horses except in frosty weather." Specially bred horses called "everlasters" and excellent saddles allowed fifty miles "to go so easy [that they won't tire] a man so much as 20 or 30 . . . in England." It probably also had something to do with the fact that colonial miles were shorter than English ones.

With so much of the significant economic function of major marketing and home production of everyday goods handled on individual large plantations, there was no real need for town building. Necessary community institutions and gathering places were dispersed along the roads or at crossroads where they were most central to the population that used them. Eighteenth-century southern maps reflect this geographical reality, with place names that almost always end in "Church," "Court House," or "Corners," and only rarely in "-town" or "-burg."

Churches often stood alone at a crossroads or atop a rise, usually lacking a bell tower since few of their congregants would have lived close enough to hear the ringing. On Sundays, after the service, the community met around the church to exchange greetings and gossip, the men discussing politics and settling minor community problems among themselves. Courthouses rarely stood entirely alone; it was almost always accompanied by a lockup (jail), at least one tavern, and often a store, if none of the taverns provided "convenience" merchandise. Once a month, when court was in session, this area came alive, creating the atmosphere of a fair. Militia muster was held, peddlers offered their wares along the road, and great quantities of alcohol were consumed. There was much laughing, arguing, and personal tests of strength and skill—as well as just plain fighting—along with horse racing, cockfighting, and all sorts of other games and opportunities for gambling. However, outside of Sundays at the church and court days at the courthouse, there were few signs of neighborhood life around these public facilities.

At many crossroads closer to individual neighborhoods, a lone tavern that operated as a general store or, conversely, a general store that also provided "spirits" by the drink might attract a more steady and predictable stream of customers. The crossroads stores, in particular, were unlike any shop or general store in New England towns. They took up all the slack for missing institutions, sometimes accommodating travelers, often acting as post offices. They extended credit and acted as banks by also accepting deposits; they took in merchandise in trade, arranged for orders of special goods direct from Charleston or Baltimore, and aided local exchange within the far-flung neighborhood, buying grain, for instance, from a farmer who had grown too much, and selling it to another neighbor whose crop had come up short. Storekeepers often brewed their own beer or distilled their own corn "likker," or whiskey, which they sold in quantity. They offered the most incredible assortment of goods, from "Pershon silk" to matches, from chamber pots to tennis racquets. One French traveler even despaired of finding a translation for the word "store" as it was used in America, especially in "places thinly inhabited."

The frontier was the largest region of all in eighteenth-century America, but by its very nature it was never geographically permanent. What constituted the frontier in the perspective of the colonists and their British government was negative: lack of control over indigenous Amerindian populations or failure to remove them entirely; lack of contiguous European settlement; lack of the extension of British institutions and governmental control over colonial communities; and a predominance of "uninhabited," uncultivated "virgin" land. Compounding this absence of civilization were the isolation of each discrete settlement that had been "planted" and a dearth of known paths or waterways safe and reliable enough to ensure continual connection and communication. For Amerindians who had lived on the continent for centuries, the word "frontier" made little sense, unless regarded as the line between themselves and the encroaching Europeans—and it was in the very nature of the frontier that no such line existed.

The difference in perception is apparent in the different reactions of John Lawson, an Englishman, and his "Indian Pilot" to a night in the Santee River swamp in the Carolinas at the start of the century: "In the Beginning of the Night," wrote Lawson, "we were awaken'd with the dismall'st and most hideous Noise that ever pierc'd my Ears . . . our [guide] (who knew these parts very well) acquainted us, that it was customary to hear such Musick along that Swamp-Side, there being endless Numbers of [wild animals] which take this Swamp for their Abode . . . coming in whole Droves to hunt the Deer [and] making this frightful Ditty 'till Day appears, then all is still as in other Places."

Lawson's virgin "wilderness" was home to Native Americans of the southern colonies, a home long since disrupted and changed by successive waves of European explorers and settlers. Removed from their original lands and decimated by disease, the local population had combined in survival groups, forming a new culture that combined many elements that had been common to their precontact ancestors. Maize and tobacco still played central roles in their lives and their towns gathered around "square grounds," where each side represented one of the four sacred points of the compass.

Although town layout varied, William Bartram, the well-known naturalist, had described a typical town or *talwa* when he traveled through the South just before the Revolution. In addition to the square ground, the central space in the talwa included a plaza, the council house or rotunda, a *tvlwv* (sacred fire), and a tall ceremonial ball pole which, like the spire of a colonial church, could be seen by congregants living miles away. Each family plot formed a small square ground of its own, with a cookhouse and winter residence on one side, a skin house for the summer on another, a provision house on a third, and a place for storage and entertaining on the fourth. Although many of the houses were located along regular streets stretching back from the central square ground, by the eighteenth century many of these Amerindians, who were settled agricultural people, had followed the European example, fencing their fields and living on individual farms or ranches.

During the same period, Native Americans in the North were perhaps even more deeply affected by European contact than their brothers to the south. Each community continued to be identified by a particular tribal name, but its population included the members of many other tribes: sometimes there as captives or slaves, sometimes married in, sometimes refugees, like the victims of internecine "Fox Wars" that sent the Mesquakie of Wisconsin "to live with the Iroquois in New York and Pennsylvania." Native American communities also included Europeans and Africans captured as children or adults, as well as French, Scottish, or Irish traders who lived there with their Indian families. The mobile nature of everyday life among the woodland Amerindians created towns that, while permanently sited, might be almost entirely vacant when the community moved to winter fishing and hunting camps, leaving the elderly to serve as caretakers. Over the course of the century, the traditional building styles of the communities were frequently modified to the "more comfortable" log cabins with glazed windows and stone fireplaces that were the hallmark of European settlement. The last home of the famous Mohawk leader Joseph Brant, who led the Iroquois into the Revolution on the side of the British during the Revolution, was, to judge by a contemporary sketch, a model of Georgian civilization in the wilderness.

Colonial farmers of European background who settled wilderness lands were generally moved by two factors: the push and pull of migration. In New England, many landless poor families and single young men felt "pushed" to migrate from communities that were already overcrowded and offered little opportunity to provide for their own children. Others were "pulled" by the hope of commercial success rather than pushed by depressed conditions. Real estate speculators did not migrate themselves but bought up hundreds of thousands of acres to hold in an unimproved state until the coming of "civilization" caused them to rise in value. As the first settlers arrived in a new location, these claims often stood in the way of their dreams. Ignoring paper deeds as legal technicalities, "squatters" marked out and settled on a piece they fancied, trusting that the improvements they made to the property—cleared fields, crops planted, houses, barns, and fences erected—would gain them eventual ownership. They propounded arguments like those of Maine's attorney general in 1795: "[Property derives] from man's annexing his labour to some part of the great mass of matter, and by thus separating it from the common stock . . . [therefore a poor man can] seize upon [unimproved land] as his own . . . because the earth belongs to the sons of men indiscriminately until there is an exclusive appropriation."

Failure to conform to established legal niceties gave frontier settlers and their communities an aura of lawlessness, only magnified by a life-style containing very few of the institutions and amenities considered indispensable in both Europe and the longer-settled parts of the colonies. Lack of churches and ministers led to some of the most obvious problems, including self-marriage, in contemporary terms, "after the Negro fashion." Visitors complained of the quality of life: ". . . cabins quite open and expos'd. Little or no Bedding, or anything to cover them—not a drop of anything, save Cold Water to drink— . . . No Shoes or Stockings—Children run half naked." Worse yet was the behavior of the girls who went "bareheaded, barelegged and barefoot with only a thin Shift and under Petticoat. [They draw] their Shift as tight as possible to the Body, and pin it close, to shew the roundness of their Breasts, and . . . their Petticoat close to their hips to shew the fineness of their Limbs . . . they expose themselves often quite naked, without Ceremony . . ." But the most common criticism of all was that the people behaved like savages, or as George Washington put it in his journal for 1748:

"[they were] a parcel of barbarians and an uncouth set of people, as ignorant as the Indians."

The remarkable thing about the frontier was its tendency to disappear. At the beginning of the century, large stretches of "unimproved" land settled with Indian villages, paths, and waterways occurred in every colony, from Massachusetts to Virginia. By the time the Constitution had been signed, Indian settlement had virtually disappeared east of the Alleghenies, partly as a result of the Paris Treaties of 1763 and 1783, which redistributed the Indian nations out of their lands. As the danger of Native American attack was neutralized in huge stretches of land from Lake Erie and western Pennsylvania southward through western Kentucky to Georgia, white settlements that had once been forts became rural towns, as did trading posts that had once done direct business with Indians or white traders. Sometimes the "town" was no larger than five or six houses surrounding a church, store, or mill, but the whole ambiance changed. Whereas Moncks Corner, only thirty miles from Charleston, South Carolina, had been a frontier village on the wagon trail in 1750, by 1771 the *South Carolina Gazette* counted "113 Wagons on the Road to Town, most of them loaded with Hogsheads of Tobacco, besides Indico, Hemp, Butter, Tallow, Bees Wax and many other articles; who all carry out on their Return, Rum, Sugar, Salt and European Goods." Further from the coast, isolation continued to create a problem; English traveler Isaac Weld passed judgment on the people of Lexington, Kentucky, noting that, "Of all the uncouth human beings I met with in America, these people from the western country were the most so; their curiosity was boundless." Yet, in questions like, "What might the price of bacon be [in the low country]?" we can recognize a legitimate need for communication.

Descriptions of the change of Fort Pitt into Pittsburgh give a fair picture of the process of transformation from frontier to established settlement. 1772—"The Village . . . consists of about 40 dwelling houses made up of hewed logs . . ." 1783—"[Pittsburgh] numbers at this time perhaps 60 wooden houses and cabins, in which live something more than 100 families. . . .

However little to be regarded the place is now, from its advantageous site it must be that Pittsburg will in the future become an important depot for the inland trade." 1788—"It is an irregular, poorly built place. The number of houses, mostly built of logs, about 150." 1794—"Pittsburg . . . great throughfare for the emigrants to the western country, is a large and handsome town . . ." 1797—"The place consists of wide straight streets . . . the houses number over 300, without the warehouses are in part of brick but many of them are still of wood. [Public buildings include] the courthouse, the jail, the school, the Presbyterian church, and a German Lutheran church . . . the number of inhabitants is 1480." Less than twenty years later, wilderness had become despoiled environment. 1816—"Pittsburgh was hidden from our view. . . . Dark dense smoke was rising from many parts, and . . . rendered it singularly gloomy."

By the arbitrary demographic yardstick that requires an urban place to have a population of at least three thousand, early nineteenth-century "smoky Pittsburgh" was not yet a city, despite its growth in numbers, institutions, and pollution. There were only twenty-three or twenty-four such cities in Anglo America by the first United States census in 1790: all but five lay north of the Mason-Dixon line. Together they were home to about one in twenty Americans, and, with the exception of Lancaster, Pennsylvania, were all located on Atlantic coastal harbors. Some we would find difficult to classify as cities since, like Gloucester and Marblehead, Massachusetts, large commercial fishing centers just north of Boston, they contained virtually none of the business establishments, cultural institutions, or style in architecture and living patterns that we think of as essential to urban life.

Smaller places occasionally offered may of the elements of city life, despite the lack of critical mass. Williamsburg, capital of Virginia, for example, fell below the required three thousand permanent residents, but appeared quite sophisticated, at least when the government was sitting. Not only was there a fine "palace" for the Governor, as well as other "handsome, brick buildings" and wide, straight streets—all definitely part of an urban landscape—there were newspapers, silversmiths, a Society for the Promotion of Useful Knowledge, a college, a full social calendar of balls and theater and musical entertainment, and a collection of some of the finest thinkers and orators on the continent. Out of session, some question arose as to its true urbanity, at least earlier in the century, when William Byrd reported in frustration to his diary several times: "I endeavored to pick up a whore but could not find one"; "I walked after two women but in vain"; or, again, "I walked a little to pick up a woman and found none so I went home."

At the time of the Revolution, only Philadelphia, New York, Boston, Charleston, South Carolina, and Newport, Rhode Island, were large enough and sufficiently urbane to awaken colonial pride in progress and culture, and visitors from the major centers of Europe continued to see these five, for the most part, as "quaint" and unsophisticated. Philadelphians still tethered cattle in their yards, and a cowherd made a living by ringing his bell at the corner of 2nd and Pine each morning, collecting and driving the cows to graze out in the fields past Fifteenth Street. The modesty of Bostonians in the 1750s brought something of a snicker: despite a population of almost sixteen thousand and a variety of truly urbane buildings and organizations, the largest number of newspapers and magazines printed in the western hemisphere, and one of the most prestigious and oldest of the colleges, the town government responded with alacrity to a "Great Complaint made of many Persons Washing themselves in Publick and frequented Places to the Great Reproach of Modesty and good Manners." An ordinance was passed ordering that "no Person whosoever above the Age of Twelve Years, shall in less than an hour after Sun-set undress themselves and go into Water within ten Rods of any Dwelling House in this Town, . . . nor shall any Person being in the Water, swim to such parts of the Town, as to be plainly within Sight of any Dwelling House." New York, on the other hand, took a much more European view of morality. In the district known as the "Fields," there were so many prostitutes that young men were constantly approached in the street by women like the one who "displayed her Breast . . . with a most artful smile" to young Alexander Anderson. For those who wanted a little more privacy or a more regular relationship, New York offered a large number of bawdy-houses like those of Mother Carey, or Mother Giles or Mother Gibbons.

Of the five major population centers in colonial America, Charleston was urban by virtue of its genteel opportunities for upper-class social life rather than for any outstanding quality of the exciting, "gritty" life that made other cities magnets for country folk. Called by one historian "the Ellis Island of America's black populations," and by another "most elegant . . . with more costly mansions than those of any other city," it provided a moving picture of the stark contrast between owners and owned. During the glittering "season," Charleston offered all the cultural advantages of theaters, musicales, dancing assemblies, and soirees. Church services were well attended by the "best people," and a constant round of visiting and shopping allowed display of what one English gentleman in 1774 described as a "marvel" of southern gentility: "Most People of Property," he wrote, "keep single horse chairs . . . but many of the genteeler sort keep handsome Four Wheel'd Carriages, and several Carry this luxury so far as to have Carriages, horses, Coachmen, and all imported from England." At the other extreme, for those from Europe or the northern colonies who had never seen a slave auction or, for that matter, as many Africans and African-Americans in their whole lives as they saw in the streets on a single day in Charleston, it was a scene that both fascinated and repelled.

Newport had a lot in common with Charleston, although many of the traits of its year-round residents were considered peculiarly northern. It was not exactly Sodom or Gomorrah when it came to vices of "low character" like prostitution or bathing naked in public, but the "better sort" of the tiny metropolis were thought of as even more unsavory than the usual run of sharp Yankee merchants. Many of the greatest fortunes had been built on privateering during the French and Indian War, when one-third of the adult males, including slaves, were involved at one time or another in this legal form of piracy. With the advent of closer British regulation of colonial trade after the war, Newporters turned to smuggling as did most of

the merchants in America, but they turned out to be a lot better
at it. The Vernons, an important merchant family, set the pattern, bringing in goods from East India disguised as herring,
and wines and silks from Spain under cover of Lisbon salt, a
legitimate cargo. The price, according to William Vernon,
amounted to bribes in the amount of $6,000 Spanish per year
to the local customs collector.

Other moral values and life-styles espoused by Newport's
inhabitants were sharply at odds with those of the surrounding
colonies. They carried religious toleration even further than the
Philadelphia Quakers, who welcomed all Christians: in Newport there were no restrictions at all, and one of the finest
buildings in the town was a Jewish synagogue designed and
built by an Anglican in the latest Georgian style. Furthermore,
nowhere north of New York were slaves—Indian and black—
more in evidence, serving the needs of the West Indian and
Carolina planters who came by the shipload every May to October, desperate to escape the "killing" summers at home. During
the height of Newport's popularity as a resort, in the years just
preceding the Revolution, the local newspaper printed the
names of arriving summer tourists, with those of the most distinguished in capital letters, those of the "middling sort" in
regular type.

While the word "urbane" is suited to the general ambiance
of Newport and Charleston, Boston, although it fell from the
largest to third-largest colonial metropolis during the eighteenth century, exhibited something of the gritty sense of urban
life along with its small-town quality. Although resident Bostonians were fairly homogeneous, sailors from merchant ships
provided a touch of variety, as did Native Americans abroad in
the streets, attending meetings on the Commons, like the "parade of Indian chiefs marching up the street . . . [in] laced hats,
and . . . laced matchcoats and ruffled shirts, [followed by] a
multitude of the plebs of their own complexion." The economy
of Boston presented an urban prospect that was occasionally
bleak, with its large population of widows and orphans whose
husbands and fathers had been lost in one of the many colonial
wars, and with its recurring bouts of recession, depression, and

inflation. On the other hand, it could point to its rich, elegant, and even occasionally debauched upper class of gentility who understood the meaning of consumerism, even though the word was not yet invented. Yet, somehow, Boston never glittered: when it was still the largest of the Anglo-American cities, a visitor noted that "the streets of this town are very quiet and still a'nights." There was a determinedly intellectual cast to its public life: even in the taverns, one was able to attend lectures like that on the "properties of electricity," and as the Revolution approached, its leaders were middle-class intellectuals like the Adamses, not elegant gentlemen, many of whom, along with governor Thomas Hutchinson, headed to England when the trouble started.

It was, in some respects, the seamy side of city life, and the great variety of people speaking different languages, wearing different costumes, and hawking exotic merchandise, as well as the sheer numbers that jostled each other along the crowded waterfront streets, that provided the attraction of the two largest cities, Philadelphia and New York. Both had been virtually born in duality—Dutch in New York, German in Philadelphia—and, as principal ports of entry for new immigrants, were continually enlarged by these and other new nationalities as they arrived. Although many merely passed through on their way to the rural lives they had come to build, there were always those who never got further than a couple of blocks from the wharf on which they landed. Those with a skill, a little capital, or a few good connections became part of the American success story or, more likely, of the "happy mediocrity," as Benjamin Franklin termed the basic citizenry of the colonial world. Although most learned to transact their business and express themselves in English, they retained the accent of their homelands and were constantly augmented by newcomers whose "strange tongues" raised the decibel level of the streets along with the sounds of saws and hammers, iron wheels on paving stones, the barks, whinnies, and porcine grunts of the many animals running loose, and the semimusical cries of hucksters and streetmongers.

Alexander Hamilton, a Scots-born doctor from Maryland who

traveled from his home in what he called a "progress" as far
north as Maine, left many of the sharpest pictures we have of
the communities of the continent at midcentury, although his
prejudices occasionally got the better of him. His description of
an evening in a Philadelphia tavern summarizes the polyglot
nature of city life as well as providing proof that this is not just
something we notice in hindsight, but that was of particular
interest to contemporaries. On Friday, June 8, we read that Dr.
Hamilton "dined att a tavern [in Philadelphia] with a very
mixed company of different nations and religions. There were
Scots, English, Dutch, Germans and Irish; there were Roman
Catholics, Church men, Presbyterians, Quakers, Newlightmen,
Methodists, Seventh day men, Moravians, Anabaptists, and one
Jew."

While there were occasionally sharp differences between the
religious groups and "high words arose among some of the
sectaries," for the most part ethnic elements coexisted fairly
harmoniously, although one New Yorker, early in the century,
reported to the Royal Society in London that "our chiefest
unhappyness here is too great a mixture of Nations, and English
ye least part." On the other hand, the Reverend John Sharp
looked at it more optimistically, feeling that it was an advantage
for the English in New York that they had to learn both Dutch
and French, "which are very useful accomplishments," and
there was much to be said for the opportunity "to learn Hebrew
here as well as in Europe, there being a Synagogue of Jews, and
many ingenious men of that nation from Poland, Hungary, Germany, &c."

The large black populations of these cities were less well
tolerated and, except that they were out there on the street
along with everyone else, were not really included as part of the
mix. Both New York and Philadelphia had black populations,
part slave, part free, of over 10 percent before the Revolution,
saw the number drop significantly during the war years, and
then rise again precipitously when their states adopted abolition. Philadelphia in particular became a magnet for southern
blacks escaping slavery, partly because it was so close to the
slave states, and partly because it was justly known as the home

of the abolition movement. When the Revolutionary leaders John Jay and Alexander Hamilton founded the New York Manumission Society in 1785, many prominent Philadelphia Quakers had been working to free and educate African-Americans for decades. In 1787, at the very time that the Constitutional Convention was in progress, members of the black leadership community of Philadelphia, many of them former slaves like Absalom Jones and Richard Allen, formed the Free African Society to take charge of their own lives, instituting, among other things, a "visiting committee to inspect the conduct of fellow city dwellers."

In general, black folk in northern cities spent far more time in the streets than did most other inhabitants, since most of them were servants living in the homes of white employers or masters and there was no private space in which they could get together. In Philadelphia, the "Negro burial ground" became a gathering place where those of varying African backgrounds could be found "on Sundays, holidays, and fair days . . . dividing into 'numerous little squads,' 'dancing after the manner of their several nations in Africa, and speaking and singing in their native dialects.' " This high visibility—they also used the courthouse square as a favorite hangout—made whites nervous, and laws calling for the repression of their "Riott & tumultous manner" were passed at least six times in the century. In New York, where there was a much larger slave population, resentment among blacks and fear among whites ran much higher, and there were two major alleged slave conspiracies—in 1712 and again in 1741—followed by draconian punishment and tightening of the slave codes.

Many of the laws against gathering were to some extent unenforceable and unenforced, except when the trouble was specifically racial, since street activity was an integral part of life for all except the most aristocratic. An eyewitness account of a street procession put together on the spur of the moment in Philadelphia in 1744, to celebrate the proclamation of war against France, can give us the flavor of a myriad of urban "events" that took place during the eighteenth century. "There were about 200 gentlemen attended Governour Thomas," the observer reported. "Coll Lee of Virginia walked att his right hand, and Secretary Peters upon his left; the procession was led by about 30 flags and ensigns taken from privateer vessel and other in the harbour, which were carried by a parcell of roaring sailors. They were followed by 8 or 10 drums that made a confounded noise, but all the instrumental musick they had was a pitifull scraping negroe fiddle which followed the drums and could not be heard for the noise and clamour of the people and the rattle of the drums. There was a rabble of about 4000 people in the street and great numbers of ladies and gentlemen in the windows and balconies. . . ."

Many other street "happenings" were regular affairs, often with a tinge of class antagonism, like Pinkster's Day in New York, and Mummer's or Shooter's Day in Philadelphia. As the Revolution approached, mob activity often turned to mob destruction and violence, sometimes controlled and directed by leaders of the "Cause," sometimes not. After the war, and particularly after the adoption of the Constitution, these activities, once thought of as semilegitimate political demonstrations, lost their legitimacy, and were put down by force of governmental arms. Public festivals became orchestrated events like the Fourth of July, celebrations that took place throughout the new nation, with planned sermons and orations along with municipally funded fireworks.

At the beginning of the eighteenth century only about one in twelve colonials were city dwellers. Although urban populations increased, rural areas grew faster, and by 1800 only about 5 percent of Americans lived in cities. Yet urban centers exerted an ever more powerful influence on the reality of everyday life in politics and economics, and perhaps exercised a still greater pull on the American imagination. The lure of the city with all its excitement and color was counterbalanced by a fear and suspicion of its seductiveness. There was something unnatural about the urban way: the prevalence of artificial lighting in cities seemed to stand things on their heads; time was measured in hours rather than by the sun; tasks were done by the tick of the clock, not the crow of the rooster.

A basic kind of antagonism developed between the people

who inhabited two such very different realities. City folk were so knowing, as if they had a key to the workings of the world that was lacking to their rural cousins. Both sides felt it, although to rural people the distinction was one of morality, while to urban dwellers it was one of brains and ability. One man who had served in the navy during the Revolution looked back years later on his shipboard relationships during the fateful year of 1779: "I had received some little moral and religious instruction, and was far from being accustomed to the habits of town boys . . . [who] thought themselves vastly superior to country lads. . . . My diffidence and aversion to swearing, rendered me an object of ridicule to those little profane chaps. I was insulted and frequently obliged to fight [an activity at which they were also better]."

The suburban ideal that became the hallmark of nineteenth-century American life was previewed in the diary of Sally Logan Fisher in 1785, as she looked forward to moving out of Philadelphia to the family's suburban estate in Germantown: "[May the children] be preservd in innocent simplicity and kept free from the pollutions of the World, but how [difficult] it is to stem the torrent in a great City, where there is so many temptations, so many avenues to Vice."

8

ℳ

Iɴ 1751, the British made a fatal mistake: They decided it was time to improve trade and commerce within their American possessions by creating a postal service that integrated communications from Boston to Charleston with established routes and regular deliveries. To be honest, until that time, there was very little—geographical or cultural—that held the colonies together. During times of war, when there was need for quick communications, the Admiralty encouraged private shipowners to run packets (boats that handled only mail rather than mixing it with merchandise) back and forth to London, but this meant that it was more efficient to send messages from the Carolinas to Massachusetts by way of England than directly from colony to colony. While there were numbers of what we might call tourists, Europeans or Americans, who traveled the length of the continent and occasionally ventured some few miles inland on scientific expeditions or just out of curiosity, they were, for the most part, reporting rather than communicating.

The second major mistake on the part of the British was to appoint Benjamin Franklin postmaster general of the new service. Here was one of the few colonials of midcentury who already thought like a man of the continent rather than a Bostonian or a Philadelphian or any other narrow bit of colonial territory. He was even willing to entertain the idea that Native Americans might be people to deal with rather than animals to be removed: "Savages we call them because their Manners

236

differ from ours, which we think the Perfection of Civility; they think the same of theirs." Although the plan on which he collaborated—to unify the colonies and establish friendly relations with the Iroquois tribes—failed in Albany in 1754, it carried the idea of intracolonial networking into the realm of the possible. For the next twenty years, until dismissed by the British on the eve of the Revolution, Franklin was part of a team that oversaw the development of the postal network as an effective means of communication among Americans.

The service provided relatively reliable contact between Philadelphia and New York on a three-times-a-week basis, from New York to New Haven twice a week, and from there to Boston and points north or west only once. Many more routes were covered only once every two weeks, and although southern post riders set forth from Williamsburg to Charleston twice weekly, the service was considered particularly poor; the post office continually lost revenue due to bad roads and worse accommodations, uncertain delivery, and carelessly handled mail. "[The route was] in every respect the most tedious and disagreeable of any of the Continent of North America," wrote Hugh Finlay, an English inspector, in 1774. Not that the roads in the North were a whole lot better. Of one stretch in Connecticut, Finlay reported, "The road is one continued bed of rocks, and very hilly. . . . It is impossible for a Post to ride above four miles an hour on such roads, and to do even that he must have a good horse, one used to such a path."

The post failed to turn a profit largely because the British government never took control of the building, maintenance, and regulation of these awful roads over which it had to travel. They were, and remained, strictly under local purview, and even individual colonial administrations steered clear of them whenever possible. If a road was considered of sufficient value to the whole community, linking it to market towns or commercial centers like Boston or Baltimore, the town or county might allocate taxes for the project. Otherwise, building and maintenance were the duty of those who benefitted directly. In cities, it was local government, in the name of the public good and private profit, that regulated and controlled street paving, lighting, and cleaning, at least in theory, and at least in the main streets in the better part of town.

Many, if not most, roads were not built intentionally at all, but were created by usage; local folks went the most convenient way from one place to another, often cutting across someone's land, sometimes skirting a field, widening in extralegal fashion first a footpath, then perhaps a cartway, one that might even be incorporated into the route of through travelers, like the post riders. Farmers across whose land such roads were cut sometimes complained, usually unsuccessfully. More often, they put gates across the road to keep their animals in and stray livestock out. Gates slowed the passage of a rider significantly: he had to alight, open the gate, lead his horse and, perhaps, a vehicle through, go back and reclose the gate, remount, and only then proceed ahead. Nor was this an occasional event; in a single day, one traveler from Philadelphia riding through Maryland in 1777 counted thirty-two gates. Only rarely did a community consider the plight of outsiders. In 1774, Gottfried Reuter, the roadmaster of Dobbs Parrish in the Carolina backcountry, posted signs on all nearby crossroads giving direction and distance to the nearest settlements "to the great satisfaction of travelers." More often, farmers like John Gresham, who "lost to the hogs . . . all of the Corn then planted . . . ," took matters into their own hands and "turned the road," "stopt it up," sometimes rerouting it, sometimes just ending it, leaving strangers stranded in the middle of a cornfield.

In most places, improvements in travel depended not only on better roads but also on additional ferry service and more bridges. As the century progressed, these facilities were, more and more frequently, both instituted and regulated by local or county governments. Control of the ferries augmented tax revenue and was occasionally exercised on behalf of social policy, like the ferry in Anne Arundel County, Maryland, which took all churchgoers free on Sundays between nine and eleven in the morning and again from two to four in the afternoon. Of course, in the thinly settled regions to the west, water travel continued to be the only viable alternative to any elaborate combination of roads, ferries, and bridges. Near the end of the eighteenth century, the Ohio River was "dotted with flat boats and keel-boats bringing troops and supplies . . . to the forts such as Fayett and McIntosh," and prospective settlers jammed themselves onto riverboats so that one described that "we are closely crowded having 27 men on board, 2 cows, 2 calves, 7 hogs, and 9 dogs, besides 8 tons of baggage."

Part of the vision of the founding fathers when they wrote the Constitution included a recognition, expressed by James Madison in Number Fourteen of the *Federalist Papers,* that "intercourse throughout the union will be daily facilitated by new improvements" in roads, canals, and bridges. Along the coast, lighthouses, long recognized as vital to local community interests, became acknowledged as part of an overall network that would "speed communication everywhere . . . [and allow] the will of the people . . . [to] travel quickly to Congress, undelayed by storms and swamps." By 1789, the first Congress had assumed responsibility for a dozen lighthouses and had instituted a Lighthouse Service that would erect dozens more by the end of the century. Equal expansion took place in the postal service and, during the 1790s, the number of post offices increased from 75 to 903, and the number of miles of post route expanded from 1,875 to 20,817. Like the British before them, however, federal legislators were loathe to actually involve themselves in the building of roads or canals and left implementation to local authorities and private business corporations.

Necessary as these improved facilities were to the increase of trade and the movement of goods, they did little to speed communications across the new nation. At the time of the battles of Lexington and Concord in April of 1775, it took a fast horse and rider, or a relay of them, two days to reach New Haven, five days to New York, seven to Philadelphia, nine to Annapolis, thirteen to Williamsburg. It was not until the ninth of May that news of the Revolution reached Charleston, and then it was by ship. By the end of the century, it still took over a week for a newspaper item printed in Boston to find its way into the Philadelphia press, and over two weeks for a Philadelphia report to appear in the Carolinas. Printed almanacs offered annual information to citizens in remote areas: the yearly schedule of court sittings around the state, mileage charts from one place to another, and charts to figure out the weather and the phases of the moon. These last might seem esoteric today, but were absolute necessities for travel in the days when the full moon allowed a rider to cover some ground at night, while knowledge of "ice in" or "ice out" warned travelers whether they needed to bring the runners for the wagon as well as the wheels. Specialized information on scientific advances, methods of farming, and fashion in literature, clothing, and interior decoration were disseminated as promptly as magazines from the principal cities could be distributed to their widely scattered subscribers, or letters exchanged between friends and relatives in distant settlements. Information moved most reliably, perhaps, stored in the minds and hands of craftsmen migrating from the fashion centers of Europe to the coast of the New World, or from the coast, inland.

One fact of everyday life remained unchanged by the Revolution. Given the stately pace of travel and communication, local government continued to play a major role in supporting the economic needs and lives of eighteenth-century American communities. In each region the issues of roads, ferries, and bridges were joined by other concerns of significance to the local inhabitants either between neighbor and neighbor or affecting the whole area. Property lines needed adjudication; essential services like markets, mills, docks, weights and measures, and quality control over local products all required regulation and inspection. Perhaps the greatest number of regulations was passed in relation to taverns, which, like roads, had to serve the outside world as well as the immediate neighbors. If we were able to count—which we are not, since there were more unlicensed facilities than there were legitimate ones—we would unquestionably find that taverns outnumbered any other single kind of business, convenience, or accommodation in colonial America, perhaps more than all other types added together. Some were no more than isolated farmhouses offering a bottle of cheap rum or a barrel of homemade beer or hard cider to those who passed along an almost unpopulated frontier trail; some were village inns, full of "inquisitive local rusticks";

7.1 Views of a variety of eighteenth-century community centers (pp. 214–222).

A. Detail of anonymous painting of Boston in 1730–40, indicating in perspective and scale the focus of seaport towns on their harbors. *(Worcester Historical Museum)*

B. Concord, Massachusetts, seen by a member of the Connecticut guard as the British mustered on the village green during the first battle of the Revolution, April 1775. Residences and facilities cluster around the commons, while the public cemetery is relegated to the fringes. *(New York Public Library)*

C. Eighteenth-century row housing along the main street in Germantown, Pennsylvania, with the market (far right) as the focal point. This sketch was done in the nineteenth century, and the firehouse at the far right dates from the later period. *(Germantown Historical Society)*

D. A tavern on a country road in Harlem (now the northeast corner of 8th Avenue and 120th Street), center for travelers' services in neighborhoods of scattered farms, rather than cluster settlement. *(New York Public Library)*

E. The lonely courthouse at the top of a rise was a common center of community life in the rural South, as was this example in Hanover, Virginia, in 1734, where wrestling matches were held on the green on court days. Behind the vantage point of the viewer was a tavern, once presided over by Patrick Henry. *(Virginia State Library and Archives)*

7.2 In this engraved logo from a notice of the New York Hand-in-Hand Fire Company in 1762, the ideals of volunteer private municipal services are shown in the complexity and cooperation of fighting a potentially disastrous blaze in an urban environment. Very few municipalities in eighteenth-century America could muster the equipment or the manpower to provide this kind of service (p. 228). *(New York Public Library)*

The FLYING MACHINE.

This is to give NOTICE to the PUBLIC,
THAT the FLYING MACHINE, kept by JOHN BARNHILL, in Elm ſtreet, near Vine-ſtreet, Philadelphia ; and JOHN MASHEREW, at the Blazing ſtar, performs the Journey from Philadelphia to New-York in two days, and from thence to Philadelphia in two days alſo; a circumſtance greatly to the advantage of the traveller, as there is no water carriage, and conſequently nothing to impede the Journey. It has already been performed to the general ſatisfaction of many genteel people. They ſet off from Philadelphia and New-York on Mondays and Thurſdays, punctually at Sun-riſe, and change their paſſengers at Prince Town, and return to Philadelphia and New York the following days: paſſengers paying ten ſhillings to Princeton, and ten ſhillings to Powles's Hook oppoſite to New-York, ferriage free, and three-pence each mile any diſtance between. Gentlemen and Ladies who are pleaſed to favour us with their cuſtom may depend on due attendance and civil uſage, by their humble ſervants,
§ JOHN BARNHILL and JOHN MASHEREW.

8.1 The importance of intercolonial travel was well understood by the middle of the century, and entrepreneurs made continual efforts to provide service, although lack of good roads made it an almost impossible undertaking. It is difficult to know how it was possible to get from Philadelphia to New York without "water carriage," as promised in this advertisement from the *Pennsylvania Journal* of April 16, 1767 (pp. 237–238). *(Historical Society of Pennsylvania)*

8.2 Charles Willson Peale depicted *A Representation of the Figures Exhibited and Paraded Through the Streets of Philadelphia* in 1780 as Philadelphians burned Benedict Arnold's effigy in a traditional street demonstration (pp. 253–254). *(Library Company of Philadelphia)*

8.3 An apocryphal story identifies this picture by William Birch as depicting the removal of an old blacksmith shop to a location where it could be used as the home of the newly created Bethel Church in 1794. While the legend is unlikely, its very invention suggests the importance of the founding of the church to Philadelphia's black community and to the larger community as well (p. 260). *(Library Company of Philadelphia)*

8.4 The integration of German and English culture manifested itself in material objects like this *schrank* (wardrobe) from Berks County, Pennsylvania, made in 1781. Although the construction methods, general form, and decoration of the piece are colonial German, the owner, David Hottenstein, had come to recognize the advantages of the English use of drawers, and a convenient set marches down the center of his *schrank* (p. 263). *(Henry Francis du Pont Winterthur Museum)*

8.5 Being painted in informal dressing gown with nightcap perched on shaved head made the statement that Joseph Sherburne could afford to treat an important status symbol, an oil painting by John Singleton Copley (1767), in a casual manner (p. 267). *(The Metropolitan Museum of Art)*

and others were elegant, well-equipped city establishments, where one might encounter the best in conversation, along with fine Madeira wines and imported brandies.

Obtaining a tavern license depended on several qualifications that give us an idea of how the community viewed its responsibilities to the public. Location was always part of the issue: as part of the network connecting strangers and inhabitants, taverns had to be near roads, important bridges, ferries, courthouses, and sometimes churches. As one New Jersey statute put it, taverns needed "[to provide] an accommodation of strangers and travelers, the transaction of public business and the refreshment of mankind in a reasonable manner." Most laws required that overnight facilities be provided as well: in Maryland, near the courthouse, were required "six good and substantial beds, [with] sufficient warm covering for the same"; in Rhode Island, one bed was needed for the "convenience of travelers"; while New Jersey required two spare beds and "sufficient accommodations for the stabling and pasturing of horses." Still other regulations related to the kind and amount of liquor sold, to whom it might be sold—in most places Indians, Negroes, servants, and apprentices were prohibited—and how much it was to cost. Attempts at price control were perhaps the most dismal failure, leading to the large number of illegal "tippling" or "disorderly" houses. Finally, there were what we might call "sin taxes": fees for the license and excise on the beverage served. The revenues thus generated were often designated for social uses like "repairing court houses and prisons, [and] increasing the salaries of justices," in Maryland; or for "the use, benefit, and better support of [Yale] college, its rector and tutors," in Connecticut.

One of the prime responsibilities of regulators was to pass on the fitness of the potential tavernkeeper in respect to his or her moral character and reputation for honesty and trustworthiness. At the beginning of the century, publicans were usually among the most respected members of their communities, often former deacons, assemblymen, town clerks, or justices of the peace. As the century wore on, the job began to fall to those who were less reputable, and influential men in communities throughout the colonies frequently bought up the licenses and hired someone to "keep the ordinary" (run the bar) lest the reputation of the community suffer at the hands of dishonest or price-gouging tavernkeepers. Although many officers from the Revolutionary army became bartenders as a way to try to make good on losses suffered in the service of their country and one English visitor "was impressed by the number of lawyers, ex-judges, and former members of the legislature who kept tavern in New York state," the prestige of the occupation continued to decline. More and more, the licenses were granted to widows as a way to keep them off the welfare rolls of the community, a use not calculated to enhance the social standing of the occupation.

Governmental responsibility for the character of the tavern-keeper as well as for the legitimacy of the tavern was merely one of a whole host of social services increasingly underwritten by communities rather than individual households over the course of the eighteenth century. Along with the assistance of the public sector, however, came a less welcome insistence on outside control over the lives of families and individuals. Then, as now, the best way to avoid community scrutiny and interference was to avoid being poor. The common thread that ran through the lives of all those who became "public charges" was their poverty, and except in the very largest cities where specialized "asylums" such as orphanages or "bedlams" began to function at the very end of the century, all those who could not provide for themselves were indiscriminately assigned to the poorhouse.

The poorhouse was conceived of not merely as a warehouse for those who could not support themselves, but as a place of reform for those who *would not;* the line between poverty and moral responsibility was even less well established than it is today. With the proliferation of poorhouses came repeated attempts to regulate their quality and effectiveness. In 1770, when Salem, Massachusetts, built a new facility able to accommodate over one hundred paupers, it also instituted a set of guidelines: The bedding and linens were to be aired and changed regularly; strong liquors were excluded; food was to be "wholesome and well-prepared"; and, most importantly, new arrivals were to be "deloused" on entrance.

Most of society's "sweepings" not only shared "the fault" of being poor, they shared the lack of a family that was able or willing to help them out. The reasons for poverty and lack of family support varied widely, however. In larger, more urban places, those who appeared in the poorhouse were often itinerant: down on their luck, caught by unexpected illness, a downturn in the economy and loss of a job, or destruction of their lodgings by fire, for example. They were there until their legs healed, until their husbands and fathers came back from overextended voyages, until warm weather created a need for dockworkers again, or until they were able to move on to new, more promising locations. These were the traditional "poor," temporarily dependent on society at large and for whom poorhouses had long existed in England.

The most common cause of poverty, one that reached into every community, urban or rural, increasingly becoming the responsibility of the neighborhood rather than the domestic household, arose from the "problem" of getting old. For all but the wealthiest, the preindustrial world decreed that most jobs required fairly strenuous physical labor, so that those who had not been able to save ahead before they became old were in an unenviable position. Despite public exhortations to "esteem and reverence and venerate" the elderly, Increase Mather noted that many "[treated] aged persons with disrespectful or disdainful language only because of their age [and commonly called] this or the other person 'old such an one,' in a way of contempt on the account of their age." He was right, of course, and the town records, again and again, refused to accord aged citizens the dignity of their full names, referring to them simply as "old Bright" or "old Woodward," at least when they required assistance from the community alms chest.

Although local governments, especially more rural ones, tried hard to force family members to care for their old and indigent, they were often unsuccessful. The churchwardens of Newtown, New York, sued the grandchildren of the "poor impotent old widow" Mary Martin in the Court of General Sessions which ordered the four of them "to show cause (if any they have) why they should not be assessed for the relief of their Grandmother according to law." Mary Martin's situation was more often the predicament of elderly widows or spinsters: men who were ill and old might suffer the same fate, but the facts of the ownership of property in colonial America made them far less vulnerable. Since old age was, in itself, a terminal disease, such folks usually remained in the almshouse until removed by death, and homes specifically for the elderly were an invention of a much later period. The community did not face up to the fact that it was age and not poverty that was the problem.

Illness of the indigent began to be accepted as a specific responsibility late in the century and hospitals were built in the major cities of Boston, Philadelphia, and New York. The new federal government also began to recognize its responsibility in community care. In 1798, Congress passed the "act for the Relief of Sick and Disabled Seamen." Customs collectors in each port were required to take an additional twenty cents from each shipmaster in the harbor for every month that a seaman had served on his ship. The following year, the act was extended to cover officers and sailors of the navy as well. All funds went to the Treasury Department, whose officials were made responsible for medical or custodial care of sick seamen.

Other reasoning controlled community involvement in what we call "mental illness," referred to by eighteenth-century people as "insanity," "madness," or sometimes "derangement." Before the Revolution, there was actually a rather tolerant attitude toward madness: It was seen as a recurring rather than a continuous state, so that between bouts of its outbreak, the individual was expected to perform usefully in society. Children might be warned to stay away from someone who regularly acted "crazy" on the commons, but he was unlikely to be restrained except by the family during his or her worst moments. As one historian has pointed out, colonists found the insane to be "irritating nuisances [but not] persons to be controlled, confined, or cured." As Enlightenment ideas of rationality and self-control permeated post–Revolutionary America, and as communities organized their responsibility for social services, the idea of the mad wandering around indulging in aberrant or irresponsible behavior became intolerable; they were redefined as too "dangerous to go at large" and ordered confined by their families or, failing that, in the jail or the poorhouse. While there was some faint hope that institutional discipline might "reform" them, they were not realistically judged to be "curable."

The other major function of the old domestic household left hanging in air by changes in family structure during the eighteenth century was that of the training of the young. Technical training for farm work, craftsmanship, and housewifery continued for the most part to be a household affair. The community got involved only to assign poor youngsters to private masters or to settle disputes between master and birth parent where a contract worked out badly. The question of book learning was more complex, however. In different places, at different times, and to differing degrees, the community had always had a role to play in the acquisition of the skills of literacy and numeracy, if only because so many parents lacked the time or knowledge to tackle the job themselves. At no point were parents who could afford it relieved of the financial responsibility of education, but in New England, towns built schoolhouses, hired teachers, and contributed public funds, often using "sin taxes" derived from liquor sales and tavern licenses. In the South, there were virtually no provisions made for public education, at least none that was ever put into practice. In the Middle Colonies one or more of the religious organizations in a neighborhood generally provided a schoolhouse and a place for the master to stay, while the parents paid his salary and bought the books, writing slates, and any other supplies needed by their children.

At the very end of the century, towns in New England and the middle states began to recognize that extension of traditional public education would not be sufficient to satisfy the needs of the new nation for an "educated citizenry." In fact, private schools had been increasing in number since the middle of the century, preparing middle-class youths for new jobs in the professions, merchandising, and engineering for internal improvements like bridges and roads. All who wrote about the philosophy of education, from Noah Webster in New England to Benjamin Rush in Pennsylvania and Thomas Jefferson in Virginia, expressed the need for some public involvement to provide an understanding of civic morality through the spread of literacy. This was especially important in the context of a nation in which the population shared little from one family to another in terms of the values and goals of religion, moral understanding, and societal responsibilities.

Again, the problem was framed primarily in terms of the needs of the poor, who were perceived as lacking in the proper social and moral values to be functioning members of the new nation, unable to pull their weight economically or contribute politically. In 1790, the First Day Society was founded in Philadelphia to "promote orderly habits, literacy, and skills among the children of the urban poor," since, as Benjamin Rush noted, "Who can witness the practices of swimming, sliding, and skating which prevail so universally on Sundays in most cities of the United States, and not wish for [Sunday schools] to rescue our poor children from destruction?" Jefferson, not surprisingly, saw the issue in political, rather than religious, terms: "[It is] expedient for promoting the public happiness that those persons, whom nature hath endowed with genius and virtue, should be rendered by liberal education . . . able to guard the rights and liberties of their fellow citizens, and without regard to wealth, birth or other accidental condition or circumstances [should be] educated at the common expence of all . . ."

When it came to the traditional role of the community as keeper of the peace and enforcer of the law, the system continued to rely on the structure of the institutional family, or at least on its patriarchal orientation, whenever possible. A free, married man was the "head of the family" and master of all its members, no matter how marginal his own position in society. Black slaves were thoroughly dehumanized, appearing in inventories of property along with the cattle, horses, and other livestock if they were field hands, and among the pots, pans, and "dough troughs" if they were house servants. Servants, apprentices, wives, and children were not "chattels" in the same literal sense, but they were generally not regarded as being "people" or "men" in the public arena. Only the head of the household was recognized as a fully empowered responsible member of society; only he was considered an adult, qualified to conduct legal and civil affairs; only he was, in fact, truly a human being. This legal fact of life impinged far more on eighteenth-century Americans than any lack of political rights like speaking in public, voting, or election to office.

The changing reality of American life—the dwindling role of traditional domestic households in the North, and the tiny proportion of all but slaves who lived within dynastic families in the South—gradually forced the community to deal more and more directly with individuals. In the years following the Revolution, a growing number of young people, particularly indentured servants and apprentices, frequently girls and young women, ran away from their jobs and masters. Mingling with the immigrants and sailors who clustered around the docks of the seacoast towns, they were out of the oversight of any household.

Issues that had previously been considered moral, and therefore the responsibility of the family, were either criminalized, like "drunk and disorderly conduct"; dropped entirely from the lexicon of unacceptable behavior requiring community oversight, like fornication or adultery; or transformed into a purely economic issue, like bastardy. No longer was there a concerted attempt to determine the father of an illegitimate child so as to assign blame and punishment for immoral behavior; the blame, such as it was, belonged to the woman, although economic responsibility for the child's support belonged to the father, if he could be found.

The growth of autonomous, nuclear families lacking firm economic or social bases within the community required the government to become involved in a whole host of other issues as well. Consider, for a moment, the "problem" of free blacks. To most eighteenth-century Americans, the phrase itself had the quality of an oxymoron. From the beginning of the century, southern laws had consistently aimed at tightening the identification between "black" and "slave"; where this was not the case, there were concerted efforts made to refuse residence to free blacks. A statute in Georgia in 1735, for example, had banned all blacks, slave or free, but when the ban on slaves was lifted five years later, the one on free blacks remained in effect. Those who were found could be "taken up" and as "the Sole property of . . . the said Trustees of [Georgia, were to] be Exported Sold and disposed of in such manner as the said Common Council of the said Trustees . . . shall think most for the benefit and good of the said Colony . . ." Often at risk of having their freedom "revoked" in the other colonies as well, free blacks had little confidence in their standing before the courts, and not only had trouble improving their situations, but even to hanging on to what they had. Free blacks in Virginia lost the right to bear arms and to vote, and were required to pay a special discriminatory tax after 1723; in South Carolina after 1721 they were required to leave the colony within twelve months of their manumission or risk reenslavement. Interracial marriages were generally prohibited, with special punishments reserved for cases involving white women and black men.

Although slavery as a system was rejected in the northern states by the end of the eighteenth century, many laws contained clauses that left some African-Americans in servitude well into the nineteenth. Moreover, the abolition of slavery was not related to any general repudiation of racism, and in almost every aspect of daily life, being black caused special impediments and difficulties. Fear provided the motive for much discriminatory legislation: for example, a Massachusetts statute of 1724 was passed after a series of suspicious fires, always considered the forerunner of black uprising. These so-called "Boston Articles" required that all black slaves remain indoors from an hour after dusk to an hour before dawn, carry no weapons, and refrain from "lurking" together in groups of more than two. Furthermore, they placed a draconian set of restrictions on free blacks as well. They were required to bind out their children between the ages of four and twenty-one to English (white) masters; were prohibited from entertaining nonwhite slaves in their "House, yard, garden or outhouse" unless the latter had been sent by his or her master; and were banned from selling liquor or provisions at the training field on all "Publick Days," and from receiving any goods from nonwhite servants or slaves. Failure to abide by the "Boston Articles" could result in banishment to the West Indies, a euphemism for being sold into slavery.

After abolition in Philadelphia in the 1780s, "respectable" blacks began to worry that they would be pigeonholed along with "Degenerate, flamboyant" members of their race. Black ministers and white members of the American Convention of Antislavery Societies warned them against speaking in "southern dialect," exhibiting a "sauntering gait, unrestrained singing and laughing, exuberant dancing," and, most of all, indulging in fancy dress and the "love of finery." Those aspiring to middle-class status worked hard to present the social images that white society promoted: sober, discreet, industrious, and frugal. Since many occupations were closed to them, they had to achieve this image while doing work considered fit only for the "lower sort": acting as fruitsellers, bakers, master chimney sweeps, coachmen, and oystermen, to name only a few of the jobs held by blacks who also owned property, were trustees and elders in their churches, and headed the many community beneficial associations that provided a safety net for their less fortunate brothers and sisters.

The revolutionary century did equally little to change the status of women and, like that of blacks, it got better in some places, worse in others. Women who remained single into maturity, a rare occurrence in the eighteenth century, or who were widowed in situations of affluence had certain rights to act within the legal setting; all others suffered, at marriage, what was appropriately called "civil death." Since a married couple was assumed by the court to be "one" in the most literal meaning of the word, a woman just simply disappeared into her husband, rather like becoming Adam's rib once again. Her husband had total ownership of her personal property and any wages she might receive, as well as control, if not outright ownership, of her real estate. As one historian summarized civil death: "Because [she] owned nothing, she could perform no transactions. . . . She could make no contracts; she could not sue or be sued in her own name; she could not execute a valid will; she could neither purchase nor emancipate a slave . . . she was not eligible to serve as a trustee, executor, administrator, or legal guardian."

The Revolution and the new state constitutions that emerged during the changeover from colonies to states made two changes that worked to the benefit of those women who had significant real property or could afford to go to court. In the South, the removal of the requirements of primogeniture and the right of the eldest son to a double portion, along with changes in the right of women to hold property in their own names, provided some economic cover for propertied wives. Northern women, although they lost some of their property rights, such as a widow's dower rights in uncultivated land, gained easier access to absolute divorce, including the right to remarry along with separation from bed and board. Moreover, they could seek not only alimony but also control over the property they had brought to the marriages, if they could prove that they were the innocent parties to the divorce.

Not that the system would be considered liberal from our point of view. There was no such thing as "no fault," or mutual consent for "incompatibility." There had to be a guilty party, and one guilty of a narrow range of offenses: adultery, fraudulent contract, three- to seven-year desertion, and very occasionally "cruel and barbarous treatment." No matter who was "guilty," custody of all minor children rested absolutely with the father. While in cases of desertion no doubt the mother retained her offspring, in any other situation women frequently lost not only control of their children, but all rights of visitation and any other sort of contact.

However uncomfortable and awkward it was for the community in the guise of the court to interfere in domestic life, there were always some cases about which there was no ambivalence. The Pennsylvania court, for example, had no difficulty in sending a man to prison for manslaughter in 1773 when, as the newspaper reported, "upon some Difference he threw a Loaf of Bread at [his wife's] Head, which occasion'd her Death in a short Time." Murder, manslaughter, robbery, rape, and a whole list of acts regarded as capital crimes were areas in which the individual had always been presumed to have acted in his own right rather than as part of a family hierarchy. Stretching far back into the tradition of English law, such acts were held to have been committed against the community as a whole and not merely the aggrieved individual or member of another family. Only the state, therefore, could exact punishment, and then only from the perpetrator, not from other members of the household or family. Personal responsibility for such heinous acts was often acknowledged by the condemned in a "gallows statement" which blamed the crime on failure to adhere properly to the teachings of "master" or "father."

It is important to remember that for the many Americans who were not of Anglo-European background, the criminal justice system was unfamiliar and confusing. Europeans of non-English backgrounds, such as the Dutch living in New York after its conquest by the British, were convinced that the new legal institutions were inadequate and lacked authority. "[I value] no English law no more than a Turd," asserted a Dutch justice of the peace, charged with enforcing that very law. For Americans whose culture was tribal, the whole basis of the law was unfathomable. Amerindians, for example, regarded murder as a crime against the family or clan of the victim rather than against the community at large. Retribution was the duty of the offended family to whom the life of the murderer was held forfeit. Among the Muscogulges in the Southeast, if the guilty individual escaped, another member of the clan took his place and was beaten with sticks, executed, or forced to make monetary restitution, depending on the circumstances. To Europeans, such tribal law seemed worse than savage, and when they saw that there was no such thing as written law, nor a court system, nor a policing mechanism, they concluded that the Indian tribes actually had no consistent law at all. The most the white power structure could muster in the way of intercultural understanding was to excuse the Native American on the grounds of savagery, as happened in Plymouth, when the rapist "Sam" was not sentenced to the death penalty because "hee was but an Indian, and therefore in an incapacity to know horibleness of The wickedness of this abominable act . . ."

Among African colonials, the situation was truly desperate. They not only had to unlearn a whole tribal system of justice that had formed the essence of their cultural background, they faced a white court structure still inventing a new system of justice for them. Blacks, whether slave or free, were coming to be seen as unentitled to the legal protections that the rest of colonial Americans enjoyed. In Virginia, by the beginning of the eighteenth century, a whole series of separate courts had been set up for the trial of slaves for capital crimes. As this special system was solidified and expanded throughout the century, it placed black defendants, as deviant subhumans, outside any social position at all.

The system of criminal justice in eighteenth-century America was not particularly well administered in either frontier areas or in settled communities. In South Carolina, despite proprietary and royal instructions to the contrary, the courts were "kept in Taverns, and the Prisons in private Houses" for most of the century. New England was not a good place to commit criminal acts and get caught for them since there was a high rate of prosecution, conviction, and punishment, but it was a good bit easier to get away with capital offenses in the Middle Colonies. In New Jersey the ignorance of the law by justices of the peace was legendary: one judge was in a quandary when he found that a man guilty of carrying a gun on another's property (a crime punishable by a £5 fine) had no means to pay. The law had failed to cover this eventuality. The justice of the peace made a decision worthy of Solomon: a whipping for the convicted man, and also for his accuser, since the law stipulated, after all, that informers were to receive half of the fine!

In New York not only were justices of the peace unskilled in the law, they were in short supply, as were nightwatchmen, constables, sheriffs, and jailkeepers. It was not easy to find nightwatchmen or constables to "secure . . . persons . . . they Met in their Rounds . . . [who were] disturbing the peace or lurking about or committing any theft" when seven out of every ten cases of obstruction of authority involved physical attacks by citizens on these officers of the law. The rural counties were as

ill served as the more obviously dangerous neighborhoods in
New York City. The sheriff of Ulster County was never punished for his negligence when it was charged that "There were
several persons in Jail for Felony, one of them for Murder of an
Officer in the Execution of his Duty [and all of them have] made
their escape." Even hangmen could be hard to find. Two prisoners condemned to die by the rope in January 1762 received an
inadvertent reprieve lasting almost two months when no one
would accept the job of executioner. Word had gone out that
armed friends of the condemned were going to attempt a gallows rescue. The sentence was carried out only after a "party
of his Majesty's Forces quartered in the City Barracks" was
called out "to guard the Sheriff and Civil Officers against any
Insult."

Partly, perhaps, as a result of the ineffectiveness of the criminal justice system, crimes against property, such as robbery and
theft, rose steadily throughout the century, while violence remained as prevalent as ever. In the early years, women were
frequently accused of crimes that had a particularly feminine
orientation in the eyes of the community, such as witchcraft,
adultery, and infanticide, but as the century progressed, they
were generally charged with the same offenses as men. When
married women were brought up for assault, however, it was
almost always in a domestic context where they either attacked
family members and servants, or assaulted public officials who
were attempting to "disturb," i.e. arrest, friends or relatives.
While men were clearly involved in a great deal of household
violence, cases of assault and battery against them that reached
the courts were more frequently committed as part of property
crimes or street actions. The latter might include anything from
James Sigison's offense of "drunkenness and Committing out-
rage in the Street" in Philadelphia in 1795 to the charge of
"committing a Riot in the District of Southward" brought
against Barney Kelly, James Forshee, David Connor, and Edward Dougherty late in the same year.

The charge of riot is one that resonates loudly throughout the
whole of the eighteenth century and, prior to the Revolution,
often carried with it an aura of semilegitimacy. Of course, riots

could degenerate into tumult; crowds into mobs; political intent or overexuberance into just plain vandalism. While colonial America was by no means in a continual uproar, the thinness of government institutions suggests that a great many inhabitants were involved at some time in their lives in crowd action either as participants or observers. "Legitimate" mob action, not unlike the demonstrations of the 1960s, was an expression of communal political feelings that lacked an outlet within the framework of ordinary government—the Boston Tea Party, various protests against the Stamp Act, and local uprisings against the Whiskey Tax are well-known examples.

While each disturbance differed in its details, they generally seemed to make use of certain universal symbols, such as bonfires, mock gallows, effigies, and liberty poles and hats. There was almost always alcohol in some form or other distributed to the crowd. When things turned really nasty, there might be tar and feathers for an unlucky individual who became the focus of the riot, and a rail to ride him out of town on. One of the most common forms of uprising in the colonies took place against houses as the surrogates of the people who lived in them. Although rioters shouted that they "were going to tear Brom [Phillips] all to pieces," what they did that November day in 1749 in Horseneck, New Jersey, was merely to spit in the farmer's face, pull down his fences, free his hogs, tear off a piece of his roof, and vandalize the interior of his house. When a New York neighborhood reacted against a particularly annoying house of prostitution in its midst, the crowd destroyed the beds and bedding—"tools of the trade"—and even tore down the house; the occupants themselves were left untouched.

Although racial, ethnic, and religious riots were rare during the eighteenth century, when they did occur, they were apt to be more virulent than other sorts of disturbances, and were directed against people rather than property. Fatalities could, and did, occur. Nor was there a great deal that constituted authority could do if citizens were intent on "rampaging," given the general weakness of law enforcement. Riots tended to burn themselves out, and a few ringleaders or those who stayed too long at the "festivities" might, in fact, end up in jail.

After the adoption of the Constitution, sober citizens began to feel that with English government gone and a republic instituted, there was enough scope for protest within established law and street action lost its quasi-legal status, giving way to organized civil festivals, like Fourth of July celebrations, which, of course, also occasionally got out of hand. Still, part of the feeling of the unpredictability of everyday life and its potential excitement went out of the American scene with the passing of the eighteenth century.

Those who had a squeamish dislike for crowds and the potentially dangerous emotions and actions they could arouse might satisfy their "guilty pleasure" in controversy by turning to the vitriolic literature turned out by eighteenth-century American presses. These made up in scurrilousness what they lacked in numbers, and although they reached only urban audiences in timely fashion while the controversy was still hot, sooner or later they found their way out to the countryside. The more respectable journals and papers had wide readership; at the time of the Revolution, for example, the *Philadelphia Journal* not only had occasional readers from Portsmouth, New Hampshire, to Charleston, South Carolina, and from Albany, New York, to Pittsburgh, Pennsylvania, but regular subscribers as well. Ephemeral pamphlets and broadsides including poems and cartoons hawked on street corners and nailed to trees were a common feature of everyday life in every community large enough to possess a press. Early on, partisan writers took no more inflammatory turn than to charge the opposition with being "strange and Unaccountable," "unreasonable and unjust," or, perhaps, of indulging in "bold and wilful Misrepresen tation." By midcentury, the opponents of one Boston faction were "Little pestilent Creatures . . . ready to cram [their] . . . merciless and insatiable Maw[s] with our very Blood, and bones, and Vitals, while making sexual advances on [our] wives and daughters."

Mudslinging between political opponents is certainly no novelty in modern-day America: the only surprise may be that we neither invented it, nor have we yet reached the low levels of campaign writers of the past. Consider the following critique of the writing of William Smith in 1756 as "the Vomitings of this infamous Hireling . . . betoken that Redundancy of Rancour, and Rottiness of Heart which render him the most despicable of his Species." Even in our own time of freedom of public vilification, this seems a somewhat excessive attack on a respected Anglican minister and Provost of the College of Philadelphia.

The invective expended between religious groups underlined the way in which networks of religious communities in the New World differed from those in the Old. For one thing, the idea of equal competition among churches was unknown in the traditional societies from which European-Americans had migrated. Second, since state-sponsored churches in Europe held monopolies within geographical regions, their congregants were members by accident of birth, and members they remained, no matter how little they participated. It required definite, possibly risky, action to leave the church, and there was no point in taking such a step unless one was willing to suffer for the rightness of an alternative church or meeting. This meant that established church membership remained high, even while indifference and apathy may have characterized a large percentage of the congregation. In colonial America, the situation was reversed. With the exception of the Anglican colonies in the South, there was no automatic affiliation. Those who wanted to belong to a church had to join it, and the meeting was usually not interested in accepting anything but the most avid, convinced believers. The outcome was that while the number of members remained low, the participation of congregants was high and enthusiastic.

For a few, religion *was* their everyday life. Among the Moravians, a small sect of German pietists who had been "convinced" and organized by one Baron von Zinzendorff, the church community became the family itself. For the first twenty years of their existence—from 1742 to 1764—the Moravians eschewed individual households and private property altogether, building and running their town of Bethlehem, Pennsylvania, in a completely communal manner. All land, buildings, tools, and domestic goods were owned by the congregation as a whole, part of a "General Oeconomy" which included the labor of all its members and the profits that resulted therefrom. Domestic units were not made up of married couples, their children and servants, but of carefully organized "choirs," rigidly segregated by sex and age. Since each individual stood equal before the *Heiland,* as Christ was called, since there were no males who dominated individual households, and since the choir system freed women from traditional domestic labor, Moravian women enjoyed an equality in choice of work, secular responsibility, and spiritual governance unlike any others in eighteenth-century America.

About half of the population of eighteenth-century America remained unchurched. A great many of these had no interest or belief in religion whatsoever, but many others lived daily lives of deep spiritual feeling without the assistance of any formal religious organization. It was the lack of outward church organization that fooled most contemporaries who traveled from place to place into thinking that religion itself did not exist. New England, perhaps, looked more religious than it was. Although the majority were not Puritans at all, town geography placed the meetinghouse at the center of daily life, all residents were taxed for its support, and ties of political influence between "saints" and officeholders gave organized religion the appearance of universality.

In the Anglican South, on the other hand, the thinness of the population and the siting of churches in the isolated countryside weakened the influence of the church in everyday life, even though it was actually established in English fashion. Traditional church events such as baptisms, weddings, and funerals began to be celebrated at home rather than in front of the altar, and burial plots were located on family farms, not in a graveyard by the church. The removal of much church business from the church building itself was, to New Englander Noah Webster, a sign that lack of attendance could be equated with disinterest, noting on a visit to Petersburg, Virginia, in 1785, "It seems to be the taste of Virginian[s] to fix their churches as far as possible from town and their play houses in the center."

Visitors to the backcountry and the frontier expected, and

found, a lack of organized worship. The Reverend Thomas Bacon commented sadly that "Religion among us seems to wear the face of the country, part moderately cultivated, the greater part wild and savage." Others insisted that backcountry folk were entirely dissolute, due to the lack of proper church institutions, "[going] thro' want of Churches & Ministers . . . to be Married by Magistrates, . . . which occasions . . . irregular Practices [including the supposition that such marriages] are dissoluble, whenever their Interests or Passions incite them to Separate . . . quitting each other at Pleasure, Inter-Marrying Year after Year with others; Changing from Hand to hand as they remove from Place to Place, & swapping away their Wives and Children, as they would Horses or Cattle. . . ."

In the Middle Colonies, particularly the larger cities, it was not a failure of organized religion to sign up most of the inhabitants, but rather the enormous number of churches from which one might choose that provided the particularly American quality of religious experience. In Philadelphia alone, there were eighteen organized denominations, some of which had several locations in and around the city by the time of the Revolution. Although there was a certain amount of mingling of languages and national roots within congregations—within the German-speaking, German-oriented Moravian community of Bethlehem, for example, one in every four members was either English, Scandinavian, French, Irish, Amerindian, or Black—churches tended to retain something of their national identity. The same Calvinist doctrine might be available as Anglo-Congregational, Scots-Presbyterian, Dutch Reformed, Swedenborgian, German Reformed, or French Huguenot.

National identity was not always enough to establish Old World churches across the spaces of New World soil. Maintaining tradition was hampered by the problem of acquiring ministers trained in Europe, and also by an unexpected difficulty in creating an intercolonial organization. The Reverend Henry Melchior Muhlenberg outlined the situation at midcentury when he tried to develop a central organization for the German Lutherans. It turned out, he discovered, that the Lutheran service and doctrine had not been all that coordinated in Europe either, although the smaller factor of actual mobility kept people from noticing it. In Pennsylvania, he could not satisfy the longing for tradition expressed by his parishioners by selecting a "liturgy to which each person had been accustomed from youth, because nearly every land, or town, or village possessed its own."

As the Great Awakening swept across the colonies, it touched every class, ethnic group, and region. It stimulated the growth of new congregations—Methodist and Baptist, particularly— and revitalized old ones, creating havoc where long-established ministers were scorned by their congregations in favor of itinerant preachers "who aimed . . . at frightening people out of their senses [and raising] . . . the affections of weak and undiscerning people [rather than] by solid argument . . . perswad[ing] them as reasonable men, to make their escape unto Christ," as the indignant regular preacher of Stonington, Connecticut, described a visit from James Davenport, one of the most controversial and extreme of the evangelicals.

The itinerancy of the charismatic preachers and their emphasis on a religion of the spirit rather than the mind, one that did not require wealth, education, or status to smooth the road to heaven, had the potential for creating a network among the poor and the disadvantaged that might even have come to embrace the black population as well. The style of revival worship was related in complex and subtle ways to that of African-Americans as they became converted to Christianity and fused their new insights with the traditions of their African beliefs and practices. But while we may see similarities of emotional intensity between the meeting held by James Davenport and the description of a black service where "when the preacher ceased reading, all . . . fell on their knees, bowed their heads to the ground, and started howling and groaning with sad heart-rending voices," contemporaries were unaware of any such affinity. White observers scornfully viewed such performances as one more evidence of "savagery," thrown off by many Africanisms in the emotional and expressive style, including spirituals, ring-shouts, and the antiphonal chanting of "psalms in chorus, the men and the women alternating." Southern Baptists were willing to encourage and convert black slaves, but they would not accept the adaptations that were required to accommodate African cultural patterns. They were quick to excommunicate their new adherents for sins like adultery or even "disorderly walk" when it was clear that blacks were unlikely to accept the same discipline in everyday life that was the lynchpin of white Baptist Chistianity.

Philadelphia's free black community, growing by leaps and bounds with the advent of abolition in the 1780s, was attracted to the emotional spirit of Methodism. Its members were, at first, welcomed into the local church, which recruited heavily among all the laboring people of the city. Relying on lay preachers and lay societies to carry its message, and meeting in homes and sail lofts, it was the only denomination in which integrated services were actually led, on occasion, by a black man. The growing number of free African-Americans in the city appears to have gone hand-in-hand with growing racism, however. While white leaders were upset by the black decision to build an autonomous church of their own, it was they who had created an atmosphere in which it was virtually impossible for integrated services to continue. In the autumn of 1792, at the first services held in the newly expanded St. George's Methodist Church, the black worshippers who had contributed both time and money to the building fund were informed that they must "sit in a segregated section of the gallery." Having been "pulled off his knees" during the prayer, the Reverend Absalom Jones led the other blacks "out of the church in a body, and they were no more plagued by us in the church."

At the other end of the religious scale from the enthusiasm of the Great Awakening, but just as quintessentially eighteenth-century, Deism spread a more sophisticated network across the continent. Also called "free thinkers," deists accepted a Supreme Power or Benevolent God who should be worshipped, but they also accepted the authority of human reason, rejected the miraculous, denied the Trinity and the authority of the Bible, and denied the divinity of Christ although they revered his teachings. Most importantly, perhaps, they saw organized religion as a social necessity rather than a spiritual force, and held "that the good ordering or disposition of the faculties of men constituted the best part of divine worship."

Although there were active, even vociferous lower- and middle-class "free thinkers"—Thomas Paine comes immediately to mind—most were gentlemen, probably including a large number of the founding fathers of the republic. We are forced to say "probably," since, like Thomas Jefferson, who clearly lived by the moral and spiritual principles of deism, genteel deists felt that "a man's religion was nobody's business but his own." They went quietly to established churches to set a good example, feeling, perhaps somewhat arrogantly, with Franklin that "a great proportion of mankind consists of weak and ignorant men and women . . . and youth of both sexes, who have need of the motives of religion to restrain them from vice, to support their virtue, . . . If men are so wicked as we now see them *with religion,* what would they be if without it?" Franklin bought a pew in Christ Church in Philadelphia and urged his daughter to attend, although he himself was rarely found there.

The sense of community among members of the same denomination was one that gave travelers or migrants a feeling of belonging in strange surroundings and new homes. For some, church or sectarian membership formed a real "neighborhood" even at a great distance, while those who lived next door were merely acquaintances. This was perhaps particularly true of those who were generally scorned or who suffered discrimination, even in the broadly tolerant atmosphere of the colonies. The question of marriage was key. As the vastly wealthy, genteel Charles Carroll of Annapolis counseled his son "Charley" (one day to be a signer of the Declaration of Independence) when he began to talk of marrying in 1762: "I Earnestly Recommend it to you on no Consideration to Marry a Protestant for beside the risque your Offspring will Run, it is Certain there Cannot be any Solid Happyness without an Union of Sentiments in all matters Especially in Religion." Charley, in the end, resorted to marriage with a much younger cousin: there were too few Catholics of his background available on the American scene to provide him with many options.

Friends—"the people known as Quakers"—were possibly the

closest-knit religious community in the colonies or, for that matter, in the Western world. Founded in England in the mid-seventeenth century, the Society of Friends had suffered a great deal of discrimination and outright persecution both in England and the colonies. It was, to be sure, something of a radical group in its early days, given to disruptive demonstrations like those in Puritan Boston by a Quaker man who burst into the Cambridge meeting, crashing two bottles together and shouting, "Thus will the Lord break you in pieces!" or by the Quaker woman who appeared in the Newbury meeting "stark naked in order 'to show the people the nakedness of their rulers.' " By the eighteenth century, the Friends had become the soberest of the sober, although, contrary to popular belief, their idea of "plain" consisted in avoiding the overelaboration of decoration on clothes, houses, and furniture while enjoying—in moderation—bright colors, good fabrics, good wine, and simple entertainment. Their ethic included approbation for hard work and economic success, and perhaps because of this or what was regarded as their clannishness, they continued to be disliked in many circles: an Anglican merchant at midcentury, for example, referred to them as "Vile Broadbrims," a reference to the style of hat affected by the men.

While religious networks are fairly easy to identify since they were gathered around particular people and institutions, the part played by one's ethnic background in everyday life is much more difficult to determine, although there is no doubt that its importance was understood by contemporaries. A pledge to learn English was often part of an Indian tribe's formal submission to colonial rule. One historian has pointed out that the chief of the Piscataway "began English lessons at the same time that he gave up polygamy, began dressing in English clothes, and converted to Christianity." Since religion and nationality overlapped so heavily, when people "stuck to their own kind" it is hard to know which was the real driving force. Where people of a single nationality settled together relatively removed from the pervasive English influence, like the French in upper New England, they retained the roots of their language and customs, accommodating just enough to deal economically and politically with the larger community of colony and empire or, later, state and nation. Ethnics who migrated in very small numbers, separately rather than in extended groups, were generally dispersed throughout the colonies and became acculturated, if not assimilated, relatively quickly. It was of these folks that Crevecoeur (always expressive on behalf of the romanticism of the "melting pot") wrote when he asserted that the typical late-eighteenth-century American came from a mixed family "whose grandfather was an Englishman, whose wife was Dutch, whose son married a French woman, and whose present four sons have now four wives of different nations."

German immigrants and their descendants formed by far the largest non-British white community in the colonies by the time of the Revolution: one in every ten inhabitants of the new nation. It makes little sense to call them a community, however, since their backgrounds, the dates and manner of their immigration, and their patterns of settlement in the New World gave them very little in common with each other. A few, like the Mennonites, arrived in extended families of relatives with a common religious motivation, and sought to create separate communities in which they could continue their Old World ways and remain "uncontaminated" by the evils of the world around them. Many others, particularly if they lived in urban areas or in places where there were few other Germans and no German church, disappeared into the Anglo population at large. Over the course of time their names changed: "Schmidt" became "Smith"; "Holtz" and "Zimmerman" were translated into "Wood" and "Carpenter"; untranslatable first names like "Cunnigunde" and "Ulrich" disappeared; "Johann" and "Elisabetta" became "John" and "Elizabeth."

For most, their relationship to their ethnicity lay somewhere in between, in acculturation rather than complete assimilation. In places like Reading, Pennsylvania, where the inhabitants were mostly German, with a large minority of English and smaller representations of French, Dutch, Scottish, and Irish, British as opposed to Continental origins created something of a recognition line: Dutch and French attended German churches (there were not enough of them to have churches of their own) and married German spouses, while the Scots and Irish associated and intermarried most with the English. Other formal institutions in Reading were separated as well: the Library Company was English; the Rainbow Fire Company, German; there were German and English newspapers. Beyond this, much of the rest of everyday civic life appears to have lacked any sort of meaningful ethnic division. Residential neighborhoods were mixed and people of all backgrounds mingled in the local taverns; Germans borrowed money from Englishmen and vice versa; equally, they sued each other for not paying up; when the Revolution began and militia units were formed, they were completely unsegregated.

It is hardest of all to determine the meaning and significance of ethnic identity among African-Americans, who at 20 percent of the total population of colonial America were the most numerous of all non-English settlers. Since the only common thread among black slaves was their slavery and their blackness, and since their African backgrounds varied widely in ethnicity, much of their culture was reformulated in the colonies, incorporating bits and pieces of Old World cultures. The many languages of Africa were integrated with each other, as well as with English, to form Creole languages distinctive in different parts of the southern colonies. We are familiar with the Gullah tongue of the islands off the eastern coast of South Carolina because it has survived into the twentieth century, but many contemporaries noticed that Virginia blacks spoke a special "mixed dialect between the Guinea and English," while a missionary in 1748 reported that blacks in the Chesapeake had "a language peculiar to themselves, a wild confused medley of Negro and corrupt English, which makes them very unintelligible except to those who have conversed with them for many years." It may be that the ability to converse with each other without allowing the master to understand might well have been a decided advantage, deliberately cultivated. There is also some evidence that many slave owners mistrusted blacks who spoke "good English without Idiom or Tone," considering them as potentially too smooth and manipulative. Certainly, it would seem that Africans, bilingual from the beginning, acquired great facility in slipping from standard English into one of a number of Creole tongues, as did Ned, a teenage slave in South Carolina, whose owner recognized that he could "speak good English *when he pleases*" [emphasis added].

Most of the evidence regarding ethnic or racial self-consciousness is of an indirect nature, since, while there is much mention of the community of religion, there is almost no reference to a brotherhood of national background. There is, rather, a kind of pragmatic evidence of ethnic solidarity on the local level—French names top lists of subscriptions for Huguenot causes, Germans who die without a will sometimes leave their possessions to a "landsmann." One clue to a positive sense of ethnicity may be found in the formation of ethnic societies in Philadelphia and New York to aid "fellow countrymen." There were five in Philadelphia by the time of the Revolution: the Welsh St. David's Society or Society of Ancient Britons (1729); the Scots' St. Andrew's Society (1747); Der Deutsche Gessellschaft von Pennsylvanien (The German Society of Pennsylvania, 1764); the English Society of the Sons of St. George (1772); and the Irish Society of the Friendly Sons of St. Patrick (1771). Actually, there was a certain amount of discomfort in the community over the idea of segregating oneself purely along national lines, even if for the stated purpose of helping the less fortunate. One member of the St. George remarked that such clubs were "for the most part idle and unnecessary; and when they operate so far as to make us injure or despise persons born in a different country from ourselves, they are indeed very reprehensible."

By far the most consistent mention of ethnicity or race was in prejudiced references regarding the group to which someone else belonged. Scarcely a single traveler throughout the century ran across a stranger without characterizing his (or her) background, if it could be discerned, with an unflattering epithet. Thus Dr. Hamilton found the Dutch women in Albany "both old and young . . . remarkably ugly . . . in their persons slovenly and dirty." Peter Kalm found their menfolk to be filled with "avarice, selfishness, and immeasurable love of money." The Scots-Irish, according to Charles Woodmason, were "very

Poor owing to their indolence. . . . They delight in their present
low, lazy, sluttish, heathenish, hellish life. . . . Both Men and
Women will do anything to come at Liquor, Cloaths, Furniture,
&c, &c, rather than work for it." One traveler through the
backcountry in 1788, John May from New England, was able to
find in the course of a single day a group of settlers he could not
trust since "they are Irish palaverers, and the truth is not in
them"; a backward town where "all sorts of superstitious traditions prevail here among the people, being Dutch"; and a band
of Indians, of whom he wrote, "I can not say I am fond of them,
for they are frightfully ugly, and a pack of thieves and beggars."

Of course, when it came to vilification, racism won over ethnicity hands down, indifferent to the enormous variety among
Indians and blacks. Fighting these calumnies was, for the victims, of necessity a subtle thing. Hannah Pittimee, a "praying,"
i.e. Christian, Indian of Natick, made the point when she
refused even to say "hello" to white townsfolk, "pass[ing]
by . . . with a great deal of scorn . . . with her face turned right
from us." Landon Carter may, or may not, have understood the
implications when he pointed out that "the more particular we
are in our [orders] and the fonder we show ourselves of anything the more careless will our slaves be."

To a large extent, it was a white-nonwhite issue, with Indians
and blacks grouped together, particularly where there was a
significant population of Indian slaves and therefore a fair number of intermarriages between nonwhites. Where local Indians
were free and their intermarriage was with whites, the racial
question was less clear-cut, for, as in the case of Catholics, Quakers, and non-Anglo Europeans, marriage was the real bottom
line. It was here that the basis of a new household was established, and the position of that household in the larger community became a real issue. The problem was noted in a dispassion-
ate manner by the minister of the Gloria Dei Church when
refusing to marry an interracial couple in 1800: "A negro came
with a white woman . . . I referred him to the negro minister,
not willing to have blame from public opinion, having never yet
joined black and white. Nevertheless these frequent mixtures
will soon force matrimonial sanction." Perhaps most hurtful of

all was the casual racism, implicit in the boast of a city dweller around midcentury that "he not only knew every gentleman in town, but every gentleman's black servant and dog."

By the 1760s, there was a noticeable growth of ethnic and racial antipathy, due in part to increasing contact between colonials of differing backgrounds, and to the entrenchment of slavery as the dominant labor system in the South. At the same time, however, there was an increasing awareness by Enlightenment rationalists that such social attitudes had no real basis in fact or reason. The word "prejudice" became a widely employed buzzword among the literati in both Europe and the colonies, and it was popular in these circles to quote Montesquieu's remark: "That all black persons should be slaves, is as ridiculous as . . . that all redhaired persons should be hanged." While the Virginian Arthur Lee might assert "with Aristotle that he knew not any who were so utterly devoid of any semblance of virtue as are the Africans; whose understandings are generally shallow, and their hearts cruel, vindictive, stubborn, base, and wicked," Alexander Hamilton, born and bred in the cruel slave society of the West Indies, stated judiciously that "the contempt we have been taught to entertain for the blacks makes us fancy many things that are founded neither in reason nor in experience." Lee confessed himself unsure whether black evil sprang "from a native baseness that fits their mind for all villainy; or that they never receive the benefit of education," but, curiously, he did not seem to feel that it made much difference! More sophisticated thinkers, however, did indeed see the difference, and education programs were strong components of the nascent antislavery movement as it was promulgated by the Quakers through their far-flung community network. At the end of the century, racism continued to be a driving spirit in daily life as the Constitution failed to address the issue of emancipation and only the most forward social thinkers dared to consider "separate but equal" as an alternative to institutionalized inequality.

Amidst all the factors that either divided colonial Americans from one another or gave them networks with which to identify, a new kind of community—both separator and unifier—

was slowly coming into being during the eighteenth century. This sort of fellowship lacked a universal name during most of the periods; the word "class" was only introduced into the vocabulary in the 1770s and did not come into common parlance until the next century. But it is obvious that the old division of society into the "best" and the "rest" was less and less applicable to an increasingly complex network of Americans whose wealth, occupations, education, and life-styles gave them something in common with some folks, yet set them radically apart from others. It is also obvious that while contemporaries recognized and understood the meaning of these similarities and differences, only the gentry had a sense of solidarity across distance which is the factor that turns social standing into class.

What allowed the gentry to form a positive sense of identification—of class—was the international and intercolonial nature of their community made possible by their extreme wealth. While there were about thirty-five thousand households that can be considered "rich" out of the half-million or so American families functioning at the time of the Revolution, only about ten thousand were recognized as the "better sort," and a mere forty-three hundred or so qualified as "real" gentry. Their position was defined by a complex mix of money, power, occupation, education, moral outlook, and the elusive quality of life-style; standing out on the landscape, with their social networks and responsibilities on public display. The gap between them and all other colonial Americans was not only visible, it was both broad and deep. In many ways, genteel families were tied more closely to each other than they were to their local communities, assuming a cosmopolitan identity that linked them with the ruling classes in the British Empire, and with the whole European world of taste and fashion. If Old World aristocracy saw them as provincial, they could shrug it off, playing the international consumer game to the hilt for the benefit of the folks back home, from whose awe they derived their power. Social status was exhibited in the ownership of items like carriages, silver, and second homes that no one else could afford. When they bought a musical instrument, it was the finest of pianofortes from London, not a fiddle or viol by a local maker. When they shopped for the necessities of life—clothes, furniture, bed linens—they were of the most costly fabrics and woods, in the latest styles and fashions.

The gentry made, perhaps, its most telling nonverbal statement about privilege through the clothes they wore on their backs. They strove mightily to keep themselves in the very latest European mode, while also sending the message that they never had to exert themselves physically, by donning wearing apparel that was not only elaborate and expensive, but also immobilizing and uncomfortable. So uncomfortable, in fact, that most gentlefolk wore dressing gowns for casual at-home daily life and entertaining. Corsets were a requirement for all women, however slim or well-shaped their natural bodies. These "torture chambers" extended from hip bone to armpit, forcing the breasts so high that it was necessary to insert a lace kerchief or ruffle to hide the nipples. Men also wore corsets, and perhaps false pads over their calves and buttocks, but only when needed to rectify natural defects that kept them from "cutting a fine figure."

Fashion changed continually, but basic style remained more constant, and for most of the century the biggest nightmare for the gentry rested atop their heads. Until the Revolution, powdered "big wigs" were *de rigueur* for gentlemen who had, therefore, to keep their heads shaved and spend their time at home in nightcaps or turbans. Not only were the fancy upper-class versions of the wig uncomfortably itchy and hot, they were almost impossible to wear with grace, since they were so heavy that they required special lessons to learn how to walk without stooping over. Abrupt motion loosed a shower of white around the room and over one's own suit from the heavy powder with which they were covered. A wig loosely fitted in search of a little comfort led to yet other disasters: if a gentleman bent over incautiously, the wig fell off; if he turned his head too quickly, the wig was left behind and he found himself looking ridiculous with his hair on sideways. When wigs gave way to natural hair, powdered, in 1777, and then to ponytails in the 1780s and 1790s, American gentlemen no doubt breathed a sigh of relief, and may even have felt that this change, symbolic of republican simplicity, was worth the loss of the few perks that came with appearing "special."

The Revolution worked no such magic for elite women, who had always worn their own hair as a base, adding extra pieces or "rats" to achieve the desired fullness, and covering the whole with bread flour to hide variations in color or texture. As hairdos became more and more elaborate in keeping with European fashion throughout the century, they also became so difficult to arrange that they were only attempted every few months. To make them last, women slept with their necks resting on wooden blocks instead of on pillows, and glued the "constructions" together with clotted dairy cream or flour paste. The resulting discomfort and the health risks of skin disease and vermin, to say nothing of the odor in warm weather, can scarcely be imagined.

The American gentry were well aware that reaching the very top of society required more than good clothes; it also called for "elegance of behavior; gracefulness of mien; [and] nicety of taste," according to Samuel Johnson's *Dictionary*. A smattering of culture in literature, painting, and sculpture; some ability to perform in music, dancing, and fencing; and the proper table manners, facial expression, and "carriage" were all part of the package. Parents whose sons passed a good part of their early years in the colonial countryside worried that a regional accent would doom them to a lower rank in society and searched for teachers who could "pronounce English articulately, and read [aloud] with emphasis, accent, quantity, and pauses," as James Dove promised to do in a newspaper ad in 1787.

Wherever possible, the "better sort" drew a social boundary around itself and guarded it carefully. In many cases, the difference was expressed in disgust with the ways of common folk. Dr. Alexander Hamilton, during his travels in 1744, disdained to "take vittles" with the keeper of the Susquehanna Ferry and his wife on "a homely dish of fish without any kind of sauce," explaining haughtily that he "had no Stomach. . . . They had no cloth upon the table, and their mess was in a dirty, deep, wooden dish which they evacuated with their hands, cramming down skins, scales, and all [using] neither knife, fork, spoon, plate, or napkin." At other times, the line was drawn with the aid of exclusionary policies. A Bostonian of otherwise accept-able credentials was disqualified as a justice of the peace in 1759 because "his grandfather had been a bricklayer," and a Virginia tailor was fined for entering his horse in a race and wagering two thousand pounds of tobacco on the outcome, "it being contrary to Law for a Labourer to make a race, being a sport for Gentlemen." When French merchant Moreau de St. Mery wished to attend a ball in honor of Washington's birthday in 1795, he alleged that he was denied tickets because he was a "storekeeper" and "could not aspire to this honor."

By the time of the Revolution, ordinary Americans were by no means necessarily willing to accept the gentry at their own assumption of leadership. Their distinctive clothing became an easy focal point for the republican spirit, and in a letter to the Associators (militia) of the City of Philadelphia in the spring of 1775, it was suggested that the hunting shirt be adopted as the uniform for officers and men alike, not only because it would be "within the compass of almost every person's ability, not costing at the utmost above ten shillings," but, more significantly, be-cause it would "level all distinctions." Barely concealed con-tempt for "over-civilized" gentility is evident in the incident that befell Captain Bernard Elliott of South Carolina in the same year. As related by a military historian, Captain Elliott was challenged by an enlisted man from his hometown who refused to serve under "any man he could lick. Elliott agreed to fight, used boxing [a skill he had learned as part of his elite education], beat him, and made him a sergeant before he could recover from the wonder of being whipped by a man who wore silk stockings." By the end of the century, there was even less will-ingness to accept exclusion from public events for social rea-sons. The elite of Philadelphia were unsuccessful in several attempts to ban their "inferiors" from the theater, and a Boston "mechanick" complained loudly and bitterly in the public press when he found that "From my situation in Life, I am *virtually* debarred from any of the *common amusements* of this town—I cannot attend CONCERTS, ASSEMBLIES OR CARD PAR-TIES."

No attack on the symbols of elite dominance could touch the roots of their power, however. These lay in their connections with each other and the strong alliances they forged through business and marriage. Their money and influence also gave them the ability to hedge, and hedge comfortably, against the inevitable sharp swings of income and production endemic to an agricultural, preindustrial world. They could—and their inventories show that they did—lay in large stocks of food, drink, and wood in an age when the seasonal nature of employment and the bare subsistence size of its rewards led as much as one-third of the population to occasional reliance on public assistance.

The social standing of all other eighteenth-century Americans carried no such relative security, no such sense of identity. Indians and slaves stood outside the system altogether, since their situations rendered them too different to relate in any way to the other members of the community. Free blacks, on the other hand, did enter into the system, although it was almost impossible for them to rise above the lowest class, for reasons of both racism and poverty. Likewise, the very poorest of white Americans were accorded no standing at all. "The poor man's conscience is clear; yet he is ashamed . . . he feels himself out of the sight of others groping in the dark. Mankind takes no notice of him. He rambles and wanders unheeded. In the midst of a crowd, at church, in the market . . . he is in as much obscurity as he would be in a garret or a cellar. He is not disapproved, censured, or reproached; he is only not seen," wrote John Adams shortly after the Revolution.

Between the obscurity of the poorhouse and the high visibility of the mansion lived the rest of Revolutionary America's half-million families, divided by an unclear line between the "lower" and the "middling" sorts. In the rural context, the difference probably involved the ownership of some land; in larger towns and cities, the possession of a profitable trade or skill, at least at the level of journeyman. Within the middling sort, the scale distinguished between large and small landowners in the countryside; "mechanicks," tradesmen, and professionals in urban communities. As in the case of the gentry, clothes provided a virtual lexicon of social place. City or country, most folks knew exactly who they were when they looked down in the morning at the same outer garments they had worn yesterday, put back on over the same basic shirt or shift they had worn for days or weeks on end, day and night. Those who did physical labor strived for comfort; farm managers, urban professionals, successful artisans, and small shopkeepers who aspired to more genteel status adopted a simplified version of the style, though not the fashion, of the "better sorts." Servants who labored in households behind the scenes wore lower-class clothes; those whose work took them into the family quarters, like ladies' maids, valets, housekeepers, and chefs, wore "imitation professional garb"; while "status" servants like butlers, doormen, and coachmen were decked out in costumes—fancy dress versions of long-departed fashions.

The vast majority of eighteenth-century Americans, living on farms and in rural villages, continued to derive their social status from their immediate neighborhoods. Their networks consisted of a variety of groupings related to wealth, kinship, length of residence, and political interest; all dependent, in the end, on personal relationships. Not that they were isolated or frozen in time: farmers could receive and understand the latest ideas for new agricultural technology and methods through the spread of written material and the migration of new landowners into the area; their wives could obtain information on the best ways to preserve foods and the newest styles in dress through similar channels of communication. Up-to-date, even fashionable, household goods were available in rural shops and the latest in furniture and architectural designs arrived in the knowledge and skills of immigrating craftsmen and artisans. Yet this awareness of the cultural standards and products of the wider world did not effect the essentially local character of these rural communities of culture. They adapted their old ways and goods to the new ideas and styles that interested them, creating idiosyncratic vernacular patterns that made for fascinating variations from town to town, colony to colony, and region to region.

Urban dwellers, too, continued to share local culture and

measure their standing in the world by that of their neighbors. Shoemakers swapped lasts and leather when they needed to, could understand and appreciate each other's problems, and even those of their brothers and cousins who were tailors or masons. They socialized at the closest tavern, and their tendency to live near others who not only shared their position in society but their occupations as well is seen in the names of the neighborhood dram shops: the Jolly Tar, the Mariner's Compass, the Cordwainer's Arms, or the Horse and Dray. The very local nature of these establishments increased the part they played in drawing lines of social distance within the city, and made them centers of group solidarity among the "lower sort."

Even before the Revolution, many tippling houses frequented by apprentices, laborers, and "mere mechanicks" sported this motto on their walls, expressing a sense of resentment toward their place on the social scale: "The King—I govern all; The general—I fight for all; The Minister—I pray for all; The Labourer—I pay for all." Conversation was often political, entertainment rough. Political discussion formed part of the diversion at gentlemen's taverns and coffeehouses as well, along with appropriate cosmopolitan background music like string quartets playing pieces by Corelli or Handel. Both kinds of establishments also offered pornographic entertainment, although David Lockwood's tavern in Philadelphia betrayed its appeal to an upper-class clientele when it featured Ebenezer Kinnersley, who sang to the accompaniment of his own violin, but "had the knack of being gross without being disgusting."

In many aspects of everyday life, upper- and lower-class pursuits were mirror images of each other. Both groups gambled on races, cockfights, and bearbaiting. Both played endless varieties of games, many long since forgotten: cards, dive, rowly-powly, loggats, shovegroat, shovel board, billiards, quoits, bowles, cales, cloughcalls, and ninepins, among others; and gambled on the outcome of these as well. Within their own circles, they mixed sociability, more drinking, and real services to the community by their participation in class-oriented organizations like the Militia and the Fire Companies.

What constituted a new trend among urban social groups was

the growing importance of a self-conscious set of citizens who frowned on participation in the older sort of socializing and saw themselves as a distinct group. Their position was articulated by a self-appointed spokesman of the "middling sort" who represented "a set of honest sober men who mind their own business." He saw much in common between those above and those below him on the social scale, and none of it was particularly flattering: "the first class consists of commercial projectors; those who make enormous gains of public confidence; speculators, riotous livers, and a kind of loungers who are to [be] found in every place but where their business calls them. . . . The third class are thieves, pickpockets, low cheats, and dirty sots. These are not restrained by principle but only by want of wealth and public trust, from being of the first class."

Status among these members of the urban middle class did not depend so much on background as it did on attitude, accomplishment, and life-style. They extolled the virtues of sobriety, industry, and frugality, aspired to the goal of respectability. Accepting the concept of the nuclear family, they placed affectionate marriage high on their list of priorities and took seriously their responsibilities in the training of their children as citizens of the new republic. For the most part, to be middle-class was to work with one's brains rather than with one's hands—eventually this idea would come to be symbolized in the phrase "white collar." Yet, since the middle-class canon embraced a meritocracy—an aristocracy of ability rather than inheritance—sober-minded artisans were acceptable, particularly if they were striving to increase their shops to the point where they would become managers rather than workers, and if they participated in middle-class improvement activities like the Philadelphia Junto, a club whose bylaws set forth that it meet once a week to discuss "Morals, Politics, and natural Philosophy," or joined circulating libraries, subscribed to newspapers and periodicals, and sent their children to Sunday School.

By the 1790s, a growing population and rebounding economy brought these middle-class ideals and institutions out into the countryside. Small towns hoping to become cities and villages hoping to become towns began to engage in "boosterism" to share in the skyrocketing real estate values and quickened business pace that growth could engender. They boasted of (plans for) paved, well-lighted streets, (projected) blocks of business and shop buildings, and the activities of their (proposed) academies, assemblies, and libraries. In Concord, Massachusetts, for example, in the space of a few years at the middle of the decade, local movers and shakers founded the Charitable Library Society, the Fire Society, the Harmonic Society, the Corinthian Lodge of Masons, and the Social Club, where members discussed the common subjects of the day: farming reforms, religious ideas, town improvements, and political news.

It was politics that came to lie at the heart of new networks of community for which the young nation was the soul. The creation of the Constitution in 1787 provided a focal point for national feelings of patriotism and identification that had been lacking since the early years of the Revolution. There were a rhetoric of patriotism and treatises on the importance of republican simplicity and virtue: behind the very development of two political parties lay a tacit assumption of the single system within which they contended. Huge celebrations of the Fourth of July became part of the symbolism of every community large enough to muster a few old soldiers to march, and a few horses to pull a float. Finding willing orators was never a problem.

In the true entrepreneurial spirit of America, the most obvious changes in everyday life were available first as goods in the marketplace: eagles as decorative motifs on domestic objects; common houses adorned with classical "republican" moldings and columns; engravings of everything and everyone having to do with the war or the Constitution. The century closed with a tremendous outpouring of portraits of Washington, and "mourning pictures" following his death in 1799, executed in paint, print, embroidery, and even human hair.

In some ways, everyday life changed little. Work routines in farming and crafts were barely scratched by new technologies, and those of the professions and management were not yet rationalized or systematized. Even a sense of inclusion in a new community of opportunity and independence was primarily felt by white men and their sons. Many, no doubt, agreed with

Edmund Randolph, a delegate to the Constitutional Convention, when he remarked several years later, "I am not really an American. I am a Virginian." Yet there were many more who felt a rush of belonging to something new and exciting. They were more likely to echo Dr. Benjamin Rush, who attended the parade held in Philadelphia on July 4, 1788, to celebrate the ratification of the Constitution and noted with satisfaction: " 'Tis done. We have become a nation."

EPILOGUE

In 1824, a middle-aged minister turned doctor, Joseph Doddridge, prepared his *Notes on the Settlement and Indian Wars*
for publication. He set down stories of his life as a child and
young man both on the frontier and in the settled towns of
eastern colonial America. As he looked back over what he had
written, he realized that much of what he described might
seem unattractive or irrelevant to those who expected history
to deal with great men and past politics. I would like to think
that Doddridge's justification for his book might stand for this
one as well:

> Should I be asked why I have presented this unpleasant portrait
> of the rude manners of our forefathers? I in my turn would ask my
> reader, why are you pleased with the histories of the blood and
> carnage of battles? Why are you delighted with the fictions of poetry,
> the novel and romance? I have related truth, and only truth, strange
> as it may seem. I have depicted a state of society, and manners,
> which are fast vanishing from the memory of man, with a view to
> give the youth of our country a knowledge of the advantages of
> civilization, and to give contentment to the aged, by preventing
> them from saying "that former times were better than the present."

Books and articles included here are primarily those that have been quoted in the text, or that have been particularly useful in the preparation of this book. Anthologies containing several relevant pieces are included in preference to individual articles.

Appleby, Joyce O. "The Changing Prospect of the Family Farm in the Early National Period," *Working Papers from the Regional Economic History Research Center,* Eleutherian Mills-Hagley Foundation, 1981.

Bailyn Bernard. *The Ordeal of Thomas Hutchinson.* Cambridge: The Belknap Press of Harvard University Press, 1974.

Benson, Adolph B., ed. and trans. *Peter Kalm's Travels In North America: The English Version of 1770.* 2 vols. New York: Wilson-Erickson, Inc., 1937.

Berlin, Ira, and Hoffman, Ronald, eds. *Slavery and Freedom in the Age of the American Revolution.* Charlottesville, Virginia: University Press of Virginia, 1983. Published for the United States Capitol Historical Society.

Bidwell, Percy Wells, and Falconer, John I. *History of Agriculture in the Northern United States, 1620–1860.* Washington, D.C.: Carnegie Institute of Washington, 1925.

Bowen, Catherine Drinker. *Miracle At Philadelphia: The Story of the Constitutional Convention May to September 1787.* Boston: Little, Brown, and Company, 1966.

Bray, Robert C., and Bushnell, Paul E. *Diary of a Common Soldier in the American Revolution, 1775–1783: An Annotated Edition of the Military Journal of Jeremiah Greenman.* DeKalb, Illinois: Northern Illinois University Press, 1978.

Breen, T. H. *Tobacco Culture: The Mentality of the Great Tidewater*

Planters on the Eve of the Revolution. Princeton, New Jersey: Princeton University Press, 1985.

Bremmer, Robert H., ed. *Children and Youth in America: A Documentary History.* 3 Vols. Cambridge: Harvard University Press, 1971.

Bridenbaugh, Carl. *Cities in Revolt: Urban Life in America, 1743–1776.* New York: Oxford University Press, 1955.

———. *Cities in the Wilderness: The First Century of Urban Life in America, 1625–1742.* New York: Capricorn Books, 1964.

———. *The Colonial Craftsman.* Chicago: University of Chicago Press, 1950.

———. *Early Americans.* Oxford, England: Oxford University Press, 1981.

———, ed. *Gentleman's Progress: The Itinerarium of Dr. Alexander Hamilton, 1744.* Chapel Hill: University of North Carolina Press, 1948. Published for the Institute of Early American History and Culture at Williamsburg, Virginia.

———. *Myths & Realities: Societies of the Colonial South.* New York: Atheneum, 1976.

Buel, Joy Day, and Buel, Richard, Jr. *The Way of Duty: A Woman and Her Family in Revolutionary America.* New York: W. W. Norton & Company, 1984.

Bushman, Richard L. *From Puritan to Yankee: Character and the Social Order in Connecticut, 1690–1765.* New York: W. W. Norton & Company, 1967.

Butterfield, L. H., Friedlaender, Marc, and Kline, Mary-Jo, eds. *The Book of Abigail and John: Selected Letters of the Adams Family 1762–1784.* Cambridge: Harvard University Press, 1975.

Butterfield, L. H., ed. *Letters of Benjamin Rush.* 2 Vols. Princeton, New Jersey: Princeton University Press, 1951. Published for the American Philosophical Society.

Cannan, Edwin, ed. *An inquiry into the nature and causes of the Wealth of Nations by Adam Smith.* 2 Vols. in One. Chicago: The University of Chicago Press, 1976.

Cappon, Lester J. *Atlas of Early American History.* Princeton, New Jersey: Princeton University Press, 1976. Published for the Newberry Library and The Institute of Early American History and Culture, Williamsburg, Virginia.

Carr, Lois Green, Morgan, Philip D., and Russo, Jean B., eds. *Colonial Chesapeake Society.* Chapel Hill: University of North Carolina Press, 1988. Published for the Institute of Early American History and Culture, Williamsburg, Virginia.

Copeland, Peter F. *Working Dress in Colonial and Revolutionary America.* Westport, Connecticut: Greenwood Press, 1975.

Crane, Elaine Forman, ed. *The Diary of Elizabeth Drinker.* 3 Vols. Boston: Northeastern University Press, 1991.

———. "The World of Elizabeth Drinker," *Pennsylvania Magazine of History and Biography,* January 1983.

Craven, Wayne. *Colonial American Portraiture: The Economic, Religious, Social, Cultural, Philosophical, Scientific, and Aesthetic Foundations.* Cambridge, England: Cambridge University Press, 1986.

Creel, Margaret Washington. *"A Peculiar People": Slave Religion and Community-Culture Among the Gullahs.* New York: New York University Press, 1988.

Cummings, Abbott Lowell. *The Framed Houses of Massachusetts Bay, 1625–1725.* Cambridge: The Belknap Press of Harvard University Press, 1979.

Dann, John C., ed. *The Revolution Remembered: Eyewitness Accounts of the War for Independence.* Chicago: The University of Chicago Press, 1980.

Davis, Richard Beale. *Intellectual Life in the Colonial South, 1585–1763.* 3 Vols. Knoxville, Tennessee: The University of Tennessee Press, 1978.

DeCrevecoeur, Michel-Guillaume St. Jean. *Journey Into Northern Pennsylvania and the State of New York.* Trans. Clarissa Spencer Bostelmann. Ann Arbor: University of Michigan Press, 1964.

Deetz, James. *In Small Things Forgotten: The Archaeology of Early American Life.* New York: Anchor Press/Doubleday, 1977.

Demos, John. *A Little Commonwealth: Family Life in Plymouth Colony.* New York: Oxford University Press, 1970.

Doerflinger, Thomas M. *A Vigorous Spirit of Enterprise: Merchants and Economic Development in Revolutionary Philadelphia.* Chapel Hill: University of North Carolina Press, 1986. Published for the Institute of Early American History and Culture, Williamsburg, Virginia.

Earle, Carville V. *The Evolution of a Tidewater Settlement System: All Hallow's Parish, Maryland, 1650–1783.* Chicago: The University of Chicago, Department of Geography. Research Paper #170, 1975.

Ekirch, A. Roger. "Bound for America: A Profile of British Convicts Transported to the Colonies, 1718–1775," *The William and Mary Quarterly,* April 1985.

Fairbanks, Jonathan L., Curator, and Trent, Robert F., Research Associate. *New England Begins: The Seventeenth Century.* 3 Vols.

Boston: Museum of Fine Arts, 1982. Catalogue of exhibition, May–August 1982.

Flaherty, David H. *Privacy in Colonial New England.* Charlottesville, Virginia: University Press of Virginia, 1967.

Forman, Benno M. "Delaware Valley 'Crookt Foot' and 'Slat-Back' Chairs: The Fussell–Savery Connection," *Winterthur Portfolio: A Journal of American Material Culture,* Spring 1980.

[Franklin, Benjamin]. *Poor Richard's Almanac by Richard Saunders.* Philadelphia, 1733–1766.

Gilje, Paul A. *The Road to Mobocracy: Popular Disorder in New York City, 1763–1834.* Chapel Hill: University of North Carolina Press, 1987. Published for the Institute of Early American History and Culture, Williamsburg, Virginia.

Greenberg, Douglas. *Crime and Law Enforcement in the Colony of New York, 1691–1776.* Ithaca, New York: Cornell University Press, 1974.

Greene, Jack P., and Pole, J. R., eds. *Colonial British America: Essays in the New History of the Early Modern Era.* Baltimore: The Johns Hopkins University Press, 1984.

Greven, Philip. *The Protestant Temperament: Patterns of Child-Rearing, Religious Experience, and the Self in Early America.* New York: Alfred A. Knopf, 1977.

Grey, Lewis C. *History of Agriculture in the Southern United States to 1860.* Washington, D.C.: Carnegie Institution, 1933. Reprint, 1958.

Gross, Robert A. *The Minutemen and Their World.* New York: Hill and Wang, 1976.

Gutman, Herbert G. *The Black Family in Slavery and Freedom, 1750–1925.* New York: Vintage Books, 1976.

Hardeman, Nicholas Perkins. *Shucks, Shocks, and Hominy Blocks: Corn as a Way of Life in Pioneer America.* Baton Rouge: Louisiana State University, 1981.

Harpster, John W. *Crossroads: Descriptions of Western Pennsylvania, 1720–1829.* Pittsburgh: University of Pittsburgh Press, 1938.

Higginbotham, A. Leon, Jr. *In the Matter of Color: Race and the American Legal Process, The Colonial Period.* New York: Oxford University Press, 1978.

Hindle, Brooke. *America's Wooden Age: Aspects of Its Early Technology.* Tarrytown, New York: Sleepy Hollow Restorations, 1975.

Hoffman, Ronald, and Albert, Peter J., eds. *Women in the Age of the American Revolution.* Charlottesville, Virginia: University Press of Virginia, 1989. Published for the United States Capitol Historical Society.

Hume, Ivor Noel. *A Guide to Artifacts of Colonial America.* New York: Alfred A. Knopf, 1970.

Innes, Stephen, ed. *Work and Labor in Early America.* Chapel Hill: University of North Carolina Press, 1988. Published for the Institute of Early American History and Culture, Williamsburg, Virginia.

Isaac, Rhys. *The Transformation of Virginia, 1740–1790.* Chapel Hill: University of North Carolina Press, 1982. Published for the Institute of Early American History and Culture, Williamsburg, Virginia.

Jennings, Francis. *The Invasion of America: Indians, Colonialism, and the Cant of Conquest.* Chapel Hill: University of North Carolina Press, 1975.

Jordan, Cynthia, S. " 'Old Words' in 'New Circumstances': Language and Leadership in Post-Revolutionary America," *American Quarterly,* December 1988.

Jordan, Winthrop D. *White over Black: American Attitudes Toward the Negro, 1550–1812.* Chapel Hill: University of North Carolina Press, 1968. Published for the Institute of Early American History and Culture, Williamsburg, Virginia.

Kawashima, Yasuhide. *Puritan Justice and the Indian: White Man's Law in Massachusetts, 1630–1763.* Middletown, Connecticut: Wesleyan University Press, 1986.

Kelso, William M. *Kingsmill Plantations, 1619–1800: Archaeology of Country Life in Colonial Virginia.* Orlando, Florida: Academic Press, Inc., 1984.

Kim, Sung Bok. *Landlord and Tenant in Colonial New York: Manorial Society, 1664–1775.* Chapel Hill: University of North Carolina Press, 1978. Published for the Institute of Early American History and Culture, Williamsburg, Virginia.

Kimball, Fiske. *Domestic Architecture of the American Colonies and of the Early Republic.* New York: Dover Publications, 1966 Reprint.

Klein, Rachel N. *Unification of a Slave State: The Rise of the Planter Class in the South Carolina Backcountry, 1760–1808.* Chapel Hill: The University of North Carolina Press, 1990. Published for the Institute of Early American History and Culture, Williamsburg, Virginia.

Klein, Randolph Shipley. *Portrait of an Early American Family: The Shippens of Pennsylvania Across Five Generations.* Philadelphia: University of Pennsylvania Press, 1975.

Klepp, Susan E., and Smith, Billy G., eds. "The Records of Gloria Dei

Church: Marriages and 'Remarkable Occurrences,' 1794–1806," *Pennsylvania History*, April 1986.

Kross, Jessica. *The Evolution of an American Town: Newtown, New York, 1642–1775.* Philadelphia: Temple University Press, 1983.

Krout, John Allen. *The Origins of Prohibition.* New York: Alfred A. Knopf, 1925.

Kulikoff, Allan. *Tobacco and Slaves: The Development of Southern Cultures in the Chesapeake, 1680–1800.* Chapel Hill: University of North Carolina Press, 1986. Published for the Institute of Early American History and Culture, Williamsburg, Virginia.

Labaree, Benjamin W. *Colonial Massachusetts: A History.* Millwood, New York: kto press, 1979.

Land, Aubrey C., Carr, Lois Green, and Papenfuse, Edward C., eds. *Law, Society, and Politics in Early Maryland.* Baltimore: The Johns Hopkins University Press, 1977. Proceedings of the First Conference on Maryland History, 14–15 June 1974.

Leavitt, Judith Walzer. *Brought to Bed: Childbearing in America: 1750 to 1950.* New York: Oxford University Press, 1986.

Lebsock, Suzanne. *The Free Women of Petersburg: Status and Culture in a Southern Town, 1784–1860.* New York: W. W. Norton & Company, 1984.

Lemon, James, T. *The Best Poor Man's Country: A Geographical Study of Early Southeastern Pennsylvania.* Baltimore: The Johns Hopkins University Press, 1972.

Levy, Barry. *Quakers and the American Family: British Settlement in the Delaware Valley.* New York: Oxford University Press, 1988.

Lockridge, Kenneth A. *A New England Town: The First Hundred Years: Dedham, Massachusetts, 1636–1736.* New York: W. W. Norton & Company, 1970.

Maier, Pauline. *The Old Revolutionaries: Political Lives in the Age of Samuel Adams.* New York: Alfred A. Knopf, 1980.

Mather, Cotton. *Things for a Distress'd People to think upon.* Printed sermon, 1696.

McCusker, John J., and Menard, Russell R. *The Economy of British America, 1607–1789.* Chapel Hill: University of North Carolina Press, 1985. Published for the Institute of Early American History and Culture, Williamsburg, Virginia.

McLoughlin, William G.. *Cherokee Renascence in the New Republic.* Princeton, New Jersey: Princeton University Press, 1986.

McMahon, Sarah F. "A Comfortable Subsistence: The Changing Composition of Diet in Rural New England, 1620–1840," *The William and Mary Quarterly*, January 1985.

Morgan, Edmund S. *The Puritan Family: Religion and Domestic Rela-*

tions in Seventeenth-Century New England. New York: W. W. Norton & Company, 1966. Reprint.

Morgan, Kenneth. "The Organization of the Convict Trade to Maryland: Stevenson, Randolph & Cheston, 1768–1775," *The William and Mary Quarterly,* April 1985.

Mumford, Lewis. *Architecture as a Home For Man.* New York: Architectural Record Books, 1975.

Myers, Albert Cook. *Narratives of Early Pennsylvania, West New Jersey, and Delaware, 1630–1707.* New York: Barnes & Noble, Inc., 1912.

Nash, Gary B. *Forging Freedom: The Formation of Philadelphia's Black Community, 1720–1840.* Cambridge: Harvard University Press, 1988.

———. *Quakers and Politics: Pennsylvania, 1681–1726.* Princeton, New Jersey: Princeton University Press, 1968.

———. *Red, White, and Black: The Peoples of Early America.* Englewood Cliffs, New Jersey: Prentice-Hall, Inc., 1974.

———. *The Urban Crucible: Social Change, Political Consciousness, and the Origins of the American Revolution.* Cambridge: Harvard University Press, 1979.

Papenfuse, Edward C. *In Pursuit of Profit: The Annapolis Merchants in the Era of the American Revolution, 1763–1805.* Baltimore: The Johns Hopkins University Press, 1975.

Perkins, Edwin J. *The Economy of Colonial America.* New York: Columbia University Press, 1980.

Piersen, William D. *Black Yankees: The Development of an Afro-American Subculture in Eighteenth-Century New England.* Amherst, Massachusetts: The University of Massachusetts Press, 1988.

Pruitt, Bettye Hobbs. "Self-Sufficiency and the Agricultural Economy of Eighteenth-Century Massachusetts," *The William and Mary Quarterly,* July 1984.

Quimby, Ian M. G., ed. *The Craftsman in Early America.* New York: W. W. Norton & Company, 1984. Published for the Henry Francis du Pont Winterthur Museum, Winterthur, Delaware.

Quinn, David B. *North America from Earliest Discovery to First Settlements: The Norse Voyages to 1612.* New York: Harper & Row, 1977.

Rediker, Marcus. *Between the Devil and the Deep Blue Sea: Merchant Seamen, Pirates, and the Anglo-American Maritime World, 1700–1750.* Cambridge: Cambridge University Press, 1987.

Rosswurm, Steve, ed. "Equality and Justice: Documents from Philadelphia's Popular Revolution, 1775–1780," *Pennsylvania History,* October 1985.

Rowe, G. S., and Smith, Billy G., eds. "The Prisoners for Trial Docket for Philadelphia County, 1795," *Pennsylvania History,* October 1986.

Rowe, G. S. "Women's Crime and Criminal Administration in Pennsylvania, 1763–1790," *Pennsylvania Magazine of History and Biography,* July 1985.

Royster, Charles. *A Revolutionary People at War: The Continental Army and American Character, 1775–1783.* New York: W. W. Norton & Company, 1979.

Salinger, Sharon V. " 'Send No More Women': Female Servants in Eighteenth-Century Philadelphia," *Pennsylvania Magazine of History and Biography,* January 1983.

Saunders, Richard H. and Miles, Ellen G., eds. *American Colonial Portraits: 1700–1776.* Washington, D.C.: The Smithsonian Institution Press, 1987. Published for the National Portrait Gallery. Catalogue for an exhibition, May 1987 to January 1988.

Schilpp, Madelon Golden, and Murphy, Sharon M. *Great Women of the Press.* Carbondale, Illinois: Southern Illinois University Press, 1983.

Schwind, Arlene Palmer. "The Ceramic Imports of Frederick Rhinelander, New York Loyalist Merchant," *Winterthur Portfolio: A Journal of American Material Culture,* Spring 1984.

Shammas, Carole. "The Female Social Structure of Philadelphia, 1775," *Pennsylvania Magazine of History and Biography,* January 1983.

———. "How Self-Sufficient was Early America?" *Journal of Interdisciplinary History,* Autumn 1982.

Shelton, Cynthia J. "Textile Production and the Urban Laborer: The Proto-Industrialization Experience of Philadelphia, 1787–1820," *Working Papers from the Regional Economic History Research Center,* Eleutherian Mills-Hagley Foundation, 1982.

Silver, Timothy. *A New Face on the Countryside: Indians, Colonists, and Slaves in South Atlantic Forests, 1500–1800.* New York: Cambridge University Press, 1990.

Silverman, Kenneth. *The Life and Times of Cotton Mather.* New York: Harper & Row, 1984.

Simler, Lucy. "The Landless Worker: An Index of Economic and Social Change in Chester County, Pennsylvania, 1750–1820," *The Pennsylvania Magazine of History and Biography,* April 1990.

Slaughter, Thomas P. *The Whiskey Rebellion: Frontier Epilogue to the*

American Revolution. New York: Oxford University Press, 1986.

Smaby, Beverly Prior. *The Transformation of Moravian Bethlehem: From Communal Mission to Family Economy.* Philadelphia: University of Pennsylvania Press, 1988.

Smith, Billy G., *The "Lower Sort": Philadelphia's Laboring People, 1750–1800.* Ithaca, New York: Cornell University Press, 1990.

———, and Shelton, Cynthia, eds. "The Daily Occurrence Docket of the Philadelphia Almshouse: Selected Entries, 1800–1804," *Pennsylvania History,* July 1985.

Smith, Daniel Blake. *Inside the Great House: Planter Family Life in Eighteenth-Century Chesapeake Society.* Ithaca, New York: Cornell University Press, 1980.

Soifer, Margaret K., ed. *The Autobiography of Benjamin Franklin.* New York: The Macmillan Company, 1967.

Stilgoe, John R. *Common Landscape of America, 1580 to 1845.* New Haven, Connecticut: Yale University Press, 1982.

Tanner, Helen Hornbeck. *Atlas of Great Lakes Indian History.* Norman, Oklahoma: University of Oklahoma Press, 1987. Published for the Newberry Library.

Tate, Thad W., and Ammerman, David L., eds. *The Chesapeake in the Seventeenth Century: Essays on Anglo-American Society.* Chapel Hill: University of North Carolina Press, 1979. Published for the Institute of Early American History and Culture, Williamsburg, Virginia.

Thompson, Roger. "Adolescent Culture in Colonial Massachusetts," *Journal of Family History,* Summer 1984.

Ulrich, Laurel Thatcher. *Good Wives: Image and Reality in the Lives of Women in Northern New England, 1650–1750.* New York: Alfred A. Knopf, 1980.

Upton, Dell. "Pattern Books and Professionalism: Aspects of the Transformation of Domestic Architecture in America, 1800–1860," *Winterthur Portfolio: A Journal of American Material Culture,* Summer/Autumn 1984.

———, and Vlach, John Michael, eds. *Common Places: Readings in American Vernacular Architecture.* Athens, Georgia: The University of Georgia Press, 1986.

Wallace, Paul A. W. *The Travels of John Heckewelder in Frontier America.* Pittsburgh: University of Pittsburgh Press, 1958.

Walsh, Lorena S. "Staying Put or Getting Out: Findings for Charles County, Maryland, 1650–1720," *The William and Mary Quarterly,* January 1987.

Ward, Barbara McLean. *A Glimpse into the Shadows: Forgotten Peo-*

ple of the Eighteenth Century. Winterthur, Delaware: The Henry Francis du Pont Winterthur Museum, 1987. Catalogue for exhibition, March–June 1987.

Waters, John J., Jr. *The Otis Family: In Provincial and Revolutionary Massachusetts.* New York: W. W. Norton & Company, 1975. Published for the Institute of Early American History and Culture, Williamsburg, Virginia.

Weigley, Russell F., ed. *Philadelphia: A 300-Year History.* New York: W. W. Norton & Company, 1982. Published for the Barra Foundation.

Wells, Robert V. *The Population of the British Colonies in America before 1776: A Survey of Census Data.* Princeton, New Jersey: Princeton University Press, 1975.

Wolf, Stephanie Grauman. *Urban Village: Population, Community, and Family Structure in Germantown, Pennsylvania, 1683–1800.* Princeton, New Jersey: Princeton University Press, 1976.

Wood, Gordon S., ed. *The Rising Glory of America: 1760–1820.* New York: George Braziller, 1971.

Wood, Jerome H., Jr. *Conestoga Crossroads: Lancaster, Pennsylvania, 1730–1790.* Harrisburg, Pennsylvania: Pennsylvania Historical and Museum Commission, 1979.

Wood, Peter H. *Negroes in Colonial South Carolina: From 1670 through the Stono Rebellion.* New York: W. W. Norton & Company, 1974.

Wright, Gwendolyn. *Building the Dream: A Social History of Housing in America.* New York: Pantheon, 1981.

Wright, J. Leitch, Jr. *Creeks & Seminoles: The Destruction and Regeneration of the Muscogulge People.* Lincoln, Nebraska: University of Nebraska Press, 1986.

Young, Alfred F., ed. *The American Revolution: Explorations in the History of American Radicalism.* DeKalb, Illinois: Northern Illinois University Press, 1976.

Zimmerman, Philip D. "Workmanship as Evidence: A Model for Object Study," *Winterthur Portfolio: A Journal of American Material Culture,* Winter 1981.

Zuckerman, Michael, ed. *Friends and Neighbors: Group Life in America's First Plural Society.* Philadelphia: Temple University Press, 1982.

———. *Peaceable Kingdoms: New England Towns in the Eighteenth Century.* New York: W. W. Norton & Company, 1970.

———. "William Byrd's Family," *Perspectives in American History,* 1979.

PICTURE SOURCES AND CREDITS

Frontispiece:

   A. National Portrait Gallery, Smithsonian Institution. Henry Benbridge, *Charles Cotesworth Pinckney,* 1774. Oil on canvas.

   B. National Gallery of Art, Washington, D.C. Gift of Edgar William and Bernice Chrysler Garbisch. John Greenwood, *Mrs. Welshman,* 1749. Canvas.

   C. Museum of Fine Arts, Boston. Gift of Henry Lee Shattuck. John Greenwood, *Jersey Nanny,* 1748. Mezzotint.

   D. Delaware Art Museum, Wilmington. Gift of the Absalom Jones School. Raphaelle Peale, *Absalom Jones,* 1810. Oil on paper.

   E. The Historical Society of Pennsylvania. Gustavus Hesselius, *Tishcohan,* 1735. Oil on canvas.

   F. National Portrait Gallery, Smithsonian Institution. Peter Pelham, *Cotton Mather,* 1728. Mezzotint.

1.1 Smithsonian Institution, National Anthropological Archives, National Museum of Natural History. *Tomo Chachi Mico.* Engraving.

1.2 The New-York Historical Society. Henry Dawkins, "Indian Testimonial," 1770. Engraving.

1.3 Abby Aldrich Rockefeller Folk Art Center, Colonial Williamsburg. Anonymous, *The Old Plantation,* c. 1800.

1.4 The Library Company of Philadelphia. Phyllis Wheatley, *Poems on Various Subjects, Religious and Moral* (London, 1773).

2.1 Bowen, *"Catfish,"* October 23, 1985. Reprinted by permission of Tribune Media Services.

2.2 Illustrations from Edmund V. Gillon, Jr., *Early Illustrations of American Architecture* (Dover, 1971).

2.3 A. The New York Public Library, I.N. Phelps Stokes Collection. John Joseph Holland, *A View of Broad Street, Wall Street, and the City Hall,* 1797. Watercolor.

   B. William L. Clemens Library, Ann Arbor. Edwin Walsh, *Last Home of Joseph Brant on Burlington Bay at the Head of Lake Ontario.*

2.4 The New-York Historical Society. *New York Gazette and Weekly Mercury,* advertisement, May 23, 1774.

3.1 The Henry Francis du Pont Winterthur Museum. *Fraktur: Cutwork Love Letter,* 1779. Watercolor & ink on paper.

3.2 A. The New-York Historical Society. John Watson, *Captain and Mrs. Johannes Schuyler,* 1725–30. Oil on canvas.

　　B. The Henry Francis du Pont Winterthur Museum. Henry Benbridge, *John Purves & Wife, Anne Prichard,* 1775–77. Oil on canvas.

3.3 The New-York Historical Society. "A New Touch on the Times. Well Adapted to the distressing situation of every seaport town. By a daughter of Liberty, living in Marblehead." Woodcut detail.

4.1 Pennsylvania Academy of the Fine Arts. Gift of John F. Lewis. James Peale, *The Artist and His Family,* 1795. Oil on canvas.

4.2 Philadelphia Museum of Art. Gift of the Barra Foundation, Inc. Charles Willson Peale, *Rachel Weeping,* 1772–76. Oil on canvas.

4.3 The Baltimore Museum of Art. Gift of Alfred R. and Henry G. Riggs, in Memory of General Lawrason Riggs. John Hesselius, *Charles Calvert,* 1761. Oil on canvas.

4.4 The National Museum of American Art, Smithsonian Institution. Museum purchase and gift of Mr. and Mrs. Murray Lloyd Goldsborough, Jr. Charles Willson Peale, *Matthias and Thomas Bordley,* 1767. Watercolor on ivory.

5.1 John Carter Brown Library at Brown University. Patrick Campbell, *Travels in the Interior Inhabited Parts of North America* (Edinburgh, 1793).

5.2 Massachusetts Historical Society, Boston. Eliza Susan Quincy, *Adams Homestead,* 1822. Watercolor.

5.3 The Library Company of Philadelphia. William Tatham, *An Historical and Practical Essay on the Culture of Tobacco* (London, 1800).

5.4 Maryland Historical Society. Benjamin Henry Latrobe, Sketch done near Fredericksburg, Maryland, 1798.

6.1 The Library Company of Philadelphia. William Birch, *Arch Street Ferry, Philadelphia,* 1800. Engraving.

6.2 New Bedford Whaling Museum. *The Little Navigator.* Shop sign. Paint on wood.

6.3 The Metropolitan Museum of Art. Bequest of Susan W. Tyler, 1979. Ralph Earl, *Elijah Boardman,* 1789. Oil on canvas.

6.4 Haverford College Library. Thomas Anburey, "A View of a Saw Mill & Block House upon Fort Anne Creek the property of Gen. Skeene which on Gen. Burgoyne's Army advancing was set Fire to by the Americans," *Travels Through the Interior Parts of North America in a Series of Letters* (London, 1789). Copperplate.

7.1 A. Worcester Historical Museum, Worcester, Massachusetts. Anonymous, detail, *View of Old Boston,* c. 1730. Oil on wood.

　　B. The New York Public Library, Bancroft Collection. Anonymous, *A View of the Town of Concord* [Massachusetts, seen during British Muster], c. 1775. Colored engraving.

　　C. Germantown Historical Society. John Richards. *Market Square,* undated. Reproduced in *Quaint Old Germantown in Pennsylvania,* 1915.

D. The New York Public Library, Emmet Collection. Archibald Robertson, *In Harlem Lane*, 1798.

E. Virginia State Library and Archives. Courthouse in Hanover, Virginia, built around 1734.

7.2 The New York Public Library, Stokes Collection. Henry Dawkins, engraver (?). Detail, *Certificate of the Hand-in-Hand Fire Company*, 1753. Engraving.

8.1 Historical Society of Pennsylvania. *Pennsylvania Journal*, advertisement, April 16, 1767. Woodcut.

8.2 The Library Company of Philadelphia. Charles Willson Peale, *A Representation of the Figures Exhibited and Paraded Through the Streets of Philadelphia*, 1780. Engraving.

8.3 The Library Company of Philadelphia. William Birch, no title, 1799. Engraving.

8.4 Henry Francis du Pont Winterthur Museum. *Schrank*, Pennsylvania, 1781.

8.5 The Metropolitan Museum of Art, Lazarus Fund, 1923. John Singleton Copley, *Joseph Sherburne*, c. 1767. Oil on canvas.